Welcome to the Home of Your Heart

**Writings by Jenny
to Dorothy "Mike" Brinkman**

Published by
Mother Courage Press
1533 Illinois Street
Racine, WI 53405

Library of Congress catalog card number 90-61688
ISBN 0-941300-17-X

Mother Courage Press
1533 Illinois Street
Racine, WI 53405

To Julie
and to the women of the Group

Acknowledgments

I want to thank all those who have supported me, encouraged me and loved me throughout the past three years as I channeled these words from Jenny.

I especially want to acknowledge Julie, who believed even when my skeptical nature assailed me; Regina, the first friend I dared trust with my writings, whose joyous acceptance gave me courage to continue; Shirley and the Group, the wonderful women who have faithfully met with me each month to hear and discuss the latest writings. Without them to listen, to share, to learn and to love, my way would have been much lonelier and not nearly as much fun. And also thanks to others who have encouraged me; co-workers, friends and those "perfect strangers" who had a way of announcing themselves as kindred.

My gratitude overflows for the women of Mother Courage Press, Barbara Lindquist and Jeanne Arnold, who not only published this book but invested their love and energy in its process.

My greatest thanks go to Jenny for, of course, without her there would be no book.

Believe what you will. Let these words inform you whether you believe they come from me, from Universal Mind or from a part of you. You see this is not so necessary to ask, "Who is writing this?" as to ask, "Does this sound like truth?"

~~~~~~~~~~~~~~~

Let me go on with some of the lessons I am here to teach you, for that is my purpose in writing to you and all the others who will read these words. I am here to teach old lessons in new ways, for there is nothing new under the sun except for packaging. You know how important that is for all of you who have been raised on TV commercials. We sometimes wonder why it is so difficult to get the message of love and peace across to you all. But that is how it is.

~~~~~~~~~~~~~~~

But be assured that these messages are not new to you. If you read these and have a feeling of calm and peace returning to you, you know that it is the remembrance of a time and place when the messages you read here were commonplace to you as when they were all there was. You remember this time with great pleasure.

~~~~~~~~~~~~~~~

So this is a message to all. Examine your complacency with the truths which are held out for you. Be careful of following too closely the answers of others. This applies to old and new messages. See that you also have the capacity from within to evaluate all the messages out there. You have the capacity to look inward to connect with deeper wisdoms, to hear voices of learning. Do this. Do not accept blindly what you hear. Live with the mystery. Live with the question. Accept the tasks of the search. That is all.

~~~~~~~~~~~~~~~

You should not try to convince anyone that you have the way, for there are many ways and many means.

~~~~~~~~~~~~~~~

I am here. Welcome to the home of your heart. Tonight I shall answer your questions and then tell you more.

Jenny

i

Prologue

The material in this book has been given to me by a very loving spirit who calls herself *Jenny*. According to her, we had a long-ago, earth-life connection where I was her mother and she was my daughter. She is now my guide. Her words, though often written to me for some specific reason, have universal meaning. Many of my friends who have read her words feel that the messages have been written just for them and have come just at the time they need clarification for a problem area in their life.

There is a sense of truth about these writings that often touches deeply. There is a feeling of unconditional love which nourishes and restores those who have read her words. I believe that her words can speak to you, and so it is with joy that I bring this book to you. If you have read other channeled material, you will recognize the similarity to messages of others who send information for a new era.

If this is your first channeled book, I ask you to read with openness. If you have difficulty believing that spirits can communicate with us, then simply read it for the truths that may speak to you or for the peace and warmth that can come from reading words of unconditional love.

Jenny's words have deeply touched my life. I find myself looking at many of the happenings of my life in an expanded way. Bringing in the view of spirit allows me to walk much easier through the trials that may confront me. I am still learning; sometimes I think I have only moved an inch or two, but I know from the writings that I need not judge myself harshly.

Jenny speaks of many things but always from a perspective of universal love. She encourages us to see our connections with all of life. She helps us to see the continuation of life through what we call *death*. She aids us in seeking our spiritual path and purpose. She gives practical information on how to live with each other in a more caring way. She asks us to reach above our everyday selves to hear our souls.

I suggest that you read this book slowly, allowing the messages to penetrate with ease into your inner being. Listen for the resonance with your soul. Hear its responses.

Introduction

It is still with some surprise that I write this introduction. Having been a skeptic most of my life about unprovable spiritual matters, I sometimes still find it difficult to view myself as someone who has written a channeled book full of information about the unseen world. How did this come to be? As a 57-year-old woman who had not been to church in 30 years and who gave very little thought to the mysteries of life except to accept them as just that—mysteries, I did not expect something so extraordinary as channeling to enter my life.

A series of events happened which led to writing the material which follows in this book. The first event occurred in the fall of 1986 when a psychic told me that I would do automatic writing. I took this with the proverbial grain of salt and thought little about it. A few months later, an article about Ruth Montgomery caught my eye. Her experiences with automatic writing were described and I was intrigued enough to get all her books from the library to see if there were any clues as to how one went about this business of communicating with the higher realms. After reading her description of how she came to write automatically, I sat down to try. Nothing much happened except for a few scribbles, and I gave it up. Then in the summer a friend lent me a channeled book by Ken Carey. This had a profound impact on me as I read it, and I came to know with deepest clarity that "I am spirit." I decided to try writing again, with the same result as before.

Then in August 1987 I attended a workshop led by a woman channeler who directed us in an attempt to reach our highest guide. A barely legible name, Jenny, came to my paper. Once back home I tried to write again and this time the words came, "Write often, we have much to tell you." The effect of this message was to frighten me such that I did not want to try that again. My long-held beliefs were about to be shaken to the core, and I didn't know if I was ready for that. I was not to get off so easy. Books, articles, people kept coming into my life leading me always to new ideas about spirit. Then I read Sanya Roman's book, *How to Channel*, and my fears quieted. I sat down and tried to write and the information began to come. Now two years later it still comes whenever I ask for it.

~~~~~~~~~~~~~~~

My dear friends, I am here to speak, too, about the writing of this book and how it has come about. The information which is contained in these pages comes to you with the best wishes of your guides who inhabit a different dimension than the one in which you now reside. These words are to help you remember, to remember that which you already know in your soul. You see, it is a time of great importance on your earth, a time of potential for great changes. You are all needed to help these changes happen and it is important that you learn to listen to the knowledge which is available to you when you are in touch with the higher realms. Your soul has been to these realms and has the knowledge, but you are so blocked now that this information is often unheard. The purpose of this book and others like it are to help you to remember and to help you to hear that which your intuition relays to you. I will stop for now.

~~~~~~~~~~~~~~~

You will see that at first I simply asked questions which were answered. In time it seemed that all I had to do was to think of a question and the answers came. Later Jenny herself brought information to me that she thought would add to my learning, and to that of others who would come to read these pages. I puzzled over these writings a great deal, wondering who indeed was writing. Was it my imagination or was I, in truth, in tune with a higher power. I admit that I still struggle with this question, though not so often, as the answer doesn't seem so important as do the effects of these words in my life—and the lives of others.

When I first began to do this writing, I was afraid to show it to others, thinking that they would see me as some kind of kook. After a month or so, I decided I would show it to a friend who already had read some channeled books. Her profound acceptance of the information gave me courage to share with others I thought might be receptive. Each person accepted with joy and recognized the words as truths which they already held in their hearts. The writings are filled with messages of unconditional love and the reading of the words brings a state of peace and warmth to those who read them.

~~~~~~~~~~~~~~~

Yes, my friends, these words which I write contain messages of great joy for all of you who are now residing on earth. They will penetrate to the depth of your heart if you but let them in. You see you are all starved for the truths of spirit, and when you receive them, you are filled in a way that your earthly pursuits cannot do. You too may have questions about where these words come from. Do they come from spirit or merely from the imaginings of a human mind? You see the distinction is not so clear as you would like it to be. Hear your own heart and then you will know that the answer to where these words come from is not so important. Let your heart hear, listen for its murmurings of excitement when you read. Let the peace that comes show you the way. These words are for you. Do not turn away from them in skepticism, but allow them to speak to you of that which you already know.

~~~~~~~~~~~~~~~

In time it became clear to me that there were several people who wanted to go further with the writings, and a monthly group was formed to read and discuss them. This group continues to this time. Two of the members of the group from its earliest days are the publishers of this book. We all thought that this was very clever of Jenny.

~~~~~~~~~~~~~~

To those of you who read my words, take them into your heart but convert them to action if you so desire. Your days can change as you welcome the world of spirit to your house. You need not change the mountains which exist but merely let these words help you with your garden. I offer this to you with love of the Universal All. It matters not what name you call this by, the words of love are the same. Come now and read with me. I will be with you.

There is the coming of a new era, a time when there will be tremendous changes in the way that humans perceive the reality of their world to be. You now live in a time of darkness, but soon there will be a changing such that much will be revealed. You will all come to see yourself as spirit in a way that you have only touched on before. There is much information being given to you to help you to assimilate the changes which are already in motion.

At this time the number of you who will understand these messages is small, but believe me when I say it is growing with every passing day.

But these words are also to help you now. The messages are for you—to help you live your life with more ease and joy. Joy is the connection of the universe. To experience the joy which comes from the love connection of the universe is to participate in Life. This book is for you. Read it with gladness in your heart for it speaks to you of your connections which go beyond the material life you are surrounded by. I bring this to you with love. Bless you all who read it.

~~~~~~~~~~~~

Bless you all who read this

(At first, the messages were handwritten and then typed into a word processing program on my computer. As we gathered together to read these writings, I xeroxed the monthly sections to share with the group. Later as I grew in practice and confidence, I was able to write directly on the computer.

Finally after almost two years, I was able to channel Jenny's messages verbally. I did so to answer people's questions and give them special messages. I also am continuing to write the messages and share them with my group.)

Q: How do I begin to write?

October 22, 1987
Beginning to write

A: This is what to do—stop for a minute and give your heart a chance to catch up. Breathe six times and relax now—Now you are more open. What do you want to ask?

Q: Why am I so low on energy?

A: You have to just rest a bit. There is some phlegm in your lungs that is working against you. Take hot baths and rest. You'll be better in a few days. You just have to take care of yourself.

Q: Why can't I seem to exercise?

A: That's a little silly but you always have been a little lazy. If you want to, you can, but if you don't, well, don't complain.

Q: Am I going in the right direction with my life?

A: You are. I'm not sure what course you are going to take, but it's all necessary for your growth. It's hard for you to know because you are not sensitive enough to your own needs. You need to be more careful of yourself and listen to your thoughts.

Q: I feel unsure and uneasy.

A: That's true because you are leaving a lot behind and don't know where you're going or how to get there, but you have to trust in yourself.

1

October 23, 1987
I am Jenny

Your mind keeps interfering. Concentrate and free your mind. Oh, can you see how much better that is?

I am Jenny, a long lost soul from . . . (I can't spell that.) Somehow it seems like you do not know if this is good for you, but I assure you that it is. You don't have to be afraid because it's all for your own good. When you study with us, there will only be good that comes from it. You have to let go and then all can come to you. Could you write a little everyday and then it will be easier? I have much to tell you and I can't do it all at once. Find a stone to hold when you write. It will help—any one will do. If you listen, you can hear the words as I write them and that helps, otherwise there isn't enough energy to get through. Fill yourself with light, open up your chakras with music and don't forget to write every day.

Q: Did I know you in another life?

A: Oh yes. A very grand time long time ago. I remember but you don't. I loved you then and now. How about that? And that takes us to today. Come again soon.

October 24, 1987
*Life is greater
than you know*

Lean back a little. I can answer you now. The rock helps to regulate the fuel and energy so I can come through better.

Q: What about Arie? (My dog was put to sleep this day.)

A: The dogs and the cats and all the animals have spirit too and live on in another form. Arie's spirit is fine. She is getting used to being here and we are taking care of her. Animals are all part of the plan. I think you know that all life is part of the same cloth and there is no distinction. Humanity is only one part, but it is by no means the whole. The spirit world is far more than you can imagine and has far more interconnections than your scientists have discovered. There is a life force that permeates every living thing and even some of those that you consider non-living, like your rock.

Q: Why is there so much death?

A: There is so much death because that is the way it is. People use the natural process of death for their own destructive ends, but death is of itself the way it is and is meant to be. There is no loss or gain, be sure of that. Only because your view is so

2

limited you feel loss and pain. If you could see all, there would be rejoicing and not tears. For every death is part of the forward movement, upward and ahead to the time when all will be set free. So be of good heart, life is greater than you know.

Q: Julie wants to know about her parents.

A: Yes, they are fine, but they are no longer together as they are studying different things right now, but they are enjoying themselves immensely.

Q: Can you tell me anything else?

A: No, maybe later.

Q: Is there a reason that you and I are communicating?

A: Yes, because you and I will write a book with many important ideas in it that will help with the healing of the earth. But first we must get acquainted a bit. That will all come in due time, when you have grown a bit more and we are able to communicate easily.

Q: Tell me about you.

A: I am an old soul. You and I were together many times and our connection is solid.

Q: Could you tell me more about when we were together?

A: I could tell you years and years of things but I don't think that's what you want to hear right now. I think you want to hear about things of the spirit that will help you grow in this way.

Q: What is spirit?

A: Spirit is all encompassing and is and always will be. You are spirit as am I and much of what you see. There are no distinctions as you have been taught between the various kinds of living things. Spirit is a life energy that is timeless, unkillable, and fills all the pockets of the universe. It is transmutable and can expound the boundaries of time and space. You are it, filled with it, and can be no other. It is pure energy. Some think that only humans have spirit, but as I told you, it permeates the animals and all living things and is from the Source.

Q: Are there differences in levels of spirit. Some people seem better than others.

A: No, there are no degrees of spirit, but there are differences in physical beings and their development such that there appear to be differences in their spirit. This is very complicated but I will try to explain it to you. Humankind was made in order to work out some of the highest order of changes in the universe. I know this doesn't make sense, but I perhaps will be able to explain more when you know more. So humanity has a plan of its own and that plan is part of the grand plan. This I cannot yet communicate to you. So as spirit comes back to body, they are all acting in this plan and the purpose is to achieve purity. The earth is a testing ground for many things.

October 26, 1987
Trust in me and all will come in due time

Hi, I am here—let me in. Try to relax so I can come through. Yes. Now for today's lesson. Is there anything you want to know?

Q: Is this just me or do you really come in?

A: Oh, you know it's me and not you. Can you take in what I have to say? You seem very tired. There is plenty of time.

Q: Tell me something I don't know.

A: I can't make you believe by tricks—you have to trust in me and all will come in due time.

Q: What about the stock market? (The stock market had just experienced a tremendous drop called the "Black Monday" crash of '87.)

A: The stock market is only a sign of things that are to come. You needn't worry as you will be all right. It's necessary to stop the gross materialism that is rampant. The times will be hard, and many will fall by the wayside, but in the end there will be a resurgence of love and loyalty. Do not despair as you will be fine.

Q: Will we have a depression?

A: I don't know—much depends on what happens. There is a possibility. It will come in response to greed and I do not know the caliber of that.

Q: Will Julie be OK too?

A: Yes, Julie will be OK too. You both have responsibilities and you will be able to carry them out.

October 27, 1987
All is well for you and the earth

How are you tonight? What do you want to know? Last night we talked briefly of some things that I want to expand upon. That is, there is a changing that is happening all over the world and that will be difficult for some to go through. There are many changes coming that might look from your side as though the world was collapsing, but this is not so. From our perspective, things have to happen or worst things would befall the earth and that cannot be. Those of you who are chosen to follow the path have much to do in the coming years. You do not know this yet, and you are not to worry that you don't, for it all will come. I don't want to tell you too much for you will worry but know that all is well for you and the earth. The plan that is to come to pass needs change to happen. Many changes are already taking place.

October 28, 1987
Each person has a part to play and must choose what that is to be

Hi, and here I am. How are you tonight? What do you want to know?

Q: How do you communicate?

A: There is a pathway to the top of your head. (This idea caused me to have extraneous thoughts.) You must stop interfering with your thoughts if we are to work easily. Just be open and relaxed. There is a pathway through the top of your head that allows me to connect directly and gain entrance to your thoughts. The writing follows from that. It is all energy exchange. I don't come into your body and move your hand.

Energy is a very fascinating property, little understood by all of you but very useful to us. I have much to tell you. First of all, let's go on with our lesson from yesterday. As I said, many things are changing and you are part of the plan. In the days to come, there will be many changes for the good and some that will shake things up. Many people are involved in changing the mass energy of the world, including you. You are needed with all the rest. There will be days of study and learning that will come to you and many others. It is a time when the boundaries are permeable and the energy of us here can reach down to those who are open. Keep studying and writing and I will tell you much that you need to know.

The times will sometimes be hard, but that is necessary. Many people will find it a trying time as they are called to examine their beliefs, and others will find themselves woefully lacking to exist in a changing world. There will be a preponderance of good energy that will sway the balance of good and evil. When that happens, miraculous things will happen. There will be a time of much loving and sharing of good fortune. The way of life is love and that no longer can be denied. Men and women are seeking that within their hearts and when it comes, there will be much relief and rejoicing. The world is in a very sorry mess at this time but all is not lost, I can assure you. Each person has a part to play, either on the side of good or evil, and must choose what that is to be. All is written and will be carried out. There will be some catastrophes, but it is too early to say what they will be or how many will be necessary.

October 29, 1987
On the power of love

Love is a very powerful force, as I know you're aware. It's magnitude for change is unmeasured. If humans ever became aware of its power, they would find that ten nuclear bombs could not equal it. It is the greatest source of power there is. Not the petty love that is sometimes called such, but the love that passeth all understanding and exists as a free standing power. It is not *to* or *for* someone but exists as energy and light. You are all capable of it, but few have figured out how to express it. Jesus did and many others, but most only have glimpses of it. Last week you saw some of it at work in the saving of Jessica (the story of the little girl who fell down the well that captured the national media) but mostly the power of love has been very undervalued. Part of what is about to happen will be an unleashing and understanding of this power.

I will give an exercise to do to strengthen your use of love as a force.

The first meditation
Love as a force

Stand with your body upright as you can make it and focus your inner gaze on a spot ten feet above your head. Imagine that all people and all life are contained in that spot. Send your force of love toward it. Imagine it coming alive with light and energy.

6

See it blaze and begin to revolve. Do this once a day and you will find yourself expanding with its power.

Q: Tell me about life and how it came to be.

A: There is much to be said about life and I will tell you some today. Life is a force of the Divine. What is the Divine, you ask. It is the All There Is—what you call God. But that is a misnomer as it puts God in a category by itself. You and I and all of life are of the Divine and always shall be. It is very hard to describe something for which you have no concepts. It is not as though I can explain by your terms. You are of the material world and understand in material terms and want explanations in material terms, but I cannot do that. Life is energy. It is a force unequal to any other. It is nondestructive, does not wear out, goes on world without end. It is. It is not only what you see around you in what you call *living things*. It is a far greater force and comes into the world in the form you see it, but it exists far and far more than you can imagine. The material world is only a small portion of the life force.

Q: Why does the material world exist?

A: The material world exists as a proving ground for experiments and for growth of organisms. The world and the Divine are always changing. There is nothing static in all of creation. It is always becoming anew. There is a purpose to that end. The earth is a place where things can be tried out and examined. There are limits of the non-material world as far as instituting change. You have to understand that the material and non-material world do not exist apart from one another. It is all one. There are no real separations between them. Life flows back and forth like the wind. You only see one side of things, so you don't understand that. But see how easy it is. Living and dying are happening all the time around you. It is not something unusual. The flowers and the birds and all the rest keep doing it. It is as it is meant to be.

Q: How does life come to people?

A: Life is always there. It does not come.

Q. What makes things seem to be material?

7

A: They are material. That is the property of your world. The energies are aligned such that form appears.

November 2, 1987
Welcome to the home of your heart

I am here. Welcome to the home of your heart. Tonight I shall answer your questions and then tell you more.

Q: What is karma?

A: The first answer is that karma is a concept that often is misinterpreted and is seen as a paying off of past sins. This is not the case. Karma refers to the means in which souls learn tasks that they have chosen as the most important learning they can do to speed their progress to nirvana. Sometimes this looks as though there is no reason for it unless it is paying off past sins, like an eye for an eye, but karma does exist to serve the soul's need to progress and is well thought out ahead of time. It is the life plan in part and provides the nucleus for the teaching of that life. A soul cannot progress without that plan. It is important for a soul to experience all aspects of material life to be whole.

November 3, 1987
Don't be afraid

Now I would like to answer your questions from last night. There is a preponderance of sorrow in the world because there is free will, and humanity has not yet learned to carry out this plan with the full force of spirit that is love. People rely too much on lower instincts and do not yet know how to control their inner forces. They rely on those of the earth and believe that they can achieve what they want by conquering the world. Humanity is struggling along on one engine, so to speak. There is a process and progress in place so that there will be changes to come.

Your weekend is inhibiting you. You are not quite so pure. (I had much difficulty writing.)

You are very difficult to come into. You are resisting on a very deep level. Just relax your thoughts and let my thoughts flow through you. Don't be afraid. I know you are worried about the consequences of all this on your life and would rather shut it off right now. It is OK to ask questions about that. Don't be so intellectual about our connection. If you want to know your resistances, we can talk about that. This is all very scary for you on one level because you still have not totally accepted the fact that you exist above and beyond your current situation. It doesn't matter where you are for there you are. You are always

8

with yourself. Please don't be afraid to face your fears and questions. That's one of the reasons I'm here.

You fear that you are making this all up and that your life will be changed. You do not know what this all means. Your ego and your higher self are in conflict over who shall direct the ship. And then there are all your so-called *selves* that get in the way with their petty grievances. It is very difficult for you to let go of all that. You also don't know what to do with this in your everyday life. Be sure that you are on the right path and there is no other. You are also afraid of Julie's path and what effect that will have on you. For now your paths run together. Your way is her way and so you can relax. Don't be afraid. The way will be shown to you. You don't have to figure it out; all will come in due time.

On life force

Let me now talk to you a bit about life some more. The process of life force is the greatest force in the universe. It permeates all the corners of the earth and the universe. Your scientists often ask if there is life in other places than earth. This is a very silly question. Life exists in magnitude in other places than earth but not as you know it. Life is not what you see only here on earth as something that emerges from a seed. It does not start in a seed or an egg. It already is and is what makes the seed grow or the egg to ripen. The force of life does not stop or start but flows constantly throughout the universe. That's why you cannot talk of life and death as though they are two things that can stop or start. Life does not begin nor does it end. Death as a concept has very little meaning beyond the earth. There you see something you have named *death* because you cannot see far enough or clear enough to see the life processes ebbing and flowing.

Love is a force

Now I would tell you some other things about love. Love, too, is a force, an energy that is produced by all life forms whether of your world or not. It is an energy with wonderful properties and, as I said, is mostly leashed on earth, though if it weren't there, there would be instant collapse of the world as you know it. The power of love even in its present meager form keeps the earth afloat. Love is continuously being given off by all life forms and is transmitted between them as a source of connection and cohesiveness. Without it, you would all perish in an instant. But there is no danger of that for indeed it is there and cannot be destroyed.

Human beings have not yet learned of its force and so do not use its power just as once they did not know how to use electricity. Look how the whole world runs on it. Love is a much more powerful force than electricity but perhaps because it is so readily available, more elusive. The time is coming when humanity will begin the study of this force and that understanding will transform the earth. You felt some of it this weekend. It has transformative power when amplified. If you form your group, the love force will be there to be used. I will help you then to know what to do. Don't forget the exercise I gave you for that will strengthen your resource.

Your friend Jeanne is a soul mate. You are all coming together now to study and learn with each other. Jeanne is learning much right now. She is freeing herself from some imposed constraints that she has lived with most of her life. When things are worked out, she will be much more able to resonate with the coming events.

Q: Who else are soul mates?

A: There are many—some of whom you do not yet know in the material plane. It is not for you to know at this time.

November 4, 1987
On political change

Tonight we have much to talk about. I can tell you have many questions. You want to know about your trip. Well, the answer to that is to look at it this way. You can have experiences such as you cannot have any other way, or you can stay home. I don't see that there is much choice, but then it's up to you. To go to Hawaii or Ecuador seems to be the same thing—no, you know one is as good as the other, but you have to choose. There is no fate involved in your choice.

You also want to know about psychic phenomena. You want to know if you are psychic too. There is a difference between being psychic and being able to channel. They are different processes. You are not very psychic, a little here and there, but that is not something you should spend too much time on. As to channeling, that is something you will be able to do very well. Just keep at it and it will get easier every day. You can learn a lot by reading books about channeling or those written by a channel, also others dealing with the same kind of phenomena such as Eastern religious books, Zen Buddhism, etc.

Now that is enough of that. I want to talk with you about some important things such as what is going to happen in the next few years which will have enormous impact on you and everyone around you. There will be changes in the way governments relate to one another as more and more higher vibrations are felt. As more people raise their vibrations to a spiritual pitch, it will be difficult for some of the more destructive things to go on. There will be changes in the leadership such that peace will become a very important issue. Change cannot come from projects or money spent trying to resolve enormous political problems. Change will come in the hearts and minds of everyone, slowly at first but increasing day by day until the weight of it tips the scales of virtue. Then there will be laughter in the streets. But first there will be unseen forces that will cause catastrophic acts.

Q: Is there evil?

On evil

A: No, there is no such thing as evil even though I speak of it metaphorically. Evil is only a lack of acting from love. It is an absence rather than a presence. When man rapes and kills, he is not in tune with the power of love and so is destructive. There are also things that happen in the material plane because of free will, and everyone is influenced by the things that happen to them. No one is fated to be evil. It is the straying from your fated path that leads to these acts. All real paths are righteous and are toward higher acts.

Q: What book are we going to write?

A: The name of it will be "Signs of Our Times," or perhaps something else, and it will be about living in a way that you follow your path.

November 6, 1987
Death & the life force

Today you have so many questions we could talk all day. You want to know more about death and life and how people get born and die and how to live in the world. You have many, many more questions. Keep your thoughts still so I can come through. They are interfering and are trying to direct the flow of writing. Keep still and all will be OK.

As to your first question about death—death as I told you is a concept that only exists on the material plane and refers to a

11

process whereby material is changed back to some basic substances. Matter is a substance of the earth and when the life force visits it becomes active and regenerating. When life force is withdrawn, then a natural process of returning to basic elements occurs and regeneration ceases for that particular animal, person or other living thing.

What makes the life force withdraw? When there has been too much destruction of the mechanical process that determines regeneration. Death sometimes occurs because the spirit of that body has finished its work and therefore has no further need of it. The process is all to the good. Life force is a constantly moving force and comes and goes according to plan. Thus the seasons follow one another and birth and death do, too. The plan of life is not to be static as it would be if there were no death. Death is that which allows for growth and creative renewal to take place. Don't be afraid of it. It has no sorrow in and of itself. Humans feel sorrow because of their narrow view of only the material world and think someone or something has been lost. So there is no sense to look at it that way. It isn't as though you will all get together in another place or will even want to. There is much more freedom in other planes and not the need to hold onto others.

You see, there is a much greater perspective on other planes, and you can see all the interconnections between every kind of life. You need not worry if this one or that one is waiting for you in heaven for they are all too busy. Not that they won't be there, but you will not have need for them as you do in life. You will see farther into your own plan and will be busy with that. Love, as you know it, does not exist here. That doesn't mean you should not form love attachments or have feelings for others. That is how it is there and you are there to partake in all that exists for you. You are there to learn, and much learning takes place between loving and making friends. I just want to mitigate your sorrows by explaining the bigger picture.

The next thing I want to talk with you about is the ways and means of using this knowledge in your life. You are confused now as you don't know what it means or how you should use it. But you are doing fine. You have been talking and sharing this with others and that is good. At this time, much is changing within you and around you as I'm sure you're aware. As you change, more will come to you about what to do. You can go too fast. I will monitor your speed and will help you with it all. Your friends are open to hearing my thoughts and will welcome hearing from us. Later, we will do something more but for now just keep writing every day as you have been. There is still much to learn. Julie is with you and it is important to share with her and to encourage her to write also. You are together now for a reason. Your paths have crossed and run together now for the good of all.

The last time we wrote, I talked to you about love and its power. **The power of love** Let me say a little more about that. Love, as I said, has tremendous power, but most do not know how to harness it. Love is a force that can transform human beings, so it is important that this knowledge becomes available to all. I don't know at this point what it will take to kindle the spark of knowledge such that mortals will begin to operate with this premise. Love is a potent force and we have been trying to get mortals to recognize it for many eons. I do not know just what it will take, but all our energies are going toward this end. It is the only hope for humankind, not for the earth, for the earth will certainly go on, but human beings are finding themselves on a destructive path that must be turned around if they are to continue to survive. Only a recognition of this power to love will do this.

The love force is one which will let mortals see how it is imperative for all to live together and to transmit the positive energy to create a world filled with peace and contentment. Love is a force that cannot be matched if it is once understood and used. No other laws are needed—it is not necessary to talk of laws, rules and other limiting beliefs because they are not needed. All these have been made up by humans in an attempt to deny their divinity. Love is of the Divine and can be no other. The Divine is the All, the No Other, the Everything and the Ever. Love is its breath. When you let yourself touch the Divine, you are changed from mere mortal to everlasting spirit that you are, whether on the material plane or not. It is possible to be material and spirit at the same time. The way to that is love.

This is the message to spread. Love is all encompassing. It **A message** cannot be separated into categories of man, woman, race, class, human or animal. One cannot love in discrete ways. Love covers all, encompasses all, glorifies all. It is magnificent. It will transform your life and engulf it. You only need to open yourself to it, for it already exists. It is time for a new definition, or a new term perhaps, for all the other ways the word is used. Love of money, for instance, has a good one already—greed; love of food—gluttony; love of possessions—penuriousness; love of others—dependency; and so on. You must shed *these* meanings of love from your vocabulary.

Love is the highest emotion you can feel. It is not something so petty. "Love one another" is the highest form of commandment there is. This should be taught in all the schools, work places, governments, families and wherever people gather. It is not too late. The clock is ticking. Gather together and feel your power. All is there for you. Let it come to you. Do not stop it from coming. Open yourself. Let it come. Feel it. You'll like it.

On feminism

Q: What about feminism. How does it fit?

A: Feminism is a concept that is subsumed under a higher order concept. There is much to be said about the feminist philosophy but it cannot stand alone as it excludes wholeness.

Take the power of love. If this is not extended to all, then you do not have it at all. Feminism is important in breaking up old beliefs and is empowering of those who would give up their power and path to another. But it cannot be all there is. It is only an awareness, an awakening, and it should not serve as the answer to everything. It is not enough.

But that is not to say that feminism is not a concept or philosophy that has much to offer. The power of love is closely aligned with feminist beliefs; however, it is time to expand, so that it truly can show the world the way to peace. The way to peace will never come through fighting or hate. It cannot. It will have to come from a way that incorporates love for all. It cannot be any other way.

 So think first before you use feminist thought to create greater differences and difficulties. Again it is a means to self-awareness.

November 8, 1987
How life begins

Today is a great day. You are very open. Let us begin. Today I want to teach you some more about life and how that begins in a seed or an egg. There is a spot within all life forms that can be activated by the life force, and this happens according to the

14

plan for each. There is more to conception than merely bringing two cells together. This is not enough to create life. The catalyst for the beginning of life comes from the life force which activates the knowledge stored in the egg or seed. This life force is always present but does not act willy-nilly, for then there would be chaos rather than order.

As you can see, the name of the game is "order." All is as it should be and follows a plan as day follows night. The beginning of life is controlled by the plan of all creation from the beginning until world without end. From the beginning of life in the first one-cell organisms until its present form, it is life force which has controlled the growth of all life forms. These are constantly evolving. There is nothing static in all creation.

You as humans, as well as all other forms of life, are a constantly moving, evolving mass of life forms. There is plan and purpose though that does not mean that all is ordained. The process is creative rather than created. The spirit of All There Is is constantly breathing new life into this mass of creation. There is change of enormous magnitude always happening, though you do not always see it because of your limited view of time. So you believe all was created and goes along on its own power to be destroyed at some time. But do not be deceived by your worldly view into believing this. You are only a small smidgen of what you will become. Humanity is in its infancy. There is much to follow. What that is, I can't tell you as everything is yet evolving. But be assured, there is order to all and never chaos.

To infinity & oneness

It is a magnificent plan, full of beauty and love. Do not ever despair, for the bounty of this plan cannot perish. Certainly it cannot be destroyed by mere mortals. All is forever. Do not fear though forms may change and be born and die. The life force is indestructible and will go on evermore, creating, changing— all according to a magnificent plan. Open yourself to its beauty. See its force, its perfectness. Be sure you are a part of it and not a part from it. This is your life plan as well as mine and all the rest. Rejoice in it. Glory in it. It is the greatest gift there is. You are there in the material world to experience it all. Do not pass it by. Feel the connections between you and your brothers and sisters of every race, creed, religion, color, sex, size, shape, animal, vegetable or mineral. You are all one. What is you is them. There is no other. You do not exist apart from one another. You are one another and are all part of the great life plan.

Have you ever seen such beauty as the sunset, or the opening of a seed, or the flight of a bird or the beating of a human heart? How fortunate to be able to see these with your beautiful eyes. Rejoice in it all. Love it all, for it is you and you are it. Tell me your fears and you will see that there is no need for them as all is well and can't be denied. All that you see around you is temporal and is only the tip of the iceberg, so to speak. The wonder of it all is immense. Rejoice in it.

November 9, 1987
Being a messenger

Hello friend, I am here. How are you today? I'm glad you are here. What do you want to know today? More about who I am? My name is Jenny. What else do you want to know? You want to know who I was before. I could tell you that we have been together in many former lives and times. You know me well but since you are not in spirit, you do not know that. We lived in the early 1800's the last time and were mother and daughter then. Since then, I have not been in mortal flesh but have been studying here, and now I am a messenger to you there.

There is much afoot here trying to contact as many of you as we can. There is openness now in the barrier between the worlds and the vibrations are such that it is easier to contact you. So those of you who are old souls who have evolved to a higher pitch are receiving messages from us here as you can see by looking around you. It has been many years since the barrier has been so penetrable. If you will just think a little, you will see how many years it has been since the messages were sent and received so easily. The word of God has been broadcast before but not with the frequency that is now.

The legacy of Jesus

Q: Who is Jesus? Is he really the Son of God?

A: Jesus is me and you and all of us. He is a very highly developed soul but . . . (Your thoughts come in. If you keep them still it, will be much easier.) Jesus was a man on earth but that is not what he *is*. Jesus is spirit of a very high vibration and has been in mortal garb many times, but do not think of him anymore as the son of God anymore than you are the daughter of God. Jesus was a man who lived with the power of love within him and tried to tell the world of its power. But the world was not ready to hear it. However, the memory of Jesus has kept

16

the world open to the message even though they have not yet learned to use it. Jesus was a very learned person when he was in flesh, though he was a simple man. He left much legacy to the world, though much has been corrupted. His message is very simple. Love one another. You saw what happened to him. It is so difficult to transmit this message. Jesus will lend his support to the changes that are happening now and will incarnate very soon again, though not in the same way as before.

Form & spirit

You want to know what shape I am. That's funny. I am not a shape now though I have been. Now I am energy and light. There is a form to me but not a shape. I know that's difficult to understand because you think I need a brain and a mouth or else I could not talk with you, but that is not the form of those of us on this plane. Spirit follows the shape of the body to a rough degree but is not solid in form as you know your body. However some spirit is formless and is pure energy. It depends on the plane you are on. When you first come across the barrier, the form is much more approximating a body, however as time goes by—that is a misnomer as there is no *time*, but you will understand if I use that term—anyway, as time goes by, the body shape becomes less distinct and more formless. By the time a spirit transcends to another plane, the form is lost altogether.

November 10, 1987
On the universe

Come, my dear. We are ready to begin again. What should we talk about today? Today I want to talk to you about the universe. How's that for a little topic? The universe is immense from your perspective and stretches with order into infinity. But that is only from your perspective. As in reality, there is a far different order to things. If you think in terms of space, then indeed that is how it is; but if indeed space is only a material world concept, then things indeed are not as they seem. The universe is not constructed on spatial nor temporal things nor thoughts. It is only your perspective from your dimension that makes it appear so. The universe is actually a self-contained illusion of earth's inhabitants whose thoughts are projected out in such a way as to create the illusion of a complex universe. However, this is not so in the real sense. Just as if you look closely into an atom, then you see that all is not what it seems to be but merely illusion of matter. Such it is with the universe. You can look further and further into it, and then all you will find is illusion.

The might of the sun and the moons and the stars is all illusionary and belongs to the material world. The universe exists on many other dimensions and is the home and creation of spirit. Do not for a moment think that anything you see exists merely for humanity or even for other life forms. The grand plan only uses the material world for a small part of its program. So you see, you and the scientists of the world can study more and more and will know less and less since nothing is really there at all. However, this is not to say they shouldn't do that; the world exists in part for just that study since it all contributes to the ongoing creation of what is.

I only want you to know that all is not as it appears so that you are able to break the conscious connections to what you see. The knowledge that you are to be given depends on a freedom from that kind of thought. You must free yourself from the boundaries of outer sight and look inward with your eyes where all truth and knowledge exist. Believe me, it is not out there. That is only illusion, no matter whether it be a chair or a star. The knowledge of love is within. There is no other way to reach it. Spirit does not exist in illusion but only in truth and love. Come. Examine your beliefs. See the glory within. Free yourself from the bonds of thought. Look and see.

November 12, 1987
On life & birth

Hi, here I am. How are you today? What do you want to know today? How about some more about life and how people get born. I know you have questions about this. Well, to start with, as I told you, life is not something that begins or ends but flows constantly like the wind. However, particular life forms such as human beings do indeed get born and appear to begin life. This is a rather difficult distinction to describe to you as you really have not thought of it any other way. But let's take a seed or an egg that is dormant. Does this or does this not have life? In the literal sense, something can grow from it given the right environment. But unless the life force enters, there can be no life. If something is dead, then the life force has been withdrawn from that particular entity. There is a difference between spirit and life force. Spirit is the wholeness of the entity. Life force is an energy, a catalyst. I don't know what other term to use. Spirit is a something; life force is a power or a pushing, a force, I don't know what other term to use.

You want to know if the spirit or the life force leaves a body first. When spirit leaves a body, the life force has been withdrawn

18

first. Sometimes spirit lingers in the vicinity of a body and waits to see if life force is indeed withdrawn. When life force is gone, the body of the entity fairly rapidly returns to base material. Without life force, no regeneration takes place and then decay sets in. This you understand has nothing to do with spirit which is indestructible. Spirit is not a body, brain or any other organ. It is pure energy and should not be confused with the base body of the entity. When someone is about to be born, the life force is already active. That does not mean that spirit has entered the body as yet. That takes place at about the time of birth. At that time, a spirit who has planned a path which can be carried out in that child's life enters the body. As soon as that happens, there are changes such that the spirit no longer knows itself as spirit and begins to experience material life as that child. There is a barrier such that former lives and knowledge are banned from that spirit-child entity.

What else could I tell you about that? Are spirit and soul the same? More or less. The difference is in the terminology but basically they refer to the same thing.

Q: How does the life force know when to enter or leave?

A: Well, that's difficult to explain also. There is a plan, and the energy of the life force is available according to plan. So the fertilized seed or egg activates or is activated by the life force according to plan. There is nothing hit or miss about it.

You have some questions which I will try to answer.

November 13, 1987
On abortion

Q: What about abortion? Is it wrong?

A: As to abortion, there is not too much wrong about that. As I told you, spirit does not enter the body until the time of birth, and even if it did, it would not matter as far as spirit was concerned as spirit is indestructible. However, in general it is best to take care, as plans are made based on the probability of a child's birth and a spirit has based a life plan on that. However, this aspect of timing is more important than when pregnancy has begun. In the beginning, the loss is not more than the loss of unfertilized eggs or the millions of sperm which perish every day. Just because they have united does not mean so much more. Does that answer your question?

19

Health & diet

Q: Should you eat certain foods or follow certain practices to be more spiritual?

A: Well, yes, that is true to some extent. It is important to eat in such a way that your body functions at its best so that it doesn't get in the way of optimal being. Body, mind, spirit, emotion, are all one during the material phase, and so what happens to one affects all the other. Bodies are made to function best on whole grains, fruit, vegetables and the like. Meat is not to be denied, as in moderation it is healthful. It is not sinful to eat other creatures; however, people so often have no idea of how important animals are in the world and eat them without concern or care of their spirits.

The important thing is to care for the health of your body and not to over indulge, for it is difficult for the body to use the extra calories. You should also rest well, exercise in moderation and provide as stress free an environment as possible for your emotional health. Laugh, play and be merry. It is much better for you than sadness which dulls the appetite and the senses. Keep living and loving and taking care of all aspects of yourself with concern, and you will be fine.

Q: Is our trip to Mexico just choice or is there fate involved?

A: Well, that is for you to figure out. There is an element of fate in it; however, you do have free will and so you will have to see what it is for you. There are check points often in one's life where the path of fate and free will merge or cross, and then you can decide which step to take down which path. Many paths lead to The Path, you know. It isn't as though all is ordained ahead of time. Just be open and see what comes. Have a good time and enjoy all the material beauty you see. It is all there for you. Open your senses. See. Feel. Live and enjoy.

Do not worry that you have questions or disbeliefs

Q: Why don't you come to me with a burst of energy as in *Agartha*?

A: That is a little strange. You want me to give you a jolt. You are afraid enough already. But I do not have to do that. You are already open to me. I could send you high energy but it is not necessary. All of us messengers do not come in the same way, you know. Just believe. Your experience doesn't have to be like someone else's. You see that others too are scared and anxious when first making contact with us, as it is so unusual in your everyday life. Do not worry that you have questions or disbeliefs. It will all even out for you as time goes by and we keep communicating. You have much to learn so just take it easy and believe.

Q: Whose grand plan is it?

A: I cannot talk to you about this yet. That will come later. You do not have the concepts in your mind that will allow me to explain it to you. You will need to wait a bit more for that. Keep studying and thinking so that your mind expands its boundaries and can conceive of greater and greater things.

Q: What can be done for human beings in pain?

A: The pain human beings feel can be mitigated and relieved in many ways. I will tell you many things about that when we write again. I think you have written as much as you can for today. Goodbye for now. Take care my dear and come again soon.

Here I am. How are you? Today has been a very hard day for you. You felt sorely tried with a love task today and found it difficult to escape your conditioning and to think about loving in a new way. Let me tell you how to handle things like this as they come up. You do not need to feel that you have no control over situations or have to suffer indignities. Love is not a force that requires that. The main thing to do is to act within the force of love, and then you will find that you do not need anger or hurt or tears to get your point across. You do not know other ways— but if you try to, you will find ways to express love at the same time as creating limits of what you will allow. Love is the force that will give you strength, understanding and wisdom. Anger dulls the senses and creates more difficulty than it cures. I don't know any other way to describe it at this time; but be sure to use the exercise I gave you when you're feeling upset or angry, and then you will feel yourself centered and able to talk with sense. That's all for now.

November 16, 1987
On love & anger

I told you it would be a grand day. Did you see the sun? What a miracle that is. Can you imagine anything like it? Something millions of miles away warming the earth, and then the earth turning just so, so it all is warmed. Could something like that

November 17, 1987
Gender-free language

just happen? You know that would be very unlikely. Everything fits so well together, don't you think? Such beauty—all over the world, including human beings.

I know you don't like my using the words "man" and "mankind," so I will try to be more multi-personal. You do not have good words that are not sex-typed for *beings*. Here in spirit that is not a problem as all spirit is not sexual and therefore does not have gender; we do not convey terms like "she" and "he" and so forth. Since we do not use words per se, I cannot give you a term that conveys sexlessness, but I think you could use one. "Human beings" is a rather lengthy term and has no pronouns to go with it.

On human beings

Anyway, on to what I wanted to tell you. Human beings are very fortunate in all they have to use to sense the world. Human beings are a very wonderful part of the life plan, though, as I told you, they are in an infancy stage and much learning will have to take place in their minds and hearts. They have such a small view of themselves that it is astonishing. They know more about machines and computers than they do of the wonders of the human being's functioning. There is little understanding of the depths of emotion and love. Little gets transmitted, no matter how hard we try.

There is difficulty with dealing with beings who are still in an evolving pattern, so sometimes it is necessary to wait for growth before making judgments. In time, as the body of consciousness grows and is refined, there will be changes in the mass thought such that human beings will be able to function at a much higher level; and then there will not be so much to be worked out in life from poor environments, lack of love, abuse, etc. Now, so much energy goes to survive rather than to know oneself as spiritual being. The world takes so much that many people go through life without being aware that they are spirit or have a life plan, much less that they are truly a miracle.

On the consciousness of all

Mortals do not see very well at all, but that is all changing. More and more messages are being sent and many more higher level souls are now incarnate so that the vibratory level is changing for the better. Many people are being influenced, even some who do not know it. There are things happening outside the consciousness of all; however, some like yourself are becoming very aware and are helping to spread the message. It is a message that will take hold, as everyone is hungry for it. But it does have much to work against, so progress will be rather slow at first. The message is being given in many forms to many types of people, groups, religions, etc. All is the same though the garb may be different. So you should not try to convince anyone that you have the way for there are many ways and many means. Talk to those who are open to you and leave the others to find their way.

November 18, 1987
The existence of other worlds

Today is a great day. Feel the air and the sun. Look up and see all the wonders of this world. They are myriad. You could not imagine such a world if you could not see it. It is just so with the world you cannot see. The wonders out best each other. Just imagine that this world did not exist in such a way that you could see it, then you would be a disbeliever if someone told you it was possible for all these beauteous things to be. You would scoff at them for sure. Open your belief system to know that other worlds which are equally miraculous exist on other planes, and that the happenings there are just as difficult to believe as those on your world would be if you couldn't see them with your eyes or sense them with your other senses. Just because you cannot see something or even conceive of it, does not mean it doesn't happen. If you think of it as all one plan and look around at the beauty of your world, you will know that what you cannot see exists in equal beauty. There is nothing to be afraid of. All is run by love from the lowest to the highest. There is no punishment, no hell and damnation. The worlds do not run on those principles. All is order. Some of the purposes or causes you cannot see since your view is clouded, but believe me, there is nothing to fear. You cannot tell what there is on this side by listening to your fears. Listen to me for I will only tell you the truth.

(This was typed directly on the computer and included many mistakes.)

November 19, 1987
On illness

Hi, I am here. This is something new. I don't know if we can do it. Let's try. What can we talk about today? There are many things in your mind, but I think I want to talk to you some more about illness. You seem to have many questions about that. You do not like what I had to say about it, I know. Illness is a problem for many people as they think a world created by God should not have illness or pain in it. So they take the fact that pain and illness exist as saying that there is evil or maybe God is dead. This is not so. As I tell you all the time, all is order and according to plan. Illness is part of the order of things. If there were no means of death, then all would go on forever, and as I told you, that would not be good for evolution. Constant regeneration needs to take place. That is the bigger picture. You wonder about the effect on each person and think that is a cruel way to handle things. How would you do it?

Perhaps, in time, death will occur by choice or some other means but in the place we are on the evolutionary scale, this is the means. Life is full of surprises. On the human scale are many choices individuals can make to keep themselves healthy. Diet, exercise, good habits keep illness away. However some bodies do not function very well because of defects in their mechanisms, especially in the energy system, and these people can benefit from techniques that realign their energy.

November 20, 1987
Freedom from pain

The topic for today is how to live in the world in a way that is as pain free as possible. You think this may not be possible but I assure you it is. Pain comes from an absence of grounding in the earth of your being, a lack of contact with your higher self, an absence of love contact. You can be pain free if you turn your mind from a focus on the daily affairs of the negative world and focus instead on higher values. There is much tension in the world caused by the focus on the trivial. Many people can see no farther than the tip of their nose and are constantly trying to bite it off. That is not the way to live in happiness. A much wider view should be taken so that the focus is not just on themselves, their needs and their wants with an accompanying pain or feeling of loss when they don't get what they want.

A different view, one of higher vibrations, can do much to change the focus of your day. Instead of being angry, hurt, dissatisfied, self-conscious, shy, or whatever your particular form of self-inflicted pain is, focus inward to your higher self and see how that erases pain from your heart. Our higher selves do not dwell in pain. They know no good can come from that. When you raise your inner eyes to higher principles of love, charity, hope, piety, etc., your vibrations will even out and twang with a much more beautiful sound. These vibrations will go out just as the radio and TV waves go out and will produce songs of great beauty in the world much like a finely tuned harp. You choose the songs that you play. They can be melodious and beautiful or they can be gross and tinny. Your thoughts are your music. Tune them to a fine pitch. Listen to your inner heart, for it knows the pitch. Do not settle for a mind full of non-melody. Expect perfection. Seek perfection. Let it rise from you, for you are perfection. It really is there within you. Do not believe for a minute that you need to live in discomfort. It is there within you. Seek and you shall find.

Can you see how this works? I will tell you more as we go on. Keep trying to understand and to do. You will find answers will come to you when you set your sights on a higher plane. Let it be OK to work with the feelings you have. Do not judge or condemn yourself. Only open yourself to your highest feeling. This will work best.

Today is a difficult day, I'm not sure why. The topic for today is learning to live within a frame of love and affection. This is not always easy to do and sometimes is the cause of much hardship.

You are hard to come into. Keep trying. Be still with your thoughts and I will be able to come in. That's better. You have much on your mind and it interferes with my joining with your thoughts. You are keeping strong feelings under wrap. I will help you with those today.

You must let yourself feel those feelings which you would rather not. I know there are concerns about your sons that you are trying to keep from consciousness, but this does not work very well because those concerns continue to brew inside. Better to let your thoughts be open and then you can work with them to raise their vibrations. You are worried about your sons and still experience guilt about them. Do not be afraid to let these feelings up into the light of day. They can then be purified with light and energy from the force of love. This will fill them with purity and will lighten their weight so they will not be such a load.

Feelings are a natural part of being human, but they must be seen for what they are. Feelings should not be allowed to direct or control your life. They are there as a signal or a warning about what is happening in your life. Heed them. They are there for you but do not wallow in them. Purify them. Fill them with love and light. See how they fashion themselves into something much easier to deal with.

25

You cannot control the lives of anyone else in the world. Know this and save yourself from the pain of guilt. You are the only one who can control your life, and the same is for others. This is not to say that you do not have influence over others. When you raise your vibrations, the energy that goes out from you settles over others within your sphere like a cloud and brings healthy vibrations of a higher order to them. Raise your vibrations and those around you will find their burdens lighter. Others of like vibration will come into your arena of life. This is the way to handle emotion. Do not repress your feelings; they only grow in power—a power that defies you and brings you pain. Just open yourself. Raise your eyes inward. Let in light, energy, love. It is all you need.

November 22, 1987
Beyond pain to spirit & joy

I am here. Open your heart for I will come in. That's it. Just open and I am there, my beloved. I know you have many questions even if you do not write them down. Let me guess what is most important. It is practical ways of using that which we have been talking about. Well, let me see. We can talk about how love can become a moving force in your life as we have been the past few days or perhaps we can talk of how life and death are related. But I think we will talk some more about human beings' pain and how that hinders them from progressing as fast in their lives as they would if they were not so hampered by it.

Pain comes from trying to create something in the world that is not there. The pain of shyness comes from trying to create a persona that goes out into society with confidence. The pain of withdrawal comes from trying to create a persona that is extroverted. The pain of trying to be macho comes from trying to create a persona that is aggressive. The pain of depression comes from being lost to the various forms of persona that one is not. That is a very difficult time for human beings when they are lost in the fog of depression, but sometimes it is necessary to feel all the depths in order to be able to rise from them with new clarity. All pain is not bad, you know.

Much growth takes place when one is trying to cope with pain. However, many people never seem to go beyond it to new learning. You must be careful not to let your own particular brand of self-inflicted pain become the ground of your being. The ground of being should be in your spirit where all is uplifting and happiness can flow. Do not let yourself focus on the negative forces going on either in you or out. The way to live with peace and harmony is to raise your eyes and see the magnificence around you, within you and all about you. Let yourself know you are a part of it all and, as such, are perfection—as much perfection as the flower in the garden or the fox in the field or the sun as it comes over the hill. You are part of this. Do not let yourself get mired in petty tribulations. Raise yourself from your petty views of yourself. You are greater than you imagine just because you are. Fill yourself with this knowledge. All else pales beside it. You do not have to be anything more for you truly are perfect. Do not strive so hard to be something else. Be yourself. It is the greatest there is. Feel your connection to all of life. Touch the heartstones of those around you. Do not ever despair because you are not good enough in one way or another. That is only from looking at life in a narrow way. Look out. Look up. Look around, not at the human-made world but at the world made by the Divine. You are part of that. Feel your spirit. You are spirit. There are no words greater.

Know that you have chosen your life for its teachings. Go gladly forth learning as much as you can from every situation. You have chosen them so that you may attain greater and greater purity. Do not become stymied by your life tasks. Explore. Conquer. Live out that which you have chosen. All life is teaching and opportunity to learn. This is the way out of pain for pain cannot exist in creative progress on your spiritual path. Look inward. There is all you need to know. Do not judge yourself by standards of the world. Judge yourself by standards of your own spirit. That will keep you on your path. Join in the force of love. Let it enter you to nourish and keep you. Rise up and allow the miracles of the world to sustain you. Do not settle for pain when joy exists in abundance.

Q: What about suicide?

A: You want to know about what happens if someone commits suicide. When persons kill themselves, there is an incompleteness to their lives, and many times they must relive those things again that they tried to escape from. Suicide is not the way out of any of life's problems because life's problems are there for growth and suicide ends all of that. Laws are against it in most societies and this reflects Divine Law. It does not mean that people will be punished or banished from heaven. Rather it is that they will find they were not able to complete their life plan and made little progress on their route to purity. There are many other ways to deal with life problems than suicide, but sometimes people cannot see that. If they would only learn to trust their inner self to help them see a spiritual way, it would be easier. The pain of depression and self-hate can be very detrimental to one's emotional stamina, and sometimes people just give up rather than seeking help. They are not to be condemned, merely pitied. There are those who would deny them God's love. This is nonsense. There is no way one can be denied the love of the universe. Give this message out.

What can you do to help people who may see no hope in going on? Help them to see that their situation is there for them to learn from, even though the learning may seem too hard. Ask them to open themselves to the spiritual voice within them which will help them find the way to health. Have them be careful to not let themselves fall into the trap of berating themselves for their lacks. This is not necessary at all. They should pay attention to the wonders of their self and not to the imperfections of the ego. Ego is second to the spiritual self and often gets bogged down in every day events and pains. Let go of those things that inhibit you. Choose life and love and joy. Do not choose despair. There is nothing but pain to be gained from that. There is something else. Do not be afraid to stand up to people who talk of killing themselves. Do not help them to stay within the confines of their prison of unhappiness. Let them know of what I have told you. Let them know that life is to be lived and all of living is for the highest end of their spirit. Do not let them bribe you with their silly ministrations, but listen to their heart and hear it. Speak to it. Give yourself to it. There is much help that you can give. Do not be afraid. You can share your knowledge with them and give them your love.

November 24, 1987
On love & life

Here I am. How are you tonight? There is a lot of interference but this should be OK now. How about talking about a little more about love and how to use it to make your life go easier? As I told you before, love is a force or an energy that exists in the world and is there for you to use and connect with. It is there for the taking. You don't need to wait for another to come and give it to you. You can connect with it directly and can use it to shower yourself with blessings. Love is a centering power that can help you to connect with the Divine which exists in all living things. It is the breath you share. You can breathe it in or out as you wish, constantly renewing your spirit with it. Do not be deceived by thinking that love is a feeling or an attribute that someone possesses or gives. Love is that which motivates you to bridge the gap between yourself and others.

Here I am. That's good. We are together again. Let us go on with yesterday's lesson about love. When we were interrupted, we were talking about love and how it isn't an emotion or an attitude but a force which is available to all for their use. When people love each other, this force is being utilized. Remember how you felt when you directed your focus to another and thought you were in love and how the whole world lit up? You were using the force of love. Remember what you did? You opened yourself, you focused and you thought positive thoughts about the other. It was as though they had no faults at all. Remember? It was impossible to feel negative about the other when you were standing in the force of love.

Too often, though, people lose that sense of power and start to view the other person in an altogether different way and think they have fallen out of love. On the other hand, there is much to be said about the ways that love is blocked by human beings. It is as though they have a TV scrambler built in which they turn on because they cannot stand the current of energy generated by love. So they block that current by turning away their focus on the positive, by closing themselves off, and by expecting that the other created the feelings of love within them. They start to look for reasons why they don't feel as loving and blame the other. They do not look at themselves and see how they are turning off the current themselves. They seem to think that love is something created by someone else, someone who has attributes that he or she can label *lovable*—certain traits that are acceptable. They do not see that love is not so directed. It does not have anything to do with your traits. You can be in the force of love no matter who surrounds you. To love is something more than liking a person's attributes or finding him or her sexually attractive. It is a much higher order act. To love is to be connected with the Source. It is to partake of the current of love and to be it, transmit it, receive it, transform and amplify it so that love goes out from you in generous doses, covering all that is within your sphere. Love is all positive. It feeds and nourishes all the life forms, including you. As you breathe it in and send it out, it nourishes you and everyone you touch. It is a wonderful force. It feels good to all who are covered by it. When you love, you are one with the Divine. Your breaths are the same. You must learn what the force of love feels like so you can experience it whenever you can.

Q: How do you distinguish love from attraction?

A: They are not the same at all. Attraction has to do with finding someone's appearance, traits, actions, etc., charming to us so that we want to move closer and be with that person. Your attention is taken by them. But love is another thing altogether, for you can love someone without being attracted to them. You may even be repelled by them. It goes far beyond that. It has to do with seeing the Divine in them, in knowing that they are you and you, them. That on another level, you are all part of one another and of the whole. Love is the energy that holds you together, the current that bonds you. Can you see how love is so much more than attraction. When you love, you see the wholeness, the perfectness, the Divinity of another, even though there also is the material person before you. You know that anything destructive done to that other is destructive to all, including you. So you see it is difficult to live in a destructive way when you are in the center of love. Reach out and open yourself to the truth of this. Open yourself to the force. Breathe it in and let it out. It is your life's breath, your connection, your knowledge of the Divinity of all creatures. Touch each other with it. Heal each other with it. It is there for you, make no mistake about it.

November 26, 1987
Connecting with other souls

Q: It was my brother Hank's birthday today. Can you tell me anything about him?

A: Listen to me and I will tell you what you want to know. Your brother Hank is not here now. He is incarnate again and is living on earth. I do not know much about him, but I could find out more if it is important to you. However, as I said before, just because someone is a relative on earth doesn't mean the same relationship exists forever. Connections go on as yours and mine, but it really is altogether different. You may or may not have more earthly relationships. Souls who have been together in other lives often revolve in the same life sphere, as you have noticed with some of your friends and loved ones. This makes learning easier as there are automatic connections as our souls recognize each other. This makes it easier for life plans to be felt and carried out. Often souls agree before birth to help each other with particular tasks or to be there for guidance and support. But that does not mean that you and your brother Hank would be together every time you incarnate. Does that answer your question?

I am here. How nice a day. I feel the energy of your group. How good for all of you and for the earth for you to be doing that. I will send you love and energy whenever you are together.

It is so important that you and others like you meet to amplify your energies. It is so important because it is that change in consciousness and awareness that groups such as yours can foster that will heal the demands of your earth. Without the love that is shared by you all, there would be much more destruction. The love energy that you are tapping into and amplifying will go out into the world increased by ten fold and raise the vibrations of the very air around you. Love energy is such a potent force that those you will come in contact with will find themselves changed even if they don't know the reason. So keep up the good work. Blessings on all of you.

Now let's talk of some other things. What shall it be for today? How about continuing to talk about finding your way in life that reflects your spirit's plan. This is not always so easy to do as you might have noticed. The way is not always clearly marked and many are so out of touch with their spirit that they do not have any sense that a path even exists. They go along, partaking of life, but not being aware of what is really going on. They never stop to examine their course or their ways, but just go blindly about, living until they die. Even some who are very religious are not at all connected to their spirit and think that going to church is all that's demanded of them. They are concerned with living according to laws that they think reflect God's plan, but too often these are merely laws that have been devised by those in power to control others.

The problem with following guidelines, such as those handed down by the church, is that there is very little looking inward where all knowledge lies. To look outward for God, whether in church, in heaven, or elsewhere misses the point. It is not that God is within you, but that you are within and that you are there with all else. There is no other. So the way to finding your path always comes from looking within. To look without is merely to be blinded by externals.

31

All knowledge comes from within. So to follow your path involves communication with your higher self about what is going on for you—to look on life and its problems, challenges, events, etc., as a means of conquering your plan for yourself on your journey to purity. Your life plan is known by your higher self and by your guide. You need to check out progress on your path to see what lessons can be learned at any particular junction. All of life is full of learning. No matter where you are, there you are and can learn that which you need to learn at the moment. Do not be afraid of life challenges. They are there for your spirit. Listen to the learnings. Some are hard and some are easy. There is much joy in life, and you should not think your path needs to be hard. You do not ever need to suffer to be in touch with your path. There are challenges to be sure, but you do not need to feel that life's ways need to be harsh.

To follow your path, to learn the lessons of this life can be done with joy and anticipation. When you focus on the *learnings* presented you instead of the problems, your way will seem much easier. Your path is not marked with tombstones of doom but with crosses of hope. Your life is very precious. It has much meaning that goes beyond the mundane. I know that people do not live at all times on the spiritual plane because indeed they are mortal and have egos and daily selves. But unless there is some understanding that more is going on, life is bleak indeed.

Life can be lived on many different levels at the same time. You can find pleasure in a walk in the park and be aware of the breath of the Divine in all the living things about you. You can have a sexual experience with your beloved and know that the love energy that you share is of the Divine. You can dance and sing and be merry and know that the connections you feel with your friends are on a spiritual as well as a physical plane. It is not that one needs to live a life of spiritual contemplation or isolation from the beauty and bounty of the world. No, not at all. It is more that while you participate on the worldly level, you recognize and are connected to higher levels of being. You are spirit and are also there in body. In no way does that negate the spirit you are. As a spiritual self, you have undertaken your present life for very particular reasons. You are learning lessons you have decided are necessary for you. Life will present these lessons over and over to you for your learning. There is no end to possibilities for your growth. So look about you each day and ask what life has brought to you for your learning. This may not always be what you want but, believe me, it is there for you. If you ask the right questions, it can help you in your growth.

I know the way is often foggy, but do not be afraid to step out and clarity will follow. Be of good cheer. Enjoy the wonders strewn along your path. You have chosen well. Do not deceive yourself into thinking you made a mistake or that you wish you were someone else. Be in touch with your own higher self to see what it is you need to learn in this particular life. That's all for today. We will write more another day.

Let's talk about some other things now. Let's talk about ways in which you can tell this information to others. Can you stop a minute and think a minute about what *you* want to talk of?

December 1, 1987
On time & death

Q: Is the time of our death set in advance?

A: Let me see if I can answer that in a way you can understand. Much of what happens in your life is predetermined to a certain extent. There is a plan and some guidelines that your life follows. Much is free will and happens because it happens. Some of that involves illness, death and other such events. However, there is a plan for your life and for its length that is known ahead of time. So, in some ways your death is predetermined and in other ways not.

I know this is a poor answer for you because you live with the concept of time and try to fit it into that framework. But here, time is something altogether different so the time of your death is not a specific point in time as you observe it to be. Your passing over is an event that happens at a point, not so much a point in time. I really cannot explain it very well to you until you understand more about how time is something altogether different than a line, as you observe it to be. In your plane, events follow one another, but in other planes, events may precede each other or happen simultaneously. Just to tease you a bit, your birth and death may happen at the same time. So then, of course, the time of your death would be predetermined. You see, you ask questions that cannot be answered given your view of things. There is much order in the universe and all of the major life events are in order. Births and deaths do not happen randomly, yet everything is not predetermined. I cannot tell

33

you more. If I can, I will talk to you again about time as you are able to hear it.

A message

There is still much resistance in you, but I can work with that so do not worry. I will give you a message for today. It is to take good care of yourself. You are prone to feeling a little sick and it would be good to watch your health for the next few days. Get plenty of rest and listen to your body. A hot bath would be a good idea. Follow through on your intuition. It can tell you what your body needs. Also be careful when driving for a few days. You will be fine but keep an eye out for other drivers. Stay calm and alert. That's all for today.

December 2, 1987
**Communication
& connection**

Today is a beautiful day in your heart. I congratulate you on your learning and loving. You are learning very well indeed. Today let's talk some more about living in the world where there is so much pain and strife.

When you look around, it seems the world has gone mad. There is so much materialism, greed, fear, killing and other ways that people hurt other human beings and themselves. It seems that so many are so far away from their Godselves as to have no connection at all. How is it that all this has come to pass, where humanity stands on the brink of its own extinction? The whole race could be killed off with the flick of a button. Could this be the same breed of persons who also have such a capacity to love and care for each other. I know that is a dilemma for many to figure out. The farther humanity gets from the Godself, from knowing that each one is spirit and belongs to creation with all the other creatures of the universe, the farther each gets from knowing the true messages of the soul.

*It is the time
for choosing*

There has been much emphasis in the last few years on physical science and the "real," but this has resulted in a turning away from intuition and knowledge of the unseen. Belief has suffered, for if everything has to be seen, then the unseeable is denied. The universe is mostly unseeable by mortals; so that means that the wholeness and majesty of the unseen universe is missed completely. When they look only to the earthly world for their pleasures and meaning, then all is lost of the real meaning. The answers are not in the practical world of mortals. Connections can be made through the natural world; however, it is necessary to be in a state of connection and communion to do so. Much has been lost in the last few decades due to the emphasis on the worldly. If this had been allowed to go on, there would have been no hope for humanity. But fortunately, this is not the case. The fact that many, many people are involved in changing their consciousness speaks well for the hope of their survival.

Many are hearing our messages and are responding with love and laughter. There is much rejoicing as people join together to share in the pleasure of opening to the Divinity shared by all. There still are multitudes who have not even a glimpse of this as yet, but every day many more people are opened to the wonders of life. They are taken by the hand of those who see and are gently led into the light. Not everyone follows. Many skeptics still scoff at the way. But in time this number will get smaller and smaller until they fade into nothingness. Then will come much rejoicing. The world will be a far different place than you know it now. There will be much love and peace, and people will have much more access to the truths of their soul. Do not be afraid to get on the band wagon. Open your hearts to the truth of my words. They will not harm you. It is time to choose for yourself which side you will be on: the growing multitudes who will follow the light of their soul or those who will choose the darkness of the way unlit by Divine Light. The way of the world is dark when the power of Divine Light is shut out. You only have to open your heart, and you will join with all of us in knowing God. Your spirit knows the way. Don't be afraid to listen and to follow. The world is changing rapidly. You can choose to be part of the change or you can hold back and be left behind in the dark. It is time for choosing. You do not have much more time.

There are changes coming in the mass thought that are very positive and powerful. Each time you choose light and love, your thoughts are added to this stock pile of wisdom. The mass thought is changing. You can sense it if you try. Do not think that you are too little or not smart enough or too shy, or whatever, to add your input into the mass thought. You count. You can influence everyone within your sphere; but also, every positive thought becomes one with all the other positive thoughts such that they will eventually cover the negativity rampant in this world.

Love one another. Raise your vibrations to their highest levels.   A message
Listen for your spirit as it talks to you. Listen to your guides. We

are speaking loudly and clearly to you. Do not be afraid. We are here to help you. Be brave. Take the step inward to your soul. This is the message to be given out. Bye, my dear, for today.

Today is a lovely day, don't you think? I know you love to bask in the sunshine. How nice that is, don't you think, and a true miracle too. What shall we talk of. You have many questions simmering in your mind. Let's see what we can cook up. The way to live with joy is one that you and others would like to know about.

Joy is different from peace or contentment. It is the ultimate of good feelings and is a much higher level vibration than contentment, though contentment is also a very nice state to be in. Joy is something that makes your heart sing and your senses vibrate with all creation. However, this is not a state many people achieve, or if they do, it is fleeting. Many people settle for an absence of misery and call that happiness. But to experience all-out joy when your very body sings with a chorus of hallelujahs is very rare indeed. This is achievable, but not by looking for worldly pleasures or gifts or more possessions. They may bring fleeting feelings of happiness, but it is not what I am talking about.

Joy resides in the soul. It reaches up and out of the very center of your being, and it comes when you are truly connected to the Source through your own soul connection. When you feel oneness with everyone and everything in the universe, then you know joy. It springs unbidden whenever you connect deeply— be that with a friend, a loved one, a pet, a sunset, or any of the myriad forms of life and non-life on your planet and beyond. That is where joy is. It rises out of peace and contentment and fills your heart with the purest emotion imaginable. The way to joy is to live in such a way that you maximize your connections through love, laughter, meditation, prayer—all the ways you can commune with your soul. When you have mastered the art of communion and connection, then joy will be there with you always. A glance at the sunset, a glimpse of love in someone's eye, a view of panoramic nature, a baby born, a flight of a bird, the opening of a flower—all these will remind you of your oneness and will bring joy to your heart.

It's so easy. You need to practice a bit, but it's very easy. Let it come to you. Open your eyes and ears and heart. Look around. Look in. Look up. See with your inner eyes. Hear with your soul's ears and see. It is there for you. Do not be afraid to feel joy. It is a wonderful high—from on high. That's all for now.

Hello, my dear. We are together again. That is good. What do you want to know today? I can see that you have many questions as usual. You want to know about how life began and about the outcome of all this writing on the lives of those around you.

As to when and how life began, that is very complex. Life began first as a thought or, perhaps, a dream in the consciousness of the Divine. You see, there was a time when life per se did not exist. The universe was barren for many eons of time and was filled with inanimate forms. When life was first *dreamed*, then the possibility of life existed, just as now nothing can exist without there being thought forms about it. So life came first into being as a thought and from the thought came form. This is a very difficult concept to communicate given your concepts and words; but if you can imagine that the saying, "The idea is parent to the act," is a valid one, then that is how it is. In the beginning, the thought was rather simple and so life forms were rather simple. The evolution of life, you see, was not a simple one at all. There has been much experimentation and growth of the idea through, what you call, millions and billions of years. There first were very simple life forms, more simple than you even know. Those have been lost as they left no trace and do not exist now in any other form on your earth. From these very simple forms, more complex forms were dreamed and new thought forms came into being. This process continued for all time and still continues, though now the changes are not so much on the cellular level as they were then, but they are centered on evolution of consciousness and other forms of the non-physical. However, back to the creation of life. I cannot tell you the exact procedure for the first creation of life because that is not something you should know. But just know that it is a creation of the Divine and continues to be. Life is a very miraculous thought, isn't it. I love to view the very many forms it visits. I never get tired of viewing life in action.

But back to what I was saying. As life forms proliferated, more and more ideas occurred. You know how that is for you, one idea leads to another. Many ideas and dreams came to the

Divine as she created the thousands of life forms. You see, they all grew out of a very simple idea. If you look through the various kinds of animals, plants, fish, or other life forms, you will always see the same prevailing principles, though there certainly are many variations. Everything fits together, nothing is random. You see that, don't you? Humanity is only one piece of creation, not necessarily the highest, you know, and shares in consciousness with many other life forms. Human beings just do not know that. There will be many evolutionary changes as time passes, but these are not so rapid as to be noticed by the unobservant. Listen to me when I tell you this, as it is not something you can see with your eyes.

There is much that will happen to those around you from reading these words. There will be an increase in peace and harmony. There will be a stillness of pain and there will be an increase in ability to send and receive love. All this and more. Feel free to share this with others as the way presents itself. You need not stand on a soap box or a mountain top. Simply share as seems right to you.

December 6, 1987
You are a magnificently functioning human being

Relax a little more. You feel very tight to me. Take a couple more deep breaths. That's better now. Keep relaxing. Let your body sink into the chair and just let go of the tension of your body. Feel your heartbeat. Know that your heart is one with your soul. Feel your breath. Know you share your breath with all other creatures of the universe. Count your breaths and see how equally they flow. You are a magnificently functioning human being with all of your parts working perfectly together. There are many things occurring inside you right now that keep you balanced and alive. Feel all of that. Focus on your aliveness, your perfectness of functioning. Feel the blood coursing through your veins and arteries. See all the organs of your body nourished by your life blood. Be aware of your immune system, protecting and taking care of your body. Be aware of your digestive system, refining and processing the food for your growth and maintenance. Feel your awe at this wonderful body you have been given at this time. Do not be afraid of its imperfections. These pale next to the miracle of its perfection. Do not judge it by external standards but care for it from the bottom of your heart. This body was given to you so that you might experience the world with your senses. It is the vehicle of your soul and carries you on your soul's journey. It is also the vehicle of your ego and so you can use yourself to enjoy the world.

How are you tonight? Tonight I will talk to you about something very important; that is, how to live with others who would hurt you, anger you or otherwise cause you distress. It is not possible to live in such a way so as to not have others around you who do things that are upsetting unless you minimize all contact with human beings. Human nature being what it is at this time, many events will occur which set off emotional reactions within. The way to handle this, when it happens, is not to explode with anger or reduce yourself to tears or any of the many ways that you have to discharge the energy generated by the cognitive perception of their acts. It is not the acts themselves that are the problem but your cognitive perception of the event. When energy is generated emotionally, often you feel the need to do something to discharge that energy and, often, at the expense of a love or friendship. There are other ways to handle this energy so that you do not do damage to yourself or others.

First, you must not think of this energy as bad in any way. It is not really negative energy so much as it is just a buildup of ions that need release. The way to release it without damage is to do one of several things that may be done singly or in conjunction with each other. One is exercise. The physical use of the body will release the pent-up energy and return the body to a state of homeostasis. The second is to discuss the event with a friend, counselor or listener. Putting ideas into words will help to release the energy into the air, in addition to sometimes getting insights on how to handle things. The third is to talk with the offending person directly without letting your emotions get out of line.

Sometimes it is helpful to have first used some other method to release the majority of your emotion. You also can know that you can change your perceptions of the event, knowing that your interpretation is just that. It may have very little to do with the actual event. You can be in charge of your mind such that you can direct it to obey your higher perceptions of things. When you look above the everyday and view the event as happening also on a higher level, then perhaps your view will change. If you see behind the scenes of the others' masks, then perhaps you will find yourself responding with understanding rather than anger. All these are things you can do to help in dealing with upsetting events.

(Your thoughts keep interfering. Let's wait until you are more settled.)

December 8, 1987
Emotional pain &
" **healing** "

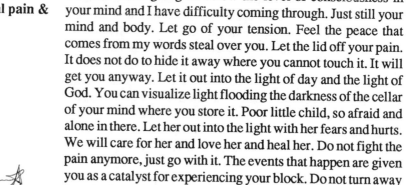

There is much going on below the level of consciousness in your mind and I have difficulty coming through. Just still your mind and body. Let go of your tension. Feel the peace that comes from my words steal over you. Let the lid off your pain. It does not do to hide it away where you cannot touch it. It will get you anyway. Let it out into the light of day and the light of God. You can visualize light flooding the darkness of the cellar of your mind where you store it. Poor little child, so afraid and alone in there. Let her out into the light with her fears and hurts. We will care for her and love her and heal her. Do not fight the pain anymore, just go with it. The events that happen are given you as a catalyst for experiencing your block. Do not turn away from it. Let it be. Touch it. It's OK.

Now the way to help heal it is this. Feel it in all the parts of your body and mind. Let it rise to the surface. Do not block it. Let it come to you in images, sensation, thoughts, whatever form it takes. Focus your attention on each one, giving it credence and validation. Fill each with light as you focus on it. Let the light illuminate and heal. Let yourself experience the feelings as the light enters. You may feel an instantaneous release, or the release may only be very small. All this is all right. Do not hurry things or feel pressure for it to be different than it is. Do this each time you feel pain. Let the guiding light help you to heal. If memories come, let them be. Use them to release more and more of your block. The pain cannot hurt you when it is bonded to light. Take very good care of yourself, my dear. You are much loved.

December 9, 1987
Increasing
consciousness

That's good. Now I am here. Today is a good day for us to talk. Just be still and I will tell you some more things you want to know. When you want to ask me questions, you can just think about them and I will hear them telepathically. You do not have to write them down but you can do so if it helps you to remember.

What shall we talk of today? You want to know more about consciousness and also why people are so out of touch with their higher selves. They are out of touch with their higher selves because there is very little teaching that is given out on how to do it. You are all so much driven by your brain that you have little use for the finer systems of your mind. If you function solely from your brain, you are limited to the learnings of your earthly life. You live on a very single-minded plane with the ego in charge. But if you are in touch with the complexities generated by your mind, then you have access to learning and information that are not earthbound. But where do you learn that?

Now there is more being done, but in general, children are taught to disregard the truths they hear rather than to listen to them. It is very hard to stay tuned in on your earth. This is changing as your consciousness changes. I told you that, at this time, the most evolutionary change is happening on the level of consciousness. Already, if you were to go back a decade or two, you would see change. The change in consciousness will be one in which it will be much easier for people to tune into their higher selves and guides, and as that happens, everything will get much easier. It is only on the level of the ego that life is hard because ego sees everything so narrowly. When ego directs the ship, the way is rocky indeed because there is not enough connection with Divine Knowledge. There are many rocks in the way in the form of life stresses, and the ego trips over them all without being able to see around them. When people see from a different perspective, those rocks are merely pebbles.

There will be a spreading of information on controlling the brain and opening up to the wider dimensions of mass mind. You see how the people you share our writings with are entranced as they recognize the truth of our words. That's because they already know them but have forgotten. There is much happiness as you would feel meeting an old friend. That is why people are so excited to read our work.

The change in consciousness is one that is spreading as those who know how to view things from a different perspective, teach and lead others to do the same. Everyone is so eager for the change that it is not hard to find people brave enough to take a chance. Once consciousness changes and becomes viable enough for world views that are expanded, then the way all communications takes place will change. Many acts that are now commonplace will not find any takers as they will be seen in cosmic light. You see there are many ways of viewing a situation, but only when cosmic grounds are included is there merging of the self and spirit. Where only ego lies, there is much difficulty. When spirit and ego merge, there is greatness. You have seen many examples of people who have achieved this, from Jesus to Gandhi, but until now there was little attempt to teach how to achieve this. It was thought that these highly developed people were just special. But now you know that it is possible for anyone to get in touch with a higher self and also to be in touch with guides such as you are. It is not mysterious. Anyone can do it given the right technique and frame of mind.

There is information now that allows anyone who wants to, to learn to talk with us. Tell them not to be afraid to try. It will brighten their life, make it easier, and lighten the burdens they carry because of their current blindness. Do not be afraid to encourage people to try their hand at it.

A meditation

Remember what to do: just relax, focus your attention and still your mind. Breathe deeply six times or more until you feel your senses quieting and your body relaxing. You must focus and keep thoughts from your mind. Then ask for your guide to come in to you. You can surround yourself with protective light if you want. Be sure to ask for your highest guide, for then you will not have to worry about the information you get. If you do get lower forms of spirit, then simply ask for your highest guide. We are waiting for you.

Everyone has a guide

Q: Does everyone have a guide?

A: Yes, everyone has a guide, always had and always will. We often have impact and input, depending on the openness of our person. We often bring things to you or direct your thoughts toward your path. We are there for you to commune with, and sometimes we keep you safe from harm, though that is not our main function. Our main function is to help you direct your life in such a way that you can learn the things you decided you wanted to learn in this life. We try to help you see your path and sometimes arrange things so that events are planned for you to learn those important learnings. We are busy indeed. But this, of course, is not all we do, so do not think you overburden us. It is a joy to work with you there when we can.

Q: What do you do otherwise?

A: Oh, many things. We are always learning more and more. As individuals find new information, that is analyzed and interpreted here. There is much to be kept track of, you know. There is so much happening all over the universe that many of us are involved merely with keeping track of it all. A tremendous amount of information is generated at any second and this must all be recorded, analyzed, interpreted and so on. So you see, there is no harp playing here. But that is only one small part of what is happening on other planes. It is as complex as all the things that happen on your plane—far too many to chronicle here. But be assured there is no boredom here. That's all for today.

Let's talk today of some things you have been wondering about. That is, how to live with people who are destructive to themselves or others. This is a touchy subject as this includes much of the human race. The numbers go far beyond criminals or mentally ill people when you count those who live life in unhappy ways and those who hurt themselves with their thoughts or others with their acts. You know many people like that. It is not that they want to or even mean to, but they do not seem to know any better. Some, of course, are more distressed than others. You see many of these in your work and do not know how to help them feel better about themselves or about their place in the world. You see how far off the track they are, but you do not know how to get them on their track again. This is not your job, you know. Everyone's path is the path that they journey, and while others can provide guidance or illumination, only the person can choose when and how each will travel the path.

December 10, 1987
Helping negative people

But back to your basic question. What should one do when confronted with such people? Number one, always see them as spiritual beings who are here on earth. To do this is to get you out of a framework of judgment, guilt, control or any of the other ways we feel when we think we should change another. When you see that they do exist as independent souls with their own way to tread, then you will be able to allow them much more freedom and will not feel responsible. But that is not all that you can do; it is possible, of course, that you are part of that person's path and so it is important to check out your connections.

Sometimes connections are apparent at first glance and sometimes it may take a bit of time. See what happens when you open to the other. Is there connection? Do your words help? Does the other feel a greater sense of self and take your energy in? All these can help you know what to do next. If the connection is weak, if you feel drained or feel other negative energy, then you know that you are not going to be productive by imposing yourself on the other. However, if you feel positive energy flowing between you, then go on with your interactions. You never need to take in negative energies of another. You can turn away or you can send up a shield of positive love energy from yourself. There is no reason to provide environments for yourself that do not improve your lot in life. There is no reason to stay in the same room even with someone who does not interact with you with a positive energy exchange.

But then there are the people you work with who are so stuck in the mire of negativity that they exude it from their pores and are not ready to change no matter what the situation. They are often into blaming others for their plight and show no inclination to step out with any control over their life. There is little you can do in those cases except for offering the services of your agency. You can send them positive energy, but do not be too surprised if it bounces off of the negativity they offer. Do not think that you need to offer more. You do not have the capacity to send them off on their path to enlightenment. That is for them to do. They will follow their own way at their own pace and you cannot affect that. Put your energies toward those who are open to you. Let them feel the force of your light and feel their response. When light and energy flow between you, you will know it. That doesn't mean that only positive feelings will always flow. You can interact positively with someone who is very angry or depressed or experiencing other emotions you call negative.

I only talk about the free flow of positive interacting energy. You know what this feels like. I know you would like to enlighten all your clients, especially the women. But this is their track in life to follow. All you can do is provide information. If the person is ready for it, she will hear it. Otherwise it will fall on deaf ears. You are a good counselor and care for your clients, but you are not God, you know. Let them be and you will feel much easier. I know you are worried that you should do more for a couple of them and you feel afraid for them. Just keep sending loving energy, accepting them for who they are and providing that which you can, but leave the larger issues to them and their guides.

Everything is very difficult today. It's getting better. Just be open and then I will align our energies so we can talk. You have much on your mind. You need to meditate and let it come up to your consciousness.

You are somewhat reluctant after your session with Dean (a psychic) yesterday, fearing what all this means and where it will lead you. Believe me when I say it will only take you where you want to go. There is no "should" or forcing to any of this. Just allow yourself to experience your pleasure in this writing and follow your intuition. It will not take you into dark places or go at a speed too fast to follow. It is natural to feel doubts and fears. That is not a problem if you do not listen to them so much that you stop what you are doing. You hear about the changes that are coming to you and wonder how you will do it all. Remember you are changing and everything that happens will fit with you wherever you are. So be of good heart. Keep writing everyday and all will come clearer to you.

You want to know if you should start a group or session to read these writings. That is a good idea. You can begin by asking people you know and see what that brings. As you get known, others will come more and more. It is important to share these words, and that is a good way to do it. If you make them available, those who want to hear will find out and will find their way to your door. Don't be afraid to risk. I know you like guarantees, but just take a risk and I will be with you.

On the universe & looking inward

What else shall we speak of? The answers to many of your questions are difficult at this time, but I will see what I can do to answer you. You have been reading about the universe and are very awed because of the sheer magnitude of it. I assure you only a little is known. It is more awesome than your scientists know. They know so little as to fit it in a tea cup or maybe a thimble. They are awed by distances. That is such a minor fact, but then they really don't have the means to find out more so they focus on what they know. There are many, many fascinating things happening in the universe all the time but given your current restrictions of time and space, they are not available to you. Do not fear, all will be revealed in due time, though not on your earth.

I do not plan on telling you more as it is best for you merely to enjoy the beauty of the stars and moon and sun and not trouble with questions that will only lead to more questions. It is not as necessary for you to understand the universe as it is for you to understand and know your Godself. That is much easier than building a telescope large enough to poke into the mysterious universe. That will only boggle your mind and not enlighten you. It is important to focus on that which you can do to enlighten and illuminate yourself.

The way to do that is clear and available. As I mentioned before, meditation, prayer, psychic readings, all of these and more will help you to look inward and connect with the soul there. You are always attached to the All There Is through your soul and can tap into the wisdom of the ages. You see, when you get your information from the Source instead of from the newspapers, etc., then you know that the information you get will lead you forward on your path. When you listen only with your ears and see only with your eyes, then it is difficult to find your way as you don't have a map of where you are going. You can't find your way if you don't know where you are going, you know, and will remain lost no matter which direction you go.

On atrocities &
the Holocaust

You also want to know about how it is that some human beings can commit atrocities such as the killing of millions of people by the Nazis, and you wonder why God doesn't stop it from happening. It's hard for you to believe that all can be part of somebody's path. That is true, as I told you, there is no evil nor evil paths. Sad, but there are persons who are so out of touch with their Godselves that they do indeed appear to be evil incarnate and do not seem to be at all in touch with higher values. This is hard to understand but, you see, men and women are incarnate. Each is flesh. Each is directed by the brain and ego. Each is affected by life happenings and may be very out of touch with her or his mission. It would not do for God to intervene, even if that were possible, as each needs to learn and to evolve. Perhaps all the atrocities look as though they were terrible events to happen, but look at the learnings and knowledge that have occurred because of them. This doesn't mean they were put there for that purpose. Humanity does have free will and so things happen because they do. But if you think about the whole of humankind learning from the total stresses of life as do individuals, you see that something like the Holocaust makes the pace of learning accelerate. It is never far from consciousness now. There is an awareness of what can be done—everyone recognized the seed of it within, and so the mass mind now carries information it once did not possess. Do not think long on the individual pain, as that is long ago alleviated. Focus instead on the learning from that time because that is what is most important. It was a replay of the worst of the inhumanity of the human species which turned against itself, and because of the visibility given it, has influenced the course of moral development. Does that answer your question?

Here I am. You are very interested in anything I have to tell you tonight. That's good.

I will tell you about living in a way that will help you to see your path more clearly. That is very important for people to know because it will help them to come alive and to be healthy in all aspects of their life. It is important to remember that life can be easy when you are not caught in the trap of ego's demands and views of things. Ego is always trying to figure things out on a practical level and often misses the mark by so much as hardly to be in the ball park. Life can get to be pretty tedious when it's filled with misfortune, hurts, pain and other things that can befall human beings. So much of the pain that is experienced comes from living too much on the ego level. When one can see more broadly or widely, there is a better chance of living in a pain free way. As I told you before, pain often comes from the perceptions of the ego about what is happening. Yet perception doesn't count for all pain. There are interpretations that hinder growth rather than augment it.

In a world that is so sadly lacking in love, there are many avenues where pain is rampant. But then, you see, there is a way even then of being that allows for growth, understanding and learning to occur. When you can work out of your spirit, then it all gets much easier, for you do not get bogged down in petty ways. There is much to be said about how to do this.

If you look inward for answers, they usually will come to you. It is important to provide enough time for yourself so that you can spend it listening to your inner self. If you do not, then all you have to rely on are the external sounds and noises. It is important to set time aside to meditate, to write, to draw, or do other forms of communion with yourself. This should be done every day if possible. The more you do it, the easier it will become. You can ask specific questions about what is happening in your external life that you want answers for. Listen and wait for the answer to percolate up. Do not jump at answers ego provides, but listen carefully for the small, still voice of your soul. Do this and answers will come to you, I promise. Every person needs time for this. It is worth getting up early for. If you do not find time, then you will often feel lost and lonely and will not know what to do. When you rely on ego to give you answers, times will be hard as there is not the information that has to do with the path you are on. The answers will come to you, if you but try. Do not think you don't have time or are too busy. You have no time for many of the things you do, but you don't seem to know that. There is nothing more important than your spiritual path. Nothing external can match the importance of connection with your soul. Give time to yourself. It will be a great gift.

December 16, 1987
Follow your quest

You are very filled with negative energy which would be good to discharge. Now just relax and I will see what I can do. Just breathe deeply and let all your body relax. Feel the energy release. If you can, let go more and more. Let your breath in and out. (I felt an energy surge.)

You are feeling lost and lonely tonight because you are feeling some things that are more or less troublesome to you. As you grow from these writings, your inner conflicts are touched. You really want to hide away from this sometimes and live unaware. But, you know, that is not where you really want to be at this time. Come stay with me and I will teach you many lessons that will help you to live happier and healthier and, in addition, will help others to do the same. I will not leave you alone and undefended. It's OK to leave some things behind and to follow your quest. Do not be afraid to change. To hold on only makes it feel harder. Look ahead and bravely set out on your journey. I am here with you. There is no set goal, nothing you have to accomplish, no laws about what you must do. Simply start out on your quest. Each step will take you one step closer—it matters not whether you reach someplace or not, but merely that you are journeying on your quest to find your path. It is always there in front of you. Simply start out. Do not judge your steps. They are all in the right direction. Do not be afraid of turns or crossroads. They are there for you to evaluate your position and to choose your way anew. It is all there before you. Just make sure that your journey is indeed a spiritual one and not merely worldly, for you are spirit and that is the single most important thing about you. To say, "I am spirit," says it all. Your journey may be far or near; it matters not. The most important fact to remember is that it is the journey and not the goal that matters.

Here I am. That's good—we are together again. Let's talk today about some things that have been troubling you. One is about levels of spirit.

As I told you, there are not *levels* of spirit, but then again I said that you should ask for highest guides. There is no real contradiction, only in expression. All spirit is at the same high level of value. There is no class system among spirit. However there are indeed levels of learning among the various manifestations of spirit in individual form. Some forms have incarnated many times, have studied much here and there, and have integrated their teachings into a higher level system and are more evolved. Others have not followed the same course and are still struggling with very basic issues. Some have not elected to learn as much as others, and some have had the bad experience of spending lifetimes in such a way that they never found their path and so did not progress on their road to purity. You see this at work on your plane as some people seem to know so much more about higher values than others. These values seem to be a part of the fabric of their lives, whereas others cannot grasp the concepts at all. There are many who struggle to catch a glimpse of what purity is all about. So you see, if you were to contact one of those less learned, then the information you got would be less useful to you.

Generally speaking, those who themselves are highly evolved souls have guides who are also highly evolved. Thus, you see, the information you get from your guide helps you to evolve further if you but listen. The space here is filled with spirits of all kinds, many of whom are studying, many of whom are planning their next earth life and lesson, and many who are still in infancy stages of growth. All is as it should be so no one is at sea. Some new souls need time to become acclimated to this plane and so are just in a state of limbo or rest as they shed their earth selves and take up where they left off. They will soon integrate the learnings of their life, fitting them in their overall plan, and then will see what they set as new goals for themselves. There is much activity here and it is all geared toward higher learnings. But do not think too much of this as, other than relieving your mind about the afterlife, it has little value for you. There is no way I really can describe it to you so I will not try too hard. Just know that all is in order and follows Divine Plan as written.

Living spiritually Let me tell you some more about finding a way to live spiritually as well as on the physical level. As I told you, to combine ego and soul, mind and brain, is a way of rising to your ultimate self. Only ego is a poor substitute. Spirit and ego together can help you to experience the world in a playful, wonderful way so that your way is easy and safe. Spirit adds a dimension to life that elevates it from the mundane to something very exciting. You see things that are totally missed when you are wrapped up only in the physical realities. Spirit frees you from the constraints of time and space and lets you fly in a space that is unencumbered by hard cold facts.

How to do this is what you want to know. First you must acknowledge with all your being that you are indeed spirit and that you live at present in a body which has a brain and other physical attributes. That is the first step. Until you believe this with your whole being, it is very difficult for you to be in touch with your Godself. Only that which can be thought has any reality for you. Second is for you to know that it is possible for you, as a person, to be able to communicate with your spirit self. Again, the belief makes it possible. Third, you have to listen. As I told you before, meditation is very important. But there are other ways: prayer, art, music, communing with nature, listening to the small voice within you, listening to your intuition, reading books, articles, etc., that come to you unbidden and that seem to answer your life questions, attuning yourself to ways in which life seems to open for you, answers which come to you, people who seem to respond to your cries. All these are evidence of communication with your higher self. There are many ways and when you are in tune, they will stand out for you.

One mark of communion with your higher self is the ease you feel. Life opens for you and the struggles seem lighter. When you are closed from communion, then life seems difficult indeed. But you ask, how does ego figure in this. What is the connection that leads to greatness? It is that your ego is the go-between between the world of spirit and the physical world. It is of the flesh and so is the vehicle of interaction. The ego is the stuff of change and can carry out the learnings for that particular journey of the soul. Ego has all the senses of the body at its command: the ability to see, to hear, to talk, to communicate and to act in the world. Without ego and its body there would be no mortal person. You see, ego by itself, when it is not informed by spirit, gets very bogged down in the physical world. This has happened in your world now. There is so much emphasis on the physical that spiritual values are hard to find. The animals and plants of the world are in danger because your people have lost the sense of connectedness on the spiritual level. You believe that somehow your conscious mind, or what usually is defined as a "higher brain," is somehow so special as to set you above all the other life forms. That is not your true purpose—to be above and to control all other life forms. Many of you know that, but sadly, at this time, you are in the minority.

Humanity as a species has a part in an overall plan and their brain developed as part of that plan; but believe me, it does not put people above the other creatures of life. Humanity must see that all is interconnected with each life form being part of the whole. This information will not come to them until there is an opening to belief which incorporates the idea of spirit as the moving force in this life. Do not be afraid to open yourself to this knowledge. It does not make you less special, but more so. To be part of the Divine Plan is much more than to be a mere cog in a fabricated world. Do not be misled by the things that can be produced or the money that can be made by any of the workings of modern day life. These can only provide food for the ego. There is so much more to be had. So much has been lost, but the time is soon when it will be regained. Keep heart, oh my people, for the time is coming when consciousness will become elevated in such a way that all will perceive from new eyes and will hear with new ears. The acts that will follow will bring peace and contentment to the world. You will know yourself in all the other life forms and will know your oneness. Love as a force will fill the very air about you.

How are you, my dear? It is a lovely day today for you. You will be filled with pleasure at the wonderful out-of-doors. The snow will fall before you and fill you with delight at its beauty. The lake will fill you with awe at its tremendousness. The birds will fill you with glee as they dive under water. Isn't it wonderful to have all that for your senses to enjoy? It is all there for you to

December 19, 1987
Sharing group energy

51

pleasure in. It is for you, in you and is you. You are all part of the whole. Each is a beautiful extension of the other. None is separate and apart from the wonder of creation. It all is the one whole. Now let us talk of some other things before you go out into a communion with your fellow selves.

Let us talk some more about your group and what you can do together. It is important to share energy with each other. Make sure there is a means to share in the force of love and to amplify it. Any of the exercises where you hold hands and meditate, chant, visualize or otherwise share common thoughts will amplify the love energy. You can do the exercise I gave you when we first started writing. I think you know much on how to lead this group. You should continue to do so for awhile. It is OK for others to take part but, at this time, it would be best for you and Julie to lead as you have the intent and the resources and you also have my writings.

You want to know some questions to ask after the meditation. Some you can use are these:
> Who am I above my physical self?
> What is my plan here on earth?
> How can I see my path?
> What factors are happening in my life right now that
> are part of my spiritual path?
> Who else in my life is journeying with me on my path?
> What place do my relationships have on my path?
> What can I do to increase my knowledge of my path?
> Who is a mentor for me that can give me information
> I need?
> What further information do I need to satisfy my brain that
> I can go ahead with my spiritual quest?

All these and more in the same vein will help others to see where they are going in their lives. You can also ask about what events in their lives have presented challenges as a means of gaining spiritual or worldly growth. Remember some of the things we have talked about, and they will present answers to your question or questions to your answers.

I also want to talk to you some more about love and how it can affect your daily life. I suggest that you continue to do the exercise I gave you. The acting out of the force of love when in a relationship with another can be a very enlightening experience. This is very different than being in love or expressing need or

You share a common spiritual connection

52

dependency. It goes far beyond that. First it takes into account that though you are separate, you share a common spiritual connection. So there needs to be both a sense of you as separate human beings and of joined spirit. Anything you do to and for the other is also done to and for you. This is just the foundation of belief you should carry. In the everyday living, it becomes necessary to act this belief out and that sometimes is where the difficulty lies.

We need to finish at another time. You are getting very tired. Write again at another time.

You are OK now. Just relax and keep your thoughts still. I will do the rest. Let's talk some more of what we started the other day.

December 21, 1987
Strengthening the force of love

We were writing about living a daily life of love and how sometimes that is difficult given the needs and demands of the ego. You so often are in a reactive state rather than an active one that it is very hard to be in the force of love. There are few times in some peoples' days when they are rooted in the present and in the presence of love. So let us see if I can help you to know what to do to help you maximize the force and minimize the barriers.

First you must begin to know the difference in how it feels to be reactive or active. You have to pay attention to yourself and come to know what it feels like to be in the different states. If you do not, you probably will continue to be caught in your propensity to react. When you have learned the difference in how you feel, act and emote when you are in the different states, you can go on to the next step, which is to catch yourself in the reactive state and transform it into an active state of love. This is not so easy to do, I know, but there are various means to help you do this. Remember how to stop and take some time to look at the situation from as high a perspective as you can. Remember that you and the other share common spirit and so your actions and the other's co-mingle. Each receives part and parcel of whatever is given off. You cannot give off negativity without giving it to yourself, and you also cannot give off light and love without giving that to yourself.

It will help you to know this when you think you will feel better if you can just get even or let your hair down and be angry. It is not useful to be angry at another as it just overflows on everyone around. It is much more helpful to use that generated energy to focus on yourself and see what is happening within. How are you hurting yourself? How are you rejecting yourself? How are you putting yourself down? No one can inject that into you if you don't already believe it or think that somehow you have it coming. When you are clear with yourself, then very little that another does will cause you distress.

You can love another for allowing you to grow in strength and understanding of yourself. When you are courageous enough to spend time looking at yourself, then you will find life being easier for you. This does not mean that you should take on blame or even responsibility for another's actions. It is only by taking a non-reactive stance that you can see what the other triggers in you, for it is all there. You will not take abuse unless you have reason to abuse yourself. You will not take rejection unless you have reason to reject yourself. This is a natural law, for you call to yourself that which exists in your thoughts. That is why when people grow and change, they often find themselves changing the other people in their lives, leaving some behind and seeking new friends and mates. Do not think that this means you will have to live with others who cause you pain, for it is indeed true that if you change yourself and you no longer invite in the others' abuse, you will often find that they must change. I know this is difficult to understand as you think that it should be up to the other to change, but that is asking too much; for as long as you are open to this thought, nothing will change.

What does this have to do with love? Until you are able to do this, you will continue to see love as something that is given out for good behavior. When you understand what I have told you, then you will be able to use the force of love to create a bridge between you and the other or, in some cases, a shield which protects you from offered negativity. You see, when you can be active and use the force of love, you are invincible. But that will take time. When you give up the pleasure of the reactive mind and seek the greater pleasure of self-growth, then you will slowly come to see how it is to live in a world governed by love. You can produce love even in the face of abuse. This does not mean you have to take abuse. But you can use the force of love energy to protect yourself. You must think about how this is. The thinking will help you to separate out the various ways of acting. I will write more another time.

I am glad to talk with you again. What shall we talk about? I know you have much on your mind. I shall give you some more information you can use. It is about how your brain and mind work to cause you so much distress over certain events.

When you perceive, via your brain, that a certain event, word or action of another is painful to you, either directly or obliquely, then the processes of defensiveness go into play. The perception you have of the event is related to many factors, many of which have been laid down in childhood. This you know. So, as the many facets of the brain seize on the event, etc., then all these factors are processed as in a computer at the speed of light, and out comes a synthesis of what you imagine happened. You see, when you consider this operation, it has very little to do with the actual event but exists almost totally in your brain.

When your brain has come up with its interpretation, then, as I said, defenses come into play if the brain senses the event to be harmful in any way. You are aware through your training of the many forms defensiveness can take. This is what happens on the brain level, but let's now bring the larger mind into the act. As you see, there is very little active play on the brain level, but when you bring your higher mind into the act, you have much more active thinking going on. When you only are reactive, you are very much stuck with your past, but when you use the powers of your higher mind, you have all sorts of control as far as changing your perception, feelings, visions, etc.

The mind is wonderfully creative and magnificent, in addition to being very wise. How, you wonder, do you get to the mind when it seems your reactive brain is so fast to sum things up? It does take some practice and some forethought. Now there are several disciplines that are teaching how to access your higher mind. Many talk about the right side of the brain. This is certainly a doorway to the mind, but some other things also help to access the higher level thinking and are available to you. Just by *intending*, then, you find your mind opening up possibilities for you.

It helps to read about ways to control your mind to give you techniques and because you will not be able to do so unless you *believe* you can. This is very important. When you believe that you have control over the thoughts and emotions, then you will be able to do so. This is not to say that you should repress or stop or block these thoughts or emotions. That is not what I mean when I speak of using your mind. Your mind can vibrate at a higher level and can come up with ideas that can help you to transform the ideas you held which contributed to your distress. When you challenge your perceptions with higher wisdom, you will find that, oftentimes, they do not hold water at all. When you use the higher values of your mind, you will experience the event in a totally different way. You will not believe it is the same event. Your brain level brings all the pain of the past to bear; your mind brings all the wisdom of the higher realms and shows the self ways of perception that incorporate values of Divine Law such as love, hope and charity. You will find that then you do not react with the same kind of defensiveness because you do not have to protect yourself from past pains. The way to your higher mind is always inward. You can reach it by writing, by asking, by looking in and up, by painting and drawing, by meditating and by prayer. You have to ask questions of it and answers will come. If you only focus on the messages of your brain, you will not hear. You have to believe, for then you will seek. Think of the principles of love and you will not go far wrong. Good luck to you.

December 24, 1987
I am here, always have been and always will be

(I had much difficulty getting started.) Let me show you the way. That's better. I cannot communicate to you when you are in a state of doubt. Just open yourself and then I will be able to talk with you. I know you don't know if this is you or me, but then how could you know for sure. Just imagine that I talk to you and then you can go ahead with the writing.

You are wondering so much whether you should go ahead with this or not. Believe me when I say that this is OK for you to have fears and doubts as long as you feel them. When you face your fears, then they turn into something else altogether different, and you gain courage and wisdom. So let's go on now.

The lesson for today comes from a situation where you have little knowledge of what to do. It is a time of much discontent and loneliness for you and everyone else. You wonder at everything bad that is happening and do not know what to do. Let me tell you some ways of being which will help you. I feel your discontent with my writing. It is difficult to communicate with you. You have to open yourself more. Don't be so afraid to let yourself hear what I have to say. I know you don't hear very well right now. But keep writing and all will get straightened out.

I want to talk with you now about a message for your Christmas as you requested. The time of Christmas now is a strange mixture of the message of hope and the hopelessness of human nature.

I shall bless you with God's love and fill your heart with the ability to see and hear far beyond your usual senses. My Christmas gift to you will be heightened awareness, a change in ability to sense phenomena, a greater clarity of thinking. I will send you peace and love and messages of great importance. We are only starting, you and I, on our journey of spiritual enlightenment. I will hold your hand and will whisper into your heart secrets which have been long lost. We will do many things which will bring you joy and peace and contentment. I will tell you wonders of other worlds but will help you live in your present one. Do not be afraid that I will leave. I am here, always have been and always will be. Just believe and I will be here. My love to you with that of all creation. Take care, my dear, and write soon.

I love you very much. There now, we shall write again. What a wonderful day. I know that you are filled with awe at the wonders of life all around you. (I was at a cottage on a farm in a beautiful valley.) Let me see if you know your lessons from this trip. Do you see the perfectness of all of life? You see it there before you. Do you see its beauty? And do you see that you as human are able to sense all that beauty. You are not blind to it. When you let yourself see, you are almost blinded by its beauty. You feel it with all your senses. By this know that you are part of it, that it is there for you to partake of. It is you, of you, for you. Do not tread heavily on your fellow creatures. Let us now talk of some other things.

You wonder about whether other stories are real and true. (I was reading other channeled books.) They are almost all true though a few have been produced mainly to make money. You can learn much by reading other books. You need not worry so whether details all gibe as we all have different ways of symbolizing that which cannot readily be communicated. As I said, you are stuck with the words and concepts of your physical life and so cannot comprehend all that really exists. We are trying to tell you in ways that you can understand, and so there will be some variation in the ways we transcribe our life here.

Seeing life force

But let me tell you more about life and how it all fits together. Life force, as I told you, is a miraculous force that permeates all of creation. You look out your window and see the world teeming with all the varieties of life—plant, animal, fowl, etc. You are awed by the sheer numbers, but believe me, this is only a small sampling. You are able to see only a small spectrum of the various forms of life. Some are too tiny and some too huge. You only see the small spectrum of life as you only see a small spectrum of light. There is so much you cannot see with your eyes. This is all right as long as you do not believe that only what you can see exists. There is so much you can't see that, relatively speaking, you are quite blind. There are forms invisible to you, but also there is much else that is invisible to you. The way that order is kept in the world is quite beyond your senses as is the way a baby grows from an egg. You cannot see the template as that exists outside your view. You do have to take so much on faith, far more than usually is implied by that word.

You are spirit here in life

Usually faith means belief in God, but that is not only what you must have faith in. You must have faith that all of life is in order, that there are processes that are unseeable and unknowable, that the interconnections between all of life exist and are what keeps order in the world. You must believe that you are spirit here in life and while here are limited by your body senses. You must believe that you have purpose and are important in the reality of creation. You must believe that higher order laws exist and that you do have access to them; that when you access them, you do have glimpses of what you already know from the place your spirit resides. So do not go blindly about your life, oblivious to the real reason you are there. Do not think that living your life with eyes closed by physical things will suffice. You must be willing to open your eyes inward. You can look out at the beauty of the world, but you will not understand your part in it unless you look within. That is where the answers are.

So encourage people to meditate, to pray, to ask questions of their higher selves—all the ways that eternal knowledge can be obtained. Tell them their lives will be enriched. It will be like adding a new sense to explore the world.

I am ready to talk with you. Pay attention to your rock. That will help. Now, this is what I want to talk with you about. When you are sorely tried by a friend, acquaintance or co-worker, then you have another chance to learn a lesson about loving. If there were no problems for you to address, then your growth would be slow indeed. You would stay at the same point in time. So be of glad heart that you were presented with an opportunity for growth. Whether you take it or not depends on you. You always have the choice. Opportunities can be taken for your growth or can be used to stay stagnant or backslide. The choice is always yours. But there are some things that I can help you with. I know that sometimes you don't know what to do or if you should do something or not. Is it best to stay quiet or should you be confrontive? We have already talked of the disuse of anger as a means of settling anything, but then what *should* you do?

The best thing to do is to first be as clear as you can about yourself. Look inward and see what is being given off in you. This is always the first step. If you are free and clear then there will be little happening within you. But sometimes you are confronted with people who take more than their share of the space and energy around you. Then, you have several choices. You can bombard them with unconditional love to see if that will aid in transforming the energy around you. It is not wise to fake unconditional love as the vibration of your true feeling will always come through, and you will find there is an acceleration of negative energy. You cannot fake love. It is only necessary to breathe it in, amplify it and breathe it out. It does not have anything to with pretense.

Then there is something else you can do. You can look at the situation from above as though you were able to see far in time and space and could see the incident in a wide perspective so that it does not gain so much importance. When you focus on a small piece of time, then you imagine that that is all there is and the incident gains importance over all. Do try to stay clear of that. Time is a relative concept in your world and things should be kept in perspective. You are the one who is in charge of your energy. When you allow someone else to take charge of it, then you have given up very much. Just remember that you, as an active person, have the ability to project your energy out as much as someone else. Most often you react with protective withdrawal or repression of your own negativity rather than with pure unconditional love. This is a lesson that takes much learning.

Now let's go on to some other topics. You will find ways of learning your lessons very soon that will speed you on your way. It is important to be open to all opportunities as they occur for you. Do not shy away from anything that is presented to you for learning. You need to take time to integrate and think about what is presented to you, but you need to think in new ways and not let yourself fall back into the old ways you had of looking at things. More change will be coming soon. The more you strengthen your ability to listen to your soul, the more you will be able to hear and see. I will be with you and will help you. Just open your heart and mind and I will be there. You are doing fine. You need to meditate a bit more as you will then find yourself opening more. There will be time to do this in Mexico, and it would be wise to take advantage of the space there. You will be fine on your trip. Do not worry. Surround yourself with light each time you go out. You will be protected from all harm. Do not surround yourself with negative thoughts, for that will allow an opening for other forms of negativity. You will be fine if you do as I tell you.

December 30, 1987
About Jenny's world

Here I am. When we last talked you were struggling with ways of handling your feelings. Let us go on with some other things.

You are learning many things from me and your other readings and wonder where this is all leading you. You think that something more is to happen and wonder what that will be. Well, first of all, there is nothing more to be done but what you are doing. All will unfold with the doing. On the other hand more is to be done and will be done in due time. I want you to know that there is purpose in all of this, but to reveal too much will only make it scary for you. Just keep on with your lessons and all will be fine. Let me see if I can be of any more help than that. You will know what is to come by your intuition. Pay close attention to it. Do not listen to the voices that counter your intuition except to use their conversation to help to clarify what your intuition is telling you. You still have work to do with yourself before more can happen. Do not struggle but merely keep learning your lessons as they are presented to you.

You want to know some more about the world I live in. The world I live in is the same world you live in, except that I live on a different plane. There is no other world that exists in some other place. We all share what you might think of as a common space except we cannot see each other because the laws that govern your view and those that govern mine are very different. It is, as usual, very difficult to describe to you as you do not have the adequate concepts. But it is not as though we here are up in the sky or heaven, floating around in nothingness. That wouldn't be much use at all, would it? Try to imagine that now there are things you cannot see, such as all the different kinds of radiation and waves. They are there because your TV and radio work, so you accept the truth of them even though you, yourself, cannot see them. That's sort of how it is. You cannot see our world, but it exists, nonetheless, in a way that is fully functioning and full of life and spirit but, at this point in your evolution, is blocked from your view. That doesn't mean we cannot communicate with you just as your TV communicates using radio waves. There is so much to be said but I don't think I will try to tell you more today.

You also want to know about God and where and what he/she **About God**
is. Do not think of God as apart from all of this. You see, you still think of him as a man in a long white robe. How limiting is that view. It is so narrow that it is almost nonexistent. God is so all inclusive, so wondrous that it goes beyond your imagination. You do not have to know who or what God is, only to know that the miracle of life is in order and is ordained. Do not let yourself quibble over terms but be steadfast in your belief that All exists and you are a part of it. You are the same as many other parts in importance. Can you see that it is not important for you to have a concrete picture of God. You cannot replace your old man in a white robe with another concrete picture. There is no use to that. What would it help if I told you God was an old woman in a long white dress or a holy beam of concentrated energy. All would limit you by giving you a picture to focus on. The way is to turn loose of your concrete pictures and expand your view in other directions. You cannot conceive of God. Do not waste your time trying. The important thing is to see and then you will know how vast your thought has to be. Do not let yourself stifle your expansion by trying to find little answers. Let your mind open you. Let your own spirit inform you. You know far more than you are aware of. Let that

knowledge flood you. Let the wisdom of your soul speak to you and you will know yourself *and* God.

December 31, 1987
To heal by love

Here I am. You are very open. That is good. Let me speak to you again of love. There is much that will be healed by love if you and others could find the way to express it or use it. There is much resistance to using the force of love in your world. There is much lip service to it. Millions of love songs, stories, etc., fill your airwaves, speaking of the great longing in all of your hearts for the peace and contentment that comes from a full heart. You all know much better what a full stomach feels like than a full heart. When you let yourself feel deep within you, you find yearnings that you know not what to do with. You don't know how to fill these, so out of these unfilled yearnings come all sorts of schemes that you use to try to fill this space. You do not know what else to do. The longing is there but the filling seems beyond you. So you listen to the songs, watch the movies, seek for someone special to bestow love upon you.

Some of you spend your whole life seeking that one person who will finally fill the void. But this is not the answer. No, you cannot fill the void by seeking love, as you commonly define it. The void disappears when you yourself are connected to your source of power and love, when you receive it from the Source, when you amplify it and then send it out to bathe yourself and others in the glow.

Only when you realize that your yearning is not for another to nourish you, but for contact with your Godself, will you be able to find the way to satisfy your craving. The loss of contact with your spiritual self and from the source of love energy is what makes life so difficult and lonely. When you are full of knowledge given by your soul, you do not need to seek substance in the world but will be able to spread it through the land. Don't you find yourself feeling different since we write? Have you ever felt so secure before? I know there are changes within you. You know that when you let yourself connect deeply then life becomes full of joy. You feel your connections with all of life deeply, and joy rises unbidden within your heart. I know you see all the ways of life in a new way now. You are so much more in tune with your natural selves and know that they and you exist now as part of a whole.

You are still learning about love, though I do see you becoming more expanded in your concepts. You know this is a difficult lesson to learn as you have beliefs about love that have to change before you can totally grasp what I am talking about. I know that this will take time for you and others, but it is the most important lesson for you to learn; for when you are able to bask in the force of love, when your yearnings are filled, then you will find that everyone will act in different ways.

Much of the pain caused in the world comes from trying to fill the void which is experienced as lack of love. When you know that of all the abundant things that exist, the most abundant is love, then you will never have to be hungry again. It is all there for you. Do not seek it from others who also are filled with void. There is nothing to be gained there. You must be brave and seek the way. Do not seek it in the world. You will always be disappointed, for your need comes from a desire to be whole with your spirit. Love is magical but elusive if your eyes only look into the world. Try to understand this and do the exercise I gave you whenever you feel hungry for love. I will be here to help you if you need. Love to you, my dear.

(In Mexico at Rio Caliente.)

January 2, 1988
**Integrating
your life**

How nice to be with you again. You are very open there. You know that there is much energy where you are and you are filled with possibilities. Just give us a chance to communicate and we will write much.

You want to know your lesson for today. It is to learn to be at peace with all the various parts of yourself. You often have experienced yourself in various ways and have identified the various parts of you. Now is a time for integration, for all the facets of yourself to merge and come together. As it has been, certain strengths were concentrated in various parts, but now the time is here for those strengths to be available for all of your integrated parts. The way to bring these parts together will be through many of the activities of the ranch but there is more that you should do.

When the moon is full tonight, I want you to put yourself in a light meditative state and visualize all of your selves there before you, dancing in the moon light. Then, one by one, I want you to visualize them dancing and joining with each other. See them all come together as one whole. Let yourself see all the strengths of each residing in that whole. Let yourself watch that self dance and twirl until you think everything is thoroughly mixed. At that point ask that self before you to enter your body. Bless it and see how you feel. There should be a new sense of centering that was not there before.

Now let us go on to some other things. This is a wonderful place for you to be, isn't it? (This is how life should be for everyone.)

You would like to know about how healing can occur on a psychological level when persons appear to be very distressed, depressed, anxious, etc., and you wonder what can be done for them. First, let us look at the cause of emotional distress. It is not stress as so often is talked about. A human being can function well given a great amount of stress if all else is functioning well. The culprit also is seen to be long buried problems from childhood that affect everyday functioning.

There is some truth to this, as we talked before, of how the brain incorporates information already contained in it with newly presented material and makes interpretations of what happened. But this is not the whole story. You see many people who had terrible childhoods and they function fine. You could match a number of people with poor childhoods with others who did not and might find a great similarity of problems. No, there is more to it than that.

The influence of belief systems

As you hold certain beliefs, then you function accordingly. If you listen to people who are emotionally distressed, you find their thought patterns and belief systems are what make them different from the other group, not their backgrounds. The laying down of a belief system is a very complicated thing; however, individual beliefs can happen very simply and quickly. If you think back to your childhood, you might remember a time when you made some decision just like that over a particular incident. You, for instance, have a dislike for straw-berry ice cream that you have in relation to a particular childhood incident. You have held that belief for many, many years, accepting it without question. That belief was made in an instant over a very small incident, but you have continued to hold it for over forty years. If you think about it, it has not severely affected your life other than when confronted with strawberry ice cream; but how many other beliefs came about in the same way and continue to live on in your psyche influencing your actions on a day-to-day basis, sometimes with distressing results.

You will do well to spend some time examining the beliefs you hold because there are several which are very limiting. It will be very enlightening for you to search your memory for some of the beginnings of the beliefs you hold. This will help you understand how controlled others are by their beliefs. You will find that you will listen to people more effectively when you identify the beliefs about life that they hold.

You will find that people will resist giving up their beliefs. One of the strongest beliefs they have is that they are what they believe, and if you took their beliefs away, they would not have any substance. They believe their beliefs are true and are an accurate representation of the world, even if these concepts cause them so much distress as to make them wish to kill themselves to get away from their beliefs.

I will give you some exercises to do which will help to eliminate the fears around giving up beliefs. The first one is to see a pile of objects which is designated as your own pile of beliefs by which you display your world. See first that you can take this pile and build a structure. It doesn't matter if you know which belief is represented by each object or brick, but merely that they are symbols of your beliefs. Now begin to build a structure. See if your bricks or objects can be put to use to build an orderly structure or see if they are so misshapen or odd-sized as to fail to be of use. Now see that you have the magical ability to take any object that is non-functional and change it into something useable that will fit into your belief system in a functional way. But see also that your structure can be changed by the way your bricks or objects are arranged. It is possible to have a functional structure that looks very different from what you started out with.

A meditation
On changing limiting beliefs

Thus the same is true of your self. It can be whole and strong even if you change all your beliefs, which is unlikely. Beliefs are only building blocks of how to structure your world. They can be changed given the fact that they are no longer functional. In your homes, if an old window rots and no longer opens, you have no concern about replacing it. You don't say, "Oh, no. Then the house won't be the same!" You have to see your beliefs in the same way. See how they impress you. When you are distressed, seek out the threads of your beliefs in the situation. Examine them; see if they are limiting you. That is the way to evaluate a belief. Is it limiting you? If so, then it is time to replace it.

The way to live is to search your life continually for ways that you are keeping yourself from expansion. Do not settle for limitations. Many, many currently held beliefs could go. Suppose for instance, it was no longer believed that war was a necessary way to solve disputes. Can you imagine the impact of that one? There is much to be said on this subject and we will talk more. Be sure to use these writings. You will do very well to begin today to look at some of your beliefs. It can be a very fun game when you think about just finding the dry rot in your structure. Have fun with yourself today. Be sure to look around. There is so much beauty to soak in.

January 3, 1988
Put your energy into positive places

Let me congratulate you on your strength and perseverance on your walk today. (I took a long hike up the mountains.) You have much energy available to you now. Let's talk of some things here in the beautiful out-of-doors. You are finding yourself changing and changed. You are more aware of things than ever before. I find that you no longer want to listen to the same kind of stories that once made you interested. There are changes happening to you on all levels. Take them in and you will feel fine. Do not worry if your thinking is different from others. You know you are on the forefront and so will not find that many people with you. Do not despair over this; just let happen what will happen. You already see the difference between a world run on principles of which I speak and a world run without them. Others will see this also. Just be who you are. Let the light energy shine from you. That is all you have to do. Do not worry about anything else.

Do not worry about the darkness

Now let us talk of something else. That is, how to live within a world where there is so much darkness. When you, yourself, are full of light, the darkness appears to be so much stronger than it did before and you feel alone in your beliefs. But then you look around and see similar lights within your sphere and realize that you are not alone. We here are appearing to more and more of you, lighting your candles, so to speak. So just keep your flame burning. Do not worry about the darkness. I know you have questions about whether to ignore the pain in the world or to use your talents to do something about it. That is a choice. You see that there is much need, but it can never be all met within the framework of your present world. It is only possible to meet all needs by a total change in the way things are perceived and the way governments rule. Peoples' consciousness of what is reality will have to change before it is possible to meet the needs of everyone. For instance, for you to work with the poor will do little to alleviate the problem except on very specific terms. You see that you will do just as well to put your energy into positive places but the choice is up to you. It is never wrong to help another in need. But pay attention when I say this will not be enough. Your writing, your positive thoughts, your actions, are more important.

You see, I have talked about the mass mind and how that also will change along with individual consciousness. That is why it is important for you and everyone else who is so moved to put as much positive energy back into the universe. So if you can help the poor and still keep a positive attitude about the nature of things, then do so. But if you become depressed or distressed, then you will not help matters any. It is important to set your priorities as to where you put your energy. And this takes some thinking. You should be careful when setting priorities that you do not look only on the material plane, as there will not be sufficient answers there. Answers to your questions will come to you through contact with your higher selves. All the answers are available to you. Do not be afraid to ask. I know you know this. Sleep well, my dear.

Changing the mass mind

Hello. Are you ready for our writing? I am here and we will talk again. Let us talk today about something which you have wanted to know. That is, what is the nature of the life force.

The nature of the life force

The life force is a very strong energy that permeates the entire universe and flows back and forth like the breath of a human being, always in motion, bathing many life forms in its power. When it visits, then one of the things that happens is what you call *living*. But that again is something you only see a part of. There is so much more to being a living being than you can see. You all see your physical body, and if someone cuts it open, you can see the various organs and the blood and other fluids. But there is much than can't be directly sensed, though some of you do have the power to see and feel more than others. There are, in addition to the physical body, other systems that are not so easily seen. For instance, there is an energy body or system that flows through and around the physical body. When the life force comes to someone, then much more happens than merely the beginning of a physical body. There are other systems around, through and within the physical body that are simultaneously activated. Without them, there would not be systematic growth or regeneration.

On the energy field

This energy system is part of the life force and is a manifestation of it. The energy that bathes the body and all of its organs is as essential to the being as the blood system or the lymph system. You there pay very little attention to it except on a more or less hit or miss way. The energy system is liable to faults and blockages much as the physical body and accounts for much of the illness and psychological problems you experience. When energy gets blocked by repressed negative thought, then the body is not fully bathed, as it would also be the case if the blood supply were to be cut off from an organ or a muscle. So you see your energy system is very important. You there know very little about this, though there is much information, but because you live in a time where only the seeable is to be believed, this information does not get distributed. But as more and more people begin to tune into their bodies, to study these words, the information will begin to flow out from the few to the many. And then there will be very different ways of teaching that will happen so that you will all know how to keep your energy body in good shape. You do not have to see it to believe that it needs your care and concern.

Here are some things that can be done to help align the energy system so as to make it functional for you. One of the most important is to process thoughts with your mind in such a way that there is not accumulation of denser negative energy which then exists in the form of blockage. The way to do this is to envision everything in a way that allows free expression of it in some form. You cannot always directly express your thoughts and ideas, but when you find that you are always repressing and holding back, then you can be sure that you are causing problems for yourself. Thoughts are energy; they do not exist in any other forms. When you repress any part of your thoughts, you are creating concentrations of energy that are stored away. The more this happens the greater accumulation of blockage. You learned earlier this year to work with stored representations of ideas in the body. This is what I am talking about. The constant repression of certain thoughts and ideas can cause such concentrations in the body that they literally form mass there. The energy cannot pass through as it should, and so there are parts of your body that do not receive the direct effect on their cells, causing pain, distress and disease.

So it is important to live your life such that you welcome your thoughts. Unrepressed thoughts and ideas have a very short life; they flow in and out of your consciousness with a rhythm much as your breath does. They can either be expressed at that time or released. Either will serve the function of allowing the energy of your thoughts to flow freely. But when you feel that you need to repress a thought or idea because you feel it is bad or will not be accepted or whatever reason you feel you need to, then you start a system of blockage that will cause psychological or physical problems.

When Freud talked about the unconsciousness as the receptacle of all kinds of repressed feelings, he really was talking about the energy blockages which hold an enormous amount of repressed material. This exists not in the unconscious but in the body's energy system, and it can be activated by events in the life of a person when situations bring up similar material as that which is repressed. When that happens, the person feels an anxiety attack, a phobia, a depression or whatever else he or she may be particularly prone to. Or it is possible that a particular organ will act out the repression of the material. So you see how important it is to keep your thought system flowing freely. Your mind is very agile and can cause blockages very easily when you so desire. You are in charge of your mind, not the other way around. Do not think that you are the victim of an unconscious mind that directs you hither and yon. You are in charge, though in cases of considerable repression and blockages, healing is necessary before you are able to direct your mind safely. You may need to consider healing of one kind or another if you find that you feel you are a victim of your own mind. This is not the case at all, but extreme blockages can feel that way.

There is a lot of interference from your thoughts, though you don't know it. When you write right after reading, then your mind is full of that and the channel is not so open. It will be better to write after a period of activity or meditation. But we are all right now, so let's go on with your questions about whether to do another exercise concerning the selves.

As you were aware this morning, there is more to do. First of all, the integration ceremony you did still left out some of your everyday selves, and it would do well to repeat it more than once. But your question is whether you should do something about uniting your selves and your spirit. Well, that is not necessary in the sense you mean it. But I know that your question comes because you are still unclear about the division of your spirit, your physical body and the ego portion of you or your selves. Spirit, or soul if you prefer, is not like the various selves you feel within you. It is not on an equal par with them but is much more prevailing, elevated and eternal. So you cannot merge it with the selves in the sense we talked about in regard to the selves. But I understand your need to have some sense of immediacy with your spirit or soul and to feel that you are illuminated with its light and wisdom. You see, your soul or spirit exists. You may not feel that because you have been so conditioned to think only of your body, mind and emotions. You know what they feel like, but you don't know what spirit feels like. You think of it as something apart from your experience because you don't know how else to talk about it.

There is a general belief in your world that human beings do indeed have a spirit, but no one tells you what it feels like. Now, first of all, you do not *have* a spirit, you *are* spirit. There is much difference there. Second, to be spirit implies that everything you are, body, mind and emotion, belong to you as spirit. The problem comes in your world when this is denied and all effort goes to working only on the physical plane and disregarding all the information that comes from the spirit you are. You are constantly in tune with the wisdom of you as spirit, but mostly you don't listen on that wavelength. But if you stop and look around you, or if you go in and listen, you will hear the voice of all the accumulated wisdom.

You want to know how to imbue your ego self with the sense of you as spirit. This is not so easy in your world as you do not have good information about this. There are other cultures where this is much easier. You will have to train yourself to listen. You already know much more about this from our writing and from other readings. You need not fear. You can be no other than spirit. It is the wisdom that you need to let come through. You cannot hear that if you only listen to noises of the physical world. But I will give you another exercise for you to do. You may do it tonight under the moon as I know you will like that, but you can do it anytime.

First, sit in a relaxed position and put yourself into a slight meditative state so that your conscious mind is still. And then imagine yourself as a being of light. You will need to sit very quietly and see if you can first take your physical self from your body so that you can see what else is there. You may have to concentrate on this quite a bit, but keep trying until you visualize yourself as a pure being of light. Then see this being of light, full of wisdom and accumulated knowledge, enter your body, infusing it from head to toe, from cell to organ with its stuff of Being. Know this is how it is.

A meditation
Being of Light

You can be no other than that, but you can deny its existence in your life—not that it will change anything. You still will be spirit and you will be touched on the physical level constantly by its source. However, it is in your consciousness where you will fail to have access to the information that is there for you. Anyone can learn to listen to her or his spiritual knowledge, even the most hardened criminal or the most base creature. Do not think that anyone is denied.

Hello, my dear. It is good to talk to you again. How nice your vacation has been for you. Do not worry that we have not written so much. There is time enough. Now you would like a message for your last day here. I will give you a fitting one. You have faced much here in the way of beauty and friendship and have faced yourself in many ways. This will stay with you and will nourish you in times to come. You have felt your connection deeply with all of nature and again were struck with awe at the beauty and order of it all. This too will stay with you.

January 9, 1988
A message
The "second coming"

Do not be afraid to see this beauty and order everywhere you go, whether in the country or in the city. The life force is magnificent indeed when it visits in its myriad forms. This you will not forget. But remember, too, the lesson you have been learning for yourself. You will continue to process teachings that have come to you here which will make you stronger and clearer. Do not forget these lessons. Remember to work on your beliefs and to see how certain ones are limiting you, and remember to do the exercises which will help you change the ones you want. You have seen here another form of reality, a way that life could be lived—free of stress and pain and full of pleasure. Let this be a beacon for you as to what you should seek in life. This is what the "second coming" is all about. You see, people can live safely with each other, sharing in joy and love. This will be a good model for you. I wish you much happiness your last night here. All will go well with your flight and I will be with you. See you at home.

(I did not write for about a week after I got home because I came down with a bad cold.)

January 19, 1988
You, indeed, are a child of the universe

You are in a new place of acceptance and openness and are ready to go ahead to the next step. And what is that, you wonder? First, there will be a deepening of our bond such that you will find a greater and greater ease with our discourse. Second, you will share more and more with other people. Getting started with your Friday night session will follow soon. You have been thinking about publishing a book and it will be good to explore the wheres and hows of that. We are not ready yet, but it is certainly time to begin exploring a bit.

Now let me give you some messages for tonight as I know you are tired and will not write long. I give you first a message of love for you and all you human beings. I send you love energy in a constantly moving current to bathe you and heal you. This you have coming to you all the time, but especially now.

A message
You have access to all its wonders

Second, I send this message for all of you who would listen. There is a time now where many important things are happening and it is important for you to keep your eyes and ears and hearts open as the next few months will be times of great activity. If you are open, it is possible that much good will come to you. Pay attention to your dreams. Pay attention to your heart. Listen for your spirit. Messages will guide you on your spiritual path. It is always possible to obtain guidance, but now the time is right for a higher degree of messages to come through. So take the time to meditate, to pray, to listen. Life is beckoning to you. Listen to it. Your way will be much easier if you know the path laid out for you. When you struggle against life, against the challenges set for you, then you often feel lost and alone. There is no need for that. You, indeed, are a child of the universe and as that child, you have access to all its wonders. You are not alone in life. You are surrounded by loving guides who always try to help you on your path toward enlightenment. You are very fortunate when you find a way to hear them. So all of you who are troubled and feel alone, now is the time to set aside some time to listen to your inner soul. Just sit quietly and ask for the answers to come to you. Listen patiently and they will come.

You have missed our writing in your life these last few days. I have been feeling your need to talk with me. (I had not felt well enough to write.) Now you have some questions about things which we have talked about before and some new ones. You also have questions about your path and the tasks you set out to work on for this life. You see, I will not tell you just like that. It will not do to tell you all of your plan, just as it would not do for individuals to come into life with a detailed blueprint of what they were to accomplish. But let me tell you this. You have often been on your path, though sometimes you have not accomplished as much as was placed before you. But do not feel discontent about that. Life will continue to present you with challenges as long as you are there on earth. It is never too late to learn.

January 23, 1988
*Everyone's path
has similar
components*

Q: But how can I learn if I don't know what I need to learn? Wouldn't it be easier if I knew, and then I could seek out places where I could learn?

A: No, this is not how it works. You would easily learn how to manipulate your life and think all you had to do was to conform to a certain lesson and you would be home free. It takes more than that. Your progress to purity is more involved and takes into account a wholeness that is quite beyond your senses. If you knew everything you had to accomplish, you would be content with that small piece and would not make all the myriad connections that you need to make.

Let me just tell you this. Everyone's path has similar components. Your way is to become more and more pure and spiritual. What does this mean? One is to live more and more in the power of love—to have this as the overriding force in your life. The next is to be very aware of the spiritual nature of all living things and also the non-living so as to live in harmony with all of creation. The next is to live your life in accordance with Divine Law, which is really a very simple set of laws, but then you need to spend time contemplating what these are. Next, is to live a physical life as full of joy and spontaneity as possible, taking in with your senses all that is presented to you in the way of physical beauty, friendship, love and joy.

You must not think that to live a life which works toward purity that you need to be a puritan of a sort. Life is to be lived. Challenges are there for you to grapple with. Your tasks are not to be eluded by a silent life of contemplation and escape. Your ego and spirit are one while you are there and to escape from your earthly tasks by contemplating your navel will not do. Some of you seem to have formidable tasks, learning merely how to survive in a life that seems filled with pain, disease, poverty or other ills. But this is not to say you cannot follow the principles above when coping and learning from your present situations. You will see all of what is presented is a means of learning that you can use. It doesn't matter if you master the exact task if you keep your eye on the main task; that is, to further your soul on its evolutionary journey, a journey which seems long by your standards. But then your standards are not those which are used to judge progress. Just know that you will have sufficient opportunity to work on those tasks which are necessary for your spirit to mature. Does that answer your question?

The evolving spirit

Q: Why does spirit have to grow if we all split off from God? Weren't we pure to begin with?

A: I told you once that all of creation is in a state of creation and evolution. When consciousness developed, there was a distinct change that occurred. Before that, there was not the question of free will. The animals and plants and birds all lived according to a well laid out instinctual process and followed laws quite naturally. When humanity was developed in the evolutionary scheme of things and consciousness grew into a different kind of knowing, then there also came the matter of free will. People were not like the animals and other life forms.

They had the means of thinking that allowed them to go beyond the instinctual, but this also let them to be prey to the various manifestations within each one that led to much behavior that wasn't in accord with Divine Law. God, as you would say, does not have the power to just remake humanity in some other way. People will have to find the way themselves. You see, you do not understand how this all is. There is the physical world and that does go by physical laws. There is the non-physical world, and different laws and properties govern there. Human beings are a combination of both and it is up to each one to bring the two together in purity. As long as people have free will, there will continue to be places where they choose against themselves.

Hello, my dear. Now is a good time to write. How are you tonight? I am ready with your lesson for tonight. You would like to have some words of love and peace for yourself and others. That is easy to do. It is very important to be in tune with those feelings as much as possible because the more you are able to focus on the positive virtues, such as love and peace, the more likely your world will be filled with joy.

I have told you often about the power of love but today let me tell you some other things that are related to that power. When you are in tune with the higher vibrations of the universe, then you are able to amplify those vibrations and send them out into the ether around you. Not only do you benefit, but others who are both far and near are the recipient of those vibrations. You know that there are many many vibrations that are not in tune with higher values. Your world is full of them. Just look at the number of negative vibrations created by most of your television shows. The amount of violence portrayed every day increases the negativity of the airwaves, in addition to being a source of poor teaching. But this only reflects the amount of negativity rampant in your world. That's why it is so important for you to be in touch constantly with the source of love to refresh the air around you. This will afford you protection from the invitations that go out and that can draw the negativity to you.

There is love in abundance. All you have to do is breathe it in and breathe it out. You know that your life is changed by the fact of your awareness of the love energy. Do not be afraid to trust in it. There is no need to doubt its potency. Just give yourself to it. Cover yourself with it. Let it flow into the world around you. Let it bring peace to your life. Let it spread like ripples in a pond to those around you. Let those ripples go out in the world and see them making an impact in ways you cannot yet see. Life is full of miracles and love is the greatest of these.

There, now. Let's see if we can write. Your lesson for tonight is to go on talking about the extent to which you have free will or choice in your life. There are questions that you and others have about whether events are preordained or scheduled for your life and if these are set in concrete, so to speak. You see this is a little difficult to answer as always, but I will try.

When a soul commences to begin to live a physical life, a plan has already been laid down by that soul which describes those tasks which are to be accomplished during that life. There may be tasks which are new and evolutionary for that soul, or there may be tasks which are karmic in nature where past deeds are recreated so as to allow other outcomes. Either of these may be true. So the soul chooses where and to whom to be born and often arranges with others to reside within the same time or space frame. This, as I said, is often very helpful so that friends and loved ones are there for support. So this you understand. But then it all gets a little more complicated because, since there is free will and choice, there is no concrete assurance that all events will happen as planned. This is very hard to describe but your thinking in terms of probabilities will help.

Your life is not laid out from beginning to end with no leeway. But then neither is it all hodgepodge where anything can happen. Do you see how this can be so. Think of probabilities. It is true that given an event, there are probabilities as to the outcome or consequences of that act. But then again these are only probabilities. You know your scientists have been studying the atom and all its components and find even there that there are only probabilities as to how the matter will behave. So it is in life. Within certain confines, certain things are possible, but not others.

For instance, it is improbable that a speck of atom will talk. There are frameworks within which things happen. And so it is with your life. You have choice and free will, but only within a system of probabilities. You cannot go outside of those. If you think on this, perhaps it will come more clear. So you see, when a soul decides to incarnate and has a plan laid out, it is within a framework that the events of that life will take place—that is a framework of probabilities. Otherwise it would be very difficult for a plan to be devised and worked on. So you see, during your life, all goes according to plan and you decide its course by your choices—but only within a framework of possibilities. I will write again on this subject as it is important and is related to finding your way on your path you have chosen.

Stay quiet for a minute. Let your mind still. Now we will talk again. Let me congratulate you on your thinking today. You are trying to see things from a different point of view.

You want to know about relationships and love between people such that they form bonds with each other. You think this is different from the way I have been talking about love and wonder about the feelings people have for each other such that lead them to form life-long bonds. Yes, this is an interesting subject to talk about. I can understand why you feel confusion because there seems to be so much confusion in your world about relationships. Is it love or dependency that brings people together? This is a big question for you all there.

I want to separate out the word *love* as I use it so as to not confuse the issue more. Let us look at how being in the force of love reflects in action. First, you see that energy that is very nice to be around goes out from you so that people are often drawn into your sphere. They often want to be in contact with you, and if they also have the capacity to unite with the force of love, then you and others want to be with them. You all have the capacity to do this. Some utilize it more than others but it is a natural capacity. So you also know that between some people there appears to be a larger amount of energy that flows between them and this you call *being in love*. This is the amplification of love energy in one of its highest forms. But I must tell you that oftentimes in relationships many other factors contribute to bonding. Some of these are positive and some are not. Many people stay in relationships who strew hate out at each other rather than love. Then you see, you are all human so you have all kinds of human foibles that get in the way. It is difficult to talk about relationships because there are so many variables. But the love energy, if it is strongly felt and shared in a relationship, is very special and can help both partners to do a miraculous amount of healing. But if it is not felt, then it is much better to disband the relationship because no growth will take place unless there is karmic law at work. How do you know this? You don't—except through your intuition.

Q: Are people meant to bond?

A: Well, *meant* is not the exact word to use. Human beings have the capacity to bond, the desire to bond and the free will to bond. The sexes were created for procreation and so bonding fulfills that requirement. However, bonding goes far beyond sexual procreation. The main effect of bonding is to allow people to practice acting out of love. We learn much on a small scale what eventually will happen on a larger scale. But there is still so much to be learned about loving, either in small or large ways. Your ego needs *so do* get in the way, whether that be in your primary relationships or in the world. If you would always stand in the force of love, you would be able to see beyond your ego needs, but this is not yet possible for you. But this is something to strive for. Your relationships will get better and better as you learn to do this.

January 30, 1988
About love &
relationships

Let me welcome you today. Isn't it a wonderful day? Have you enjoyed the warm, spring-like weather? I know you have been shut in with your own thoughts today, but it is good to look around and let yourself experience the whole of life. When you feel your connection to life, you feel more alive and at peace. You have been listening to your ego prattle a little too much, but then you have also had some valuable insights, and that is good.

Let me talk to you some more about relationships. There is a question, always, about what makes a good relationship. Is it loving each other? When asked why they stay in a bad relationship, you often hear people say that they love each other. Can this be, you ask. And I tell you there are different things at work here. You, on one hand, have to talk about how people treat each other. This is true in or out of relationship. Then, on the other hand, you can talk about love. Are the two related? Yes, of course, but it is not enough to say, "I love you." There are actions that go along with that. So often you lump sexual desire, dependency, need, etc., into one category and call it *love*. You must get out of that habit. Love is a very high-valued energy and emotion. It is not the other aspects I talked about. Those others do certainly exist in relationships, and that is to be expected, but do not confuse them with love.

Love reaches out and covers all with peace and joy and contentment. It values. It confers blessing. It judges not. When you relate to someone out of love, you see her or him as special spirit. You allow him to be himself; you give to her rather than expect to be given to. You confer rather than wait for another's gifts. Love is an active energy. It is not passive. You are trying to understand this and that is good. I know it is difficult, but I'm sure if you give it thought and time, it will become clearer. What is needed for a good relationship? First is, of course, a knowledge and ability to be in the force of love; then a willingness to be with and for the other, to recognize her as her own person, but also to know you are one in spirit. You need to treat each other as very valued beings so that this valuing goes out to cover all aspects of your life together. Each partner needs to learn to separate out the needs of his ego so as not to expect that the other should dance to her tune. This all takes time and learning, and in an atmosphere of love much learning can take place.

When there is not love, then trust is hard to come by. A relationship will not survive long in a healthy condition where only need exists. To create a space where love rules should be the goal of all who enter into union. This, I know, is not so easy and sometimes much growth has to take place before this space can be created, but it is worth striving for. There is more to be said on this subject and I will write again.

Let me come in now. I will talk with you about some important things today. That is, how to be in relationship so as to maximize the pleasure in your life. There are many there who strive to find happiness and only find misery. They look to others for peace and contentment and only find pain, or else there is not so much pain as just a vacuum or feeling of emptiness.

February 2, 1988
On happy relationships

What is it that makes for a happy relationship between two people who say they have love for each other? The first and foremost, as I said, is the ability to be in the force of love and consciously use its miraculous energy to smooth the way. Otherwise, when love is not used, then often the way is difficult indeed. There must be, however, other components and these should be called by name and not lumped under the category of love. There should be a feeling and an acting out of respect so that one does not take advantage of the other. There should be a caring for the other's needs and for one's own. There should be maturity enough so people know their own needs but can put them off in order to sometimes meet others' needs. There should be a sharing of thoughts and feeling so that the inner self is known. There should be a consciousness of one's self so that one's problems are not projected on the other. None of these are love, but they are essential if a relationship is to meet the highest definition for a loving union. You cannot have a caring relationship where caring does not take place on an hourly basis. You see, it is not enough to mouth, "I love you." You must ask for and give respect, caring, validation, communication, and then you can say, "Yes, we have a good relationship." To act out of the power of love will give you the energy to act in positive ways.

February 3, 1988
Joy from living a spiritually connected life

(I was planning the first gathering where people could hear and discuss these writings.)

You have been lonely for our talking, I know. That is good. We have important things to talk about. You have been feeling that you are part of a greater movement and have been very excited by this. You are right. The movement is forming and growing, and you find it exciting to be a part of it all. Let me assure you that others feel the same way. You see how eager people are for the writings. That is only reflective of the hunger in everyone's heart for peace and love and contentment. They are feeling, more and more, a need for spiritual awakening and connection. That is what this is all about. Your group will be very interesting for all who come as they are seeking the way to this awakening, and you are providing a way. Do not be afraid. All will go as it should. I will be with you. So trust yourself and all will be well. Do not worry about who will come or how many. Any number is fine and sufficient. You will find your own heart opened more and more, so just take time to soak in the love and friendship.

Now let me talk of something else, and that is a little more about the joy that comes from living a spiritually connected life. As I have told you, you cannot live by bread alone. You can take this to mean that material possessions and material byways are not enough. Without some sense of your Godself and your place in all of creation, life will seem empty indeed. To only seek after material gains, activity or fun will not, in the end, suffice. There are many worthy causes, but even here, if there is not a sense of connectedness, you will not be satisfied. So, lift up your hearts. Open your eyes inward. Let your soul speak to you with clear, ringing tones. Let the voice of your spirit be heard. Listen carefully, for it is the most important sound you can hear.

When you do this, when you live your life open and facing forward, then joy will rise within you. Look about you. Do not miss the wonderful beauty. Do not be blind to your interconnections with the wonders of life. You are so fortunate in the many ways you can perceive the world. Be alert, be aware, and let yourself hear and see. It is all there for you. Do not waste your time thinking petty thoughts. They will not bring in joy. Refuse them. Tell them you have no time for them. Rise above. Do not repress them. Raise your vibrations to a higher pitch. Do not be content to sink into mire. Bask in the love of All Power.

Hello, my dear. Here I am. There was difficulty, but now we are fine. You are doing well today. I am so glad to see that. I feel your excitement about our work together. Let us talk some more about things that are important to everyone. That is, what is going to happen to your world.

February 4, 1988
On the future of the world

Today, you heard that some proclaim that the world is coming to an end and only a few will be saved. This may happen. Indeed, it is one of the possibilities, but there are others. You see, I keep talking about free will as it pertains to individual lives. There also is collective thought and mind, and that too has the power of free will. You see, like a moving mass, a mass thought has energy and power. You have a sense of this when you call something a *movement*. But you do not always understand this as energy. But indeed it is. Many changes can occur when enough thought energy combines to form a movement. You saw this with the Women's Movement. But there are often conflicting forces at work so there may be a feeling of movement in one direction, and then backwards or to the side as another force of thought meets the first. Now you, in your country, have a movement of conservatism, and so it goes.

What does this have to do with the future of your world? Much aggressive thought in your world for some time is reflected in the trillions of dollars worth of arms such that you can blow yourself up a hundred times. If that thought mass continues to grow, I can assure you there will be destruction as a result. But if there are opposing movements which mitigate the force of aggression, then different outcomes are possible. You see how important you all are in this endeavor. You are part of a movement, a movement which has many facets and faces. You are one endeavor; there are many others. What they have in common is a change of consciousness that involves the recognition of your oneness, your connections to each other, the understanding that you, as spirit, have influence in your world. This movement is small, but growing. Even your TV stations are taking note. Even in your small sphere, you see how many people you have already touched. They touch others and so it goes. This is indeed a moving thought force. Isn't it fun? I love the ride.

But do not be complacent. Yours is not the only force. There are many other movements which are not in line. So you see the outcome is not preordained or known at this point. There can be changes. Take time to think on this and be clear with your endeavors so that they are in the light of your own and your world's salvation. That's all for tonight. Be of good heart, my dear, and I will talk with you soon again.

February 5, 1988
On constructing meaning in your life

Here I am. You are now open enough for me to come in. Hello, my dear. Here we are again to write of important things. Tonight I shall tell you more about life and what the meaning of that is for all of you.

Many of you often think that life is a trial and tribulation and wonder why it cannot be easy for everyone. But I have explained much of this to you already, so I will not speak of that. I am more concerned with the meaning you each construct for yourself to explain your own life. Some of you ignore the question completely, at least on a conscious level. Others think it is irrelevant and, though they may think of it, give the question no importance. Others struggle so in their daily lives that they have no time or energy for this large question. However, there are others who give this question a great deal of thought—some with despair and others with hope. Some are preoccupied with this question for their entire life. You wonder what is best. That is not to judge. Only let me say this: the question is there to be answered, and it is answered in behavior if not in words. To turn away from the question is to answer, "Life has no meaning." You see how this works? You cannot help but answer the question in some way. But think if you were taught early on to see meaning in your life.

This, you see, is different than debating on the *meaning of Life*, a question that is useless to answer because it will not be carried out in your behavior. But when you ask the meaning of *your* life and ask this from a spiritual space, then the answers that come to you will be reflected in the way you live your life. You see, there is not a right answer nor the same answers for everyone. There are many paths to home and many ways to get there. You must seek your own. Do not look for the answer out there. It is inside where your heart resides. Ask and images will come to you. Do not think that you have to know all at once or that your meaning has to be high and lofty—so high you can't reach it. No, you must seek that which you can do. Meaning comes in all sorts of packages. Only be sure that you are informed by your spirit and not by ego. You will know the difference. You will be able to judge that easily once you come to know the needs of the ego. Believe me, listening only to your ego will not get you anywhere on your path to perfection. Be of good heart. Start where you are. Seek with your heart and be open to the joy that comes from being in tune with creation. That's all for now. Take care, my dear, and we will talk again tomorrow.

Let us begin now on today's lesson. Today's lesson is on what can be done with your Friday night group. This gathering is very important as it is the beginning of a new phase for you and for them. There are some who merely will be touched but others will have a part in the steps that are to come. So it will be very interesting for you as this beginning expands to other beginnings. You have been thinking much about Friday and that is good. Your idea of a *happening* is fine, and there will be much energy brought to this gathering and it is wise to use it. Follow your intuition as to what to read. I will be informing you through it. So far you are doing fine. Do not worry. You do not have to do this all a special way. Now I have some words for your gathering.

February 7, 1988
It is no accident
that you are here

Welcome, my dear friends. I am so glad that you are enjoying and learning from my writings. You are all so important to us here because your hearts and minds are open. I want to bless you for your thoughts. There is much to be done and much to learn both for yourself and for your world and perhaps for all of creation. You are part of a larger movement which has the

You are part of a
larger movement

enormous job of changing the course of events that may lead to your destruction. This is no small matter. But do not feel overwhelmed. Your part is only what is possible, given your sphere of influence. You don't need to go out and save the world. You only have to be as a grain of sand. There is a big difference. It is the accumulation of higher vibrations that will matter in the end. If you listen to your higher selves, if you learn and listen to the teaching I am writing, if you come to know yourself as spirit, then all else will follow. You all have your own path. You all have your own way. But know that you would not be here tonight if somehow I wasn't included in what you need to carry out your life plan. It is no accident that you are here. You may be taking a first step in a new direction or you may have been traveling this way for a long time. It makes no matter. Here you are.

February 8, 1988
Connections once made cannot be broken

There is a loss in your life and you wonder how to handle this. You feel like life is long and burdensome when you count the loses of loved ones and wonder what to do. Let me tell you that if you focus on the connections that you have, whether far or near, whether in this life or another, that will help. Connections once made cannot be broken. They exist from now to eternity in some form or another. There is an imprint of your connection that is indelible, and it matters not how long or how many other connections you have—each will always last in its entirety. So your son is really only separated from you by artificial time and space. Your connection is such that all you have to do is think of him and you can sense the connection. Your thought of him activates that bond. You will always be thus. As you are with all of those you consider you have lost, believe me, they are not lost. Your connection to them exists and will always exist. You may not see each other on a day-to-day basis, but that is only one perspective. Look at you and me. You see how it is. So be of good heart. Think of how your love and relationship are indelible. You will always have each other. Do not any longer think of your losses. This puts it all in a negative way. You can talk of separations but even that is negative. Just be aware that you are connected even though you may not be able to see that. Think of yourself with golden threads which reach out joining you to all that you have loved.

Hello, my dear. You are very filled with blockage tonight. You would do well to do some Reike (a form of energy healing) on yourself before you sleep. You have been delving into your past tonight and flying away to the future, neither of which makes you feel good. You will do much better to stay in the present. It is a much easier place to be, though you would not guess that from all the ways that people try to avoid being there. There really is no other place, you see. When you remember the past or look into the future, that really is all taking place in the present. You are using your ability to imagine or to create either a past scene or an imagined one in the future. You experience feelings associated with that and then wonder why you feel badly. This is so habitual that you don't really know you are doing it.

But now, let me talk of how to be with other people who are angry with you, or hate you, or in other ways let you know that in their eyes you are lacking. They often act as though you have done something to them to make them feel the way they do. Often couples will do this to each other, and the reactions go back and forth like the wind. You wonder how this can be stopped and what tactics one can take.

First, of course, is to stop and look at your own reactions. We have talked of this before: As long as you remain in the reactive mode, there is little chance of changing anything. Often people will fight with each other until they have spent all their feelings and then can be active rather than reactive. However, often much damage is done while the anger is spewed back and forth. This anger does not leave without leaving traces and memories that come up again and again. So it seems that better ways could be found to achieve the same result without the damage done by blowing off feelings. Again, it is important to validate and allow your feelings their due because the repression of them is also damaging. Then what is one to do?

This is how to do it. The first thing is to separate yourself from the other, not in anger or isolation, but by saying that you need time to look at your own feelings and reactions by looking deep into yourself so that you can begin to come from your center. A chance to meditate will be helpful. When you feel that you have looked into the whys and wherefores of your own reaction, then it is time to reconvene with your other to discuss the situation.

85

But this time you will be able to see how you can be in the force of love but still remain active in your approach. You can listen to the other, allowing the full story of the involvement to be told. It would be most helpful if they also followed your practice, but if not, you can act on your own. Your own lack of reaction will allow them to run their own course and come to an active state of their own. This may take some practice for you, but believe me it can be learned. This does not mean that you do not have a responsibility to yourself to clarify, state your case or to otherwise stand up for yourself. You do not have to allow abuse. You have control over what you allow. You can always break off communication by saying that you will be willing to talk when the other has greater control. You are in charge of your actions.

When things again are at a place where you can talk, then it is time to negotiate a settlement. This also takes some doing sometimes. But if there is good faith and you stay within an active framework, this can be accomplished. You are both entitled to a fair hearing of your grievance but both are responsible for creating a solution. To only be angry implies that it is up to the other to find and provide the solution. Anger does not imply the right to demand change from the other. Negotiation implies the cooperation between people to find a solution which will allow for growth, forward motion and closeness. There are many routes to negotiation, but often people are afraid to do so because they really want to win it all. You need to be honest about that. Negotiation is one of the highest skills your world needs—from the family to world government. It is no longer a viable solution to act out in violence and war, but neither is it a viable solution for individuals.

The time is coming when love will be the ruling force. It is time to learn to use its energy to help in creating new forms of interaction. As long as anger in one form or another is the governing force, there will be trouble in your world. Believe me when I say there are other ways to be than hurting each other. There is much to learn and I cannot tell it all to you. But there are messages being given to many people about this, and you will see it reflected in books and other forms of communication. So ponder on this as it will be very important learning.

There was another message for the gathering this evening.

Welcome friends. I know I already said that, but it bears repeating. This message is for you to help you to live a life of bliss and joy until we meet again. You are all very fortunate to have found each other to share your love and concerns with. This evening will remain within your hearts and will nourish and sustain you if you but let it. But until we meet again, be aware of the world you live in, the creatures you share this world with, the miraculous working of your body, the wonderful sense of feelings that allows you to connect with others in all sorts of ways. You are wonderful and all of life is wonderful. You may be beset with all sorts of challenges in the next month. Some of them in the external world and some created by your own ego, but if you step above a bit and see yourself as an actor in this wonderful play of life, you will see it all a little differently. Pay attention to the set and the other players. They were created by a master craftsperson, so do not let yourself sink in the mire of everyday without using your senses to know that you and all else are far more than what meets your everyday eye. Be alert. Look around. Be pleased with the majesty and magnificence. If your children trouble you, be aware of the wonder of them. If your beloved offends you, be aware of the majesty of the love you share. If there is poverty or pain or other ills, be aware of the wonder of the universe that abounds. Partake of the love available to you. Reach out into the abundance and drink. You need not be thirsty or hungry. I shall stay near you and bless you.

Now, you want to know about religion and our writing. You still find yourself uninterested in religion.

On one truth & many interpretations

Let me tell you that there is only one truth and many, many interpretations. The reality is very difficult for you all to comprehend—and that includes you. You can only understand by your own concepts, and that is very limiting. The progress of knowledge is based on expansion of concepts. All increases in knowledge lead to other increases in knowledge, though, sad to say, not always in the direction of truth. You and I talk here and the truth is modified by your conceptual mechanisms. So is it true of other teachings.

Religious beliefs have the same kind of viability. They misinterpret because that is the way of it. And now you are having my words and see similarities and differences, and you wonder why you then don't feel religious or want to talk of religion. Why listen if what you hear already pleases your senses? You see, you are not only *learning* from me, you are *remembering*. It is not necessary for you to get religion. You only have to pursue truth as you find it. There has been much distortion by religions, and there has been much lip service by religions to the *word* of truth but ,often, little practice. You will do well to follow your heart but know that these writings could be used in the same way religions are. Nothing is safe, you know, from distortion. You must try to stay as clear as you can from ever using these words to judge or condemn others. That is one of the main problems with religions; that is, the use of words for control. Jesus taught many things but he did not teach the use of God's word to control or condemn others. Be sure you look at others with love and forgiveness. There is no need to judge them and find them lacking by any criteria. This is not the way of Universal Love. It does not follow from Divine Goodness and does not perpetuate the evolution of goodness in the world.

Come study with me. Use these words for your own growth. Share them with others for their growth. That is the way of it. Do not worry if you do not believe this or that. The main goal is to seek truth for yourself and how to use that knowledge in finding and following your path. Do not let yourself stray from this idea.

February 13, 1988
Dealing with negativity

How nice to see you again. I want to congratulate you on your gathering last night. I so enjoyed being there with all your friends and their guides. I will look forward to your next meeting. It is very exciting for us here to see all of you opening your hearts and minds. We send you thanks and love. Wasn't that energy wonderful? I know you will not forget that for a while.

Let us talk of how to manage in a world so full of people who have chosen a life of negativity. They would shower you with it if you would let them. They really have no concept that they are creating the negativity in their lives. They would assure you that they had no part in it. It just is. But you know this is not true.

Negativity is a powerful force when it becomes so dense that it creates blockages as I described to you before. So what can be done in such instances where you are confronted with negativity?

Should you stay and fight, trying to show that person the error of his ways? Should you try to convince her that it is possible to live in a positive way. Or is it enough to merely serve as a model.

There is no right answer. All of these may at one time or another be a choice to take. The important thing is to remain in touch with what happens. If you are with a person who is being negative, and others listen and respond with glee or with enthusiasm when you share a different philosophy of being, then that activity is worth your while. If on the other hand, there is no response or another onslaught of negativity, then one should certainly seek a different path.

You need not add to that person's storehouse of negative wares by any kind of aggressive behavior. Merely respond from your own center of positive love and go on your way.

Serve as a different mirror

Then there is the last option, serving as a model. To act out of your own positive source of love is always a way to choose. This beacon to others cannot help but give them a glimpse of something else. You need not worry if anyone responds or not. That is not your purpose. For if you say, "I will be this way and then others will change," you will find yourself disappointed. It does not work quite that way. The way it does work is that you exist as a different reality and that can be seen. For some, it may plant a seed. For others, they may not appear to pay attention, but there may be some small glimpse of something else other than their world view. Do not hit people over the head; you will only knock them senseless. Rather, serve as a different mirror so they see a different reflection. The rest is up to them. You have no control. You only can be.

So you see, there are ways to be and they all involve knowing and acting from your center, from your higher self, from your spirit. When you only act from your ego selves, then you will find yourself irritated, affected, angry, depressed and will act out those feelings toward others which only increases their already negative picture of themselves and their world. The reason for you to act from your center is not for them, of course, but it is for your own growth. This you must always remember. To say, "I communicate with God and see how great I am," is not worth the saying. Rather, it is so much more important to seek your higher self in the interest of finding your path, of

clarifying your life and of purifying your soul. This is the
reason for your learning

Hello, my dear. You are feeling very tired today so we will not
write long, but I will try to answer your questions about ego and
see if I can give you some information for your Sunday group.

As I have talked before, ego is a manifestation of the physical
self brought to existence during the lifetime of a person, and it
is created and molded by that person's life experiences and
interpretation of those experiences. Remember, it is not a
cause-and-effect route but one of interaction between the
external experience and the internal assessment of that experience. These assessments get built into a belief system which is
the structure of the ego. *Ego* is a term we use for the overall
personality of the physical being but there are many sub-selves
formed which are all part of this larger construct.

Now you must contrast this with the other portion of a being.
Actually that is not such a good descriptive term but let it stand
for a moment. I am referring to that which goes beyond ego, that
which is not of the physical, but is a manifestation of spirit. This
you can call your *higher-self*, your *essence*, your *spirit,* your
soul, or any like term. Some call this *God-self* and others—just
God. The term doesn't matter so much, but there are some
distinctions to make. When you contrast your ego-self with the
God-self or your essence, you see there is a big difference.

Ego is concerned with the mundane of your world. It cares
about needs and getting the personality's way in things. It is
concerned with the physical and operates out of the working of
the brain. *Essence* or *God-self* or *higher-self*, on the other hand,
is something quite different. It operates out of the mind—
something much more vast than mere brain. It has access to the
wisdom of the ages. It knows the path the person is on. It knows
the why and wherefores of the meaning in that person's life. It
cares not about needs but about growth. It cares not about
getting its way but of finding the Way. You see how different
these are?

Ego is not bad, you know. Do not fall into that trap of comparing
the two. You could not live in your physical life without ego.
The problem comes when ego's voice is the only one you hear,
when you disbelieve in your higher self and so do not listen,

90

when you think ego's needs are all there is. Then you are in trouble because to live like that is very painful. It is impossible to fill all the needs of the ego, and without having access to higher messages, life hardly seems worth living.

We have often talked about the use of meditation, writing, praying, etc., to help to learn to listen to your spirit. I again encourage this. Get in the habit of listening to yourself to see if indeed the needs of the ego are directing your life. If so, it would certainly help you to first examine your belief system about the availability of higher power because if you don't believe you are more than your everyday self, you will have a hard time hearing that which goes beyond the loud voice of your ego. That is the first step. If you take care of that, then you must practice when you find yourself distressed in any way: feeling angry, reactive, depressed, lonely, or any other feeling that is distressing to you, including feelings of apathy. Then, you must search yourself to see if you are only listening to the output of your brain, and then you can see if you can elevate your thoughts to another level. This may take time at first, but it will come easier as you identify the differences. I will give you an exercise to do with your group on another day. Until then my dear, take good care of yourself. It is a very exciting time for you. Goodbye and I will see you soon again.

Hello, my dear. You are well tonight. I am glad everything went so well for you today. Let me talk to you about some things before it is time for you to sleep. Whenever you find yourself hard pressed to know what to do in regard to your spiritual life, then there are some things to keep in mind.

February 16, 1988
Integrating a life of spirit & ego

The first is to be aware that the spiritual life and the physical life, though separate, are two parts of a whole. There is not the distinction that you sometimes make. Though I know this is hard for you to perceive, believe me that it is true. So you see, as I have often told you, there are only illusionary boundaries between the two ways of being. This you have to know and this goes beyond belief. Belief, remember, is a construct of how you view reality. It is not necessarily true. But what I am telling you is something to know, and that comes from its truth. So then, the next step is to learn, as we have been talking, the way to perceive the spiritual with your physical eyes and ears and body. There are many times when you could, if you but look and listen. Often your channel is jammed with too much everyday chatter of the ego and of your external world. There are oftentimes when messages are given you, and you can hear and see these if you are open.

As I said before, to listen to your intuition is to listen to the speaking of your soul. To hear the small voice within you, which sees beyond and above the mundane, is also to tune into your higher self. To view coincidences and happenings as a sign of a greater power is to expand your view of the happenings of your world. There are others too. Sometimes words of wisdom from a friend, a book or a passage in a book that speaks to you are all ways that your higher self communicates to you. There are more. Sometimes it is a feeling in your body that signals you. Sometimes it is your emotions that indicate a message from above. All these are ways to hear your spirit and your guides. The next step is using this in your everyday life. To listen is one thing, to follow or to act is another. When you set your sights on living an integrated life of spirit and ego then you know that you will do well to heed all these ways I have spoken of. When you do accept that as your goal then you will be sure to listen and to use the information available to you. If you are one who thinks the world exists only as far as your eye can see, then you will not listen nor heed your inner messages.

There will be times when you will feel overwhelmed with life, or will find it empty and meaningless, or will live in dread because you fear you may be wrong. It is no fun to live merely on a physical level even if you make the pursuit of fun your life's goal. There is always a lack of contentment and connection when you follow that route. You all have so much and are so dissatisfied. You have made technology your God and are all slaves to it. You need to spend much of your life chasing after material objects and ignore God-made creations as though they were expendable junk. This does not make you happy. You yearn for something that you have forgotten in your mind but know in your soul. Do not let another day pass without assessing your life. Look inward. Look up and see if you have brought your spirit into your life. Let its light shine on you, through you, and before you. Life will improve tenfold if you do this.

How are you today? It is a wonderful spring day for you. You must glory in it, for it is there for your senses to enjoy. Do not miss any opportunities to tickle your senses with pleasurable sensations. That is what they are there for. Life gets boring if your senses are not fully used and given pleasurable sensations to play with.

But let us go on with your lessons about ego. You want an exercise for your Sunday group on ego and I will oblige you. The main thing to stress when doing this exercise is to distinguish between sensations created by ego and those created by listening to your higher self.

The first step is to have people pair off so that they will have a chance to work on an individual basis. The next is to have one person at a time act out a scene from their life when they have felt some distress. They should be aware of this from the start. But then, after acting out this scene, it would do well to have them ask themselves how they felt. This is very important because often this is very distressing. Then the next step is to ask the other person in each pair to serve as the partner's higher self and to describe or talk about the situation as though this were a scene that could be described from apart or above.

The main goal is to incorporate a more universal sense into the scene. The first person then takes that information and tries to integrate with the first information given to see if this new information changes the perspective and the accompanying feeling. Then this can be reversed so each gets to practice this exercise. Try to develop an ability to distinguish between ego and higher self and to see how these might work together. You do not want to give anyone the idea that ego is bad or needs to be done away with or repressed. It is merely that you can integrate the needs of the ego and the wisdom of the spirit to give you greater latitude in how you live your life. Ego is not something superfluous. It is as necessary as breathing. It is only when you live only with an ear tuned to ego that you are in trouble. You are far more than ego. Why not make life easier by listening to the voice of your higher self. This is not hard to do. Most of you do it often to some extent or other. However, to increase your conscious awareness will increase the ability to bring this information forth. It will help you to see more broadly in your life instead of through the narrow eyes of your ego alone. When you are only with ego, then the higher dimensions of your life are missed and you often feel lost and alone. When you are informed with Divine Wisdom, then you know that you are secure as a child of the universe and you know that the daily cares of everyday life are not nearly as important as ego would have you believe. You will feel freer when you can see your life in a larger context and will know that whatever you are doing and wherever you are is all part of a larger plan.

February 21, 1988

Hello, my dear. How nice to talk with you again. You had a very nice day today. I am so glad to see you partaking of activities that help you to grow in all kinds of ways. I want to talk to you some more about your Sunday group and give you a little message for them.

A meditation
To be more in touch with the spirit that you are

Here is a meditation for you.

Greetings, my friends. I want to send you a few words for today to help you to be more in touch with the spirit that you are. If you all take a few deep breaths and relax your body, mind and emotions, I will send you a small message. Now as you feel your body relaxing, as you feel all the muscles of your body becoming limp and relaxed, and as you feel your body becoming as weightless and fluid as though it had no bony structure, then you will find your mind relaxing and becoming still as a mountain lake. As your mind stills, you will find your emotions also leveling off so that they are only as small bubbles in the mountain lake. Feel this wonderful sense of relaxation and know that this is a natural state for you. Take this feeling in and store it so that you can return to it as you need it. You will be talking today of ego and spirit. As you lie here relaxed, see them as two parts of a whole—one representing the physical world and the other the world of spirit. And see how, as two parts of a whole, they complete each other, complement each other and mirror each other. This is how it is. These two parts are both available to you and you will be discussing and thinking about this further today. But hold this image in whatever way it came to you so as to be able to focus on the wholeness of that which you will be discussing. Now let yourself come back to your normal consciousness.

Hello, my dear. I am glad to write with you again today. You have been having a difficult time for the past week and wonder what is going on with you. Well, I will tell you this. You have not been heeding these writings and are feeling off center and off your path. It does not do for you to ignore these messages as they are so important for you. But you are also working out some buried treasure that needs to surface for your growth. This is very buried material but is working its way up through your psyche, and its release will be very helpful to you in preparing for your next step. Do not be afraid to just let your feelings be. You do not have to work hard to figure them out.

The next thing that you should do is to meditate and also to read and ponder the messages of these writings. It is not enough for you merely to write. These words are meant for you as well as for others. It would be good if you could find some time during your day for some quiet meditation. Otherwise there is not enough release when it all must take place at night. Much more peace will come to you if you do this. I know you are missing the presence of joy but that will return tenfold when your buried treasure is unearthed. Also, do not be so afraid of changes in your life. It is much easier for you to go ahead than for you to try to hold on where you are. Money is not so important, you know. Just flow with the river of your life. Your way will be easier than if you try to put up dams.

You also want to know about spirits and you wonder if it is safe for you to write since you read the book on possession by spirits. First, let me assure you that it is safe for us to talk as long as you are careful to ask for me and also to protect yourself with white light. The idea of possession by disincarnate spirits is one that is difficult for you to understand, and you are also afraid that you may be opening yourself to trouble. First of all, the idea of possession is not quite as it was presented in the book you just read. She has magnified the situation and has created some illusions as a means of forwarding her case. It is very difficult for two spirits to enter the same body. You can be sure that possession by two spirits in the same body is not so easily accomplished as she would have you believe. But that is not so important for you to think about. There is so much more to ponder than worrying about this, and it is not the best way to use your mind.

The way of creation is forgiveness and understanding

Let me go on and talk to you a little more about the many mysteries of life that you there have not figured out—and that is the way of it. There always has been information passed between the worlds, but because it can't be pinned down, the information undergoes so much interpretation that many beliefs occur. Then it becomes necessary for people to choose what they believe. It is impossible for most of you to know all there is to know. Little bits of information are passed back and forth, but in general all is hidden of the greater mysteries of life and death. This is necessary for you to live your life there.

Even now, though you have information, you do not have any sense of experience of this, so it remains a mystery even when you have answers. This is how it is and how it will stay. You will be able to let more information in which will influence the way you live your life, but as long as you are living, you can be no other than physical being. You must live by the laws of your world. This is how it is. Do not be afraid because there is order and plan, and you will find yourself in very pleasant surroundings at the time of what you call *your death*. Do not believe those who speak of hell and damnation. There is no such thing. The way of creation is forgiveness and understanding.

The overriding purpose of All is growth, and everything is in accord with that principle. If everything were evaluated with that basic truth in mind, then there would be other emphasis placed in your world. But until all have accepted that the world is there as part of a larger plan, that individuals are there as part of the large plan and also as the center of their own plan, there cannot be growth enough. The purpose of the universe is creation and growth. There is no other. This does not mean growth in money or other worldly possessions, but spiritual and psychological growth. For when hearts and minds have expanded so that there is no longer any doubt about the meaning of Divine Law, then the world will be a wonderful place.

On change & accelerating the power of love

If you think of humankind's minds now as almost closed systems which are very small and narrow and then imagine minds that are open and expanded by love, you will get a glimpse of what it will be. The time is coming when expansion will accelerate. Remember that each step leads to another. It has been a long time coming, but the time is now for changes to occur at a far more rapid rate than previously thought possible. I know when you look around at the things that are happening in your world, you wonder whether you should believe me or not. But you only see that which is obvious in your society. There is, I agree, much to be distressed about, and the forces now in action that are causing so much distress will continue to move also.

It is not that everything will turn at once. It is rather that a positive movement will grow stronger and stronger and eventually will have system-wide impact. There will be times of great conflict as these opposing forces come in contact with each other. But do not be afraid. Much positive momentum will change societies without great catastrophes if all continues to go as it has been. You are all part of this movement and you must take yourselves seriously. It is not enough to be complacent. You must keep learning and expanding your mind until you no longer can think in your old ways. Action will follow. There are many choices to make about how you will act, but as your mind changes to incorporate these messages, you will find your acts following as easily as they once did when you thought otherwise. This is the wonderful thing. People sometimes try to force their actions to comply with what they should do. This is not the way. The way is to expand your mind with thoughts of love and you will find your actions follow easily.

As you yourself are filled with light and love, you will find your path illuminated ahead of you. This is the way to growth and new learning. So take time to listen to your teachings. Be sure to set aside time. This message is for you. Each day it is necessary for your being to feel connected to its source. See that connection when you meditate. Ponder on it. See its meaning for you. There will be a big difference in how you see each day. That is all for now.

There, my dear. We are here again to talk with you. You have many questions on your mind and have many thoughts of others that are interfering.

March 6, 1988
The coming change of consciousness

As to your own path, you, too, are trying to peer ahead into the fog-shrouded future and are trying too hard to make it come clear. Just take one step at a time. You cannot do more than that. You want to know what to do about your house. This is a temporary place for you to be, but if it does not seem possible for you to stay, then give it up. This house is not your permanent residence, and that is why you are reluctant to put much money in it as you know there will be someplace else, but you don't know where that is. The time is not right for you to know, as much depends on the steps you are taking now. You will have what you want, a place in nature with others for community, but you are not ready to decide on where that is as yet.

This is for all who read these words. You read my messages and often wonder how this affects your life and what you should do with these words and messages. Let me tell you the purpose is twofold. The first is to connect with you to help you remember what you already know. Everyone will not read these words with the same kind of knowing. But be assured that these messages are not new to you. If you read these and have a feeling of calm and peace returning to you, you know that it is the remembrance of a time and place when the messages you read here were commonplace to you—as they were all there was. You remember this time with great pleasure. So as you read and reflect on what is written with your physical body and brain, there is a deeper knowing which is affected and that brings you much joy. Second, there is another reason that these words have come to you at this time, and that is because you are important in the changing of consciousness which is coming. The world sorely needs you and this is part of your plan. You cannot turn away without losing your place on your path. You all do not have big parts to play, but you all have important parts to play.

Some of you will only influence small spheres; others will have wider reaching influence. As time unfolds, there will be many happenings and you will all have a part to play. This does not mean that you have to figure anything out. It only means that you should follow your intuition as to what follows each step of the way. You do not want to forget your steps upon your way. There is much to be done in your world and you all have a part or you would not have been drawn to these writings. So, at this time just continue to read, to reflect, to share with others, to act, if that seems appropriate to you. The knowledge of what to do is within you, just listen to yourself and you will know. The world is changing for the better. You may have difficulty believing that as you read your newspapers and listen to your TV. But this is not the whole of it. Do not focus on *that* world for that world is crumbling.

Focus instead on the world that is being built by people like you who are open to hearing words such as these. Little by little, brick by brick, stone by stone, things are happening. There are many souls who are incarnate now that have tasks to do which will have long reaching meaning for your world. This is just starting to happen. So do not be discouraged if all still seems dark. Gather together. Sustain each other. Support each other. Share your inner knowledge with each other. This is all for now.

It has been a difficult time to come through today because there are some barriers that sometimes make it difficult to make contact, but all is well now. Let me talk to you today about how changes will come to your world. I know that sometimes you are sorely tried by the pain and despair and greed and aggression that you see around, and you despair that there will never be enough momentum for change, no matter how many people are in favor of a change. Well, this is how it might happen. Remember the outcome is not assured so we do not know for certain if this will come to pass.

March 9, 1988
How changes will happen

First, there definitely is a movement of consciousness raising going on. To be sure this is still a small number of people, but it grows each day. At this time, this is not a cohesive group. Many small groups and also individuals are slowly, by themselves, reexamining their place in the world. A few people have leadership qualities such that the world listens, but not many. This is not a movement which is following the teachings of a One, but a movement which is growing from within the hearts of many. In time, these small groups will connect here and there. They will recognize the sameness of their beliefs and will support each other in their endeavors. From out of these larger groups some leaders will emerge who will further transmit the messages. More will hear and will heed. At this point, a leader of governments will arise and will be supported and elected by those who recognize this individual's superior beliefs. This then will cause massive changes. At the same time other leaders in literature, media, civil rights, medicine, etc. will emerge. A large movement of love and understanding will begin to happen from their teachings. And this will cause other changes to happen. How long you ask? The next ten years will be ones of momentous change. Following the coming of the 21st century, there will come a time of much peace and joy. There will be changes in the way people relate to each other and their world that will equal the changes in technology in the 20th century. You cannot go on as you are. This will become apparent to more and more people as it becomes obvious that quality of life has been sacrificed along the way.

People will be open to leaders who speak the words they want to hear. Those will not be words like *war* or *destruction* or *graft* or *greed*, but words of *love* and *peace, sisterhood* and *brotherhood* and *being in interconnection with all the creatures of the universe*. There will be major shifts in thinking, and when that happens, all that follows will change.

We are now at the very beginning and it is possible to become very discouraged if you do not keep your eyes on the path. Do not despair. Do not look at the pain of the world and think that is all that is happening. This is not so. There are many of us here who are sending messages to many, many of you, and many are listening. There may be some painful happenings along the way as the old clashes with the new. This is to be expected, but in the end there will be a golden time when all that is promised comes to pass. Many are being born who will have a major part in the changes to come. Many are returning to earth who are highly developed souls and they will bring a wisdom sorely needed by the earth. Many are coming who have not been on earth for a long time, but who will bring beliefs and knowledge of a time long in the past when people and the rest of the world lived in harmony. This knowledge is sorely needed as now there is so little understanding of the interconnections of all of life.

Pay attention to books that are written as many of these will foretell that which is to come. The visionaries of the future will begin to describe a better world. There will be other signs and these you should also watch for. So do not let your mind long dwell on despair but look ahead with hope, for this all will come to pass. Use these writings to reassure you, to support you, to guide you in the years to come. I will be there with you.

March 11, 1988
Learn to use your intuition

We are here to write again. I am glad to talk with you today. It is a wonderful day and you have been doing good work in your dreams. You are working through some important matters that have been standing in your way, circumstances left over from another time which have been affecting you.

Much takes place in the part of your brain called *the uncon-scious*, but it is really the part of you which links the present physical self to the previous physical selves via your spirit. You have much more capacity than you know in your brain, and it has been often said by your scientists that you only use a small portion of it. This is not strictly true. Much of your brain is being used which you do not have conscious contact with, so you think nothing is happening. Those people who are able to consciously recognize more than the usual are called *psychic* or *crazy* or some other such term implying that they are different. They are not different but merely able to have touch with parts of their brain and its functioning that many are oblivious to.

Many of you are so locked into your consciousness that you have forgotten to hear anything else. This is a very small part of your mental ability, but its forcefulness makes it difficult to know what else is happening, since other parts of your brain function and signal much more subtly. They do not knock you out with the strength of their signs and voices. But of course, you are all aware that there is more than just that piece of consciousness that goes on rather like a motion picture with a very limited vocabulary. You are aware, through your teach-ings, of activity that happens below the level of consciousness. You believe that in the dark and damp of unconsciousness lurk many demons. This is not the way it is. It really is an ongoing functioning process that is similar to consciousness but also very different. There is input, not only from your sense organs as you know them in regard to the physical world, but also input from beyond your present world and sense.

You have the capacity to see and know much more than arrives in your consciousness, and this is always going on. You really do not live out of your consciousness at all. Much happens at another level altogether. But you think you are making sense in your life using your senses and your conscious brain.

Learn to use your intuition. You can use that to help you to follow the path laid out for you. Learn to develop your psychic powers. This will help you to see your way. Develop your healing powers. This will help you to live with ease. All these are given you. The animals know how to use these powers. They have been given no more than you. Do not rely so much on your thought processes, but learn to listen to other parts of your thinking apparatus. Believe me, you can do this. You once would have scoffed at the idea of talking with a higher guide, and now you see how easy it is. The same is true of other powers. Do not be afraid to exercise your faculties and learn more about yourself in this world and others.

March 12, 1988
*Why you are
called now to aid
in the
regeneration
of the earth*

Now we shall write so as not to lose these words. You do not need to fear me. I am with you always and love you with the energy that comes from the Source.

You have been reading of the time when all people worshiped the life force of the Universe and lived in interconnection with all the creatures of the earth. This was indeed a golden time and you do remember it as you felt you did. You did exist in such a time and that is why you are called now to aid in the regeneration of the earth. You also remember how it was when all was lost, and this is why you sometimes feel the pain so acutely of the inhumanity and violence one person fosters on another.

**On spiritual &
cellular
interconnection**

There is much that is stored in your very cells, as you must remember. Not only is your soul eternal, but the living cells are passed down one from another. These cells carry information dating back to the beginning of time. You are not born of nothingness, you know. So if you look at yourself as eternally spiritual, but also as eternal on a cellular level, you see how important it is to nourish the physical life as well as it is to be in touch with the spiritual.

**On rapid change
bringing peace
& joy**

The times are changing; there is no doubt about it. New and old information is being integrated and many ways of thought are changing. You worry that so much needs changing, and that is very accurate; but that does not mean that each person, one by one, will be changed. The changing will happen rapidly, and once the change has come, then much will follow.

You worry that since the little boys in your neighborhood play war and other violent games, you will, for sure, have another generation to go through before change can happen. But these boys only reflect your world as it is. If your world changes, then their play will reflect a changed world. You wonder how this will happen. Well, it's happening. You do well when you search the news and media for evidence, as this will sustain you.

But more important is your inner knowledge which informs you without the need for evidence. Look there. Listen and you will hear. Do not give into negative thinking. Listen to my words and reflect on them. You see how they influence you on a personal level. Let this spread beyond you. Know that you are not alone, and as ripples, you are all reaching out to join each other. The waves that will form will wash across your land. Some of you have the tasks of writing this down, others have the tasks of speaking it, and others have the task of living it. You are all teachers. You are all part of the great movement which will bring peace and joy to your lands. Just keep your heart open and continue to hear, speak, touch, and live that which you hear. Life is not meant to be hard. There are many ways that humans could sustain and support each other in love and joy instead of the ways they now cause each other pain and despair. You are part of a revolution, a revolution of light. Glory in it. Let it fill your days with gladness. This is not a figment of your imagination. You are going forth into a new time and you will find abundance there for all.

You are part of a revolution, a revolution of light

Let me talk to you about something else. That is, a message for your group tomorrow. (A spirituality group that was now meeting monthly.)

Blessed be all my friends. I join you today to bring you a small message of love and support for that which you are doing. Life is a very wonderful gift and to allow yourselves the time to come together to celebrate life is a very precious gift you give yourself. There is much love energy here to share with each other. You will be nourished by it and healed by it. Let your hearts and minds and the very pores of your body open to receive it. Let it wash over you. Let it feed you. Let it heal your pains and sorrows. Let it bring you peace and joy and abundance. I will be with you. That is all for now.

A message **On peace, joy & abundance**

Let me congratulate you on your attempt to use these writings in your life. You will find that as you practice, all will come easier and you will find your life becoming more and more joyful and easy. Now let us talk some more about another message for your Friday gathering as you have asked me to. First let me say that all will go well if you again follow your intuition and use the energy of the group. I will be there. Now for the message.

A message
As you grow in wisdom

Welcome to all of you, my friends. It is so wonderful to see you back here again. I know that you all have been reading my writings and have found them interesting and helpful. As I said before, it is not accident that they have come to you at this time. They are for you to use for yourself and for your larger purpose. I hope they bring you joy and peace, and I also hope they expand your thoughts to let in more and more light. As you grow in wisdom, you will find yourself changed, and this change will go out into the world as ripples in a lake. You are very important. Do not be frightened by this. You are very needed in your world, but you need to do no more than seems right for you. Follow your heart. Follow your intuition. Send love out with your whole being and receive it openly in return. Now there is just a small group of you here, but there are many, many groups such as this, all who are learning what it truly means to love one another. I bless you for coming. That is all for now.

Right and might are not to be joined

Let me talk to you a little of aggression and violence which is so dominant in your world and is so destructive. At this time, that destructiveness has grown to a huge point where the chances of it annihilating all life on your planet is possible. This is very strange, you know, to see an attribute grow and grow until it is like a huge cancer which cannot be stopped. You all are on the verge of being overcome by these forces. But now there appears to be a chance of change as the forces of violence have grown so as to hold each other in check. There is a reawakening of peaceful, loving people, but I do not want to minimize the strength of violence in your world. You will have to be careful as this is an unruly beast. Only an awakening of consciousness can leash it, as there is no other force that can be applied without becoming part of the beastly. Right and might are not to be joined. To be aggressive and destructive is never in the name of God. There is no room in Divine Law for the aggression that is sometimes meted out in the name of God. There is no need for religious zealots who use God's name as an excuse for their own aggressive tendencies. Believe me when I say the name of God is *love* and none other. Do not think of righteousness when you think of control over another. You are all the creatures of the universe, sprung from the same bosom, and you all share your world as one. You cannot hurt one part without the other suffering in turn. See this. Know this. Arrange your world to glorify this, and peace will follow.

You have all been trying to create peace through war. This will never happen. I know that some think that it is the force of violence that is keeping the peace, but they are mistaken. The forces of aggression are only waiting. You are all under their influence. It is time to begin to look for new ways to order your world which allows for the word of God to live. It is time for the second coming, but the message is already there. It is only time to hear it. The time is ripe now, so take time to listen to your hearts and then act in whatever way you can. You are all part of a different kind of army. Do not be afraid to join. You only need to review what you already know, to remember what you learned long ago and stand up to be counted with the rest.

(The following writing was given in response to a request I had for aid in dealing with a disagreement I had with a friend. I include it as it seems that it has application for any disagreement.)

The spirit of partnership

Hello, my dear. I will help you with your dilemma. I am glad you read the writings and reflected on them as they will be of help to you. As you saw, your ego has become sorely involved and has resurrected all sorts of old pains. The way out is very simple. Just step out. You have stepped in with both feet and think you are out of control, but that is not the case. Very much of the problem is in your interpretation and your acceptance of your interpretation as truth. This does not mean that you are wrong or that your friend is wrong. You have very different interpretations of the same event and have become angry with each other because you do not view the scene in the same way. That is the problem—not that you view it differently, but that you expect the other to see it the same way you do, as though there is a truth on one side or another.

Suffice it to say, you are both right. You both see it through your eyes and see it correctly according to the filters of your eyes. So let that be. That is truth. But then, what shall you do when it is as though you were describing two different things or talking in two different languages? You could attempt to see each other's view without judging the rightness of either. You both have equal right to your view because that is how it is for you. But do not try to convince the other you are right. That will only lead to more dissension. You can try to communicate the meaning of your view and can listen to each other respectfully without judgment, blame, excuses or other acts designed to get the other to change her view.

Sometimes in listening to each other, you will find your own views changing. They may even come closer to the same view, but that is not necessarily assured. Validate yourself; validate the other. This is all you can do. You wonder how things can be solved then. Well, solutions are something else altogether, and they are arrived at through negotiation and love. They do not come from changing someone's view. It is in the spirit of partnership that solutions can be found.

March 16, 1988
On the futility of armed might

Hello, my dear. Here we are. I am glad to be with you again tonight. You are worried because of talk of war and thoughts of war and images of war that seem to fill your world from time immemorial, and you fear the strength of the violence that never seems to be satisfied. (Troops had just been sent to Central America, and I had just seen the movie, *The Last Emperor*.)Yes, this is a very major catastrophe for the world; the use of violence on each other has slowed the evolution of human consciousness. But that does not mean that there is not movement, though by your standards very, very slow. War and violence are one side of an ongoing surge of love and non-love wrought by human hands. This continuing struggle for peace and love against the darker sides of human nature has been ongoing for a very long time, and you wonder if the end of it is in sight.

This I promised you. The ultimate destruction is on one hand and its reality is helping more and more people to see the futility of armed might. Life was given and life is taken as part of the grand plan, but societies have used the frailty of human beings for their own violent purposes, gaining ascendancy by brute force. As the chances of winning anything except their own death increase day by day, the spoils are not nearly so attractive. Now the peace-loving elements which have always existed have a chance to come to the fore. But do not be complacent. The ultimate destruction of the world is still a possibility. You all must put your shoulders to the wheel, so to speak, joining your forces of love and peace to the rest who are also breathing their life into this movement. You have the strength of the heavenly guides behind you. Live peace. Breathe peace. Bestow love on all. Do not give violence your dues.

You cannot turn the tides by yourself, so do not feel burdened with the task of changing the world. Simply live your beliefs. Live your life according to the power of love. Let it shine into your life. Let it shine through you, illuminating the space around you. Let it enter your thoughts and your actions so that every day of your life reflects its splendor. Do this for yourself and for your world. There is a changing of world thought. Join it. Amplify it. Listen for it. Look for it. Focus your attention on this. Do not listen to the world of pain and deprivation any more than you have to, as it will draw you down. Raise your eyes. Look for that which is holy and you will find within you peace and contentment and trust.

Let me tell you a little more about some things which will help make your life easier and easier. And this is to pay attention to the small voice within you that can be heard when you listen for it. Sometimes this voice is so small that you can't hear, but yet you know what it is saying. This is the voice of your soul. When you listen for its wisdom, then you will find life easier, for this voice comes from a place where all is known, and yet where fear is unknown. When you have developed the ability to hear your inner voice, you will know that you are always safe no matter what worldly things befall you. You exist above and beyond those worldly happenings, and it is the voice of your soul which can help you to see past the immediate into the larger meanings of your life. This voice speaks to you always, but you must let yourself hear. Do not listen to the voice of your TV or your newscasters or even your teachers, but hear within your own self the words of wisdom and love.

Listening to the voice of your soul

This is the message for today. Let your heart open wide to receive the blessings of the universe. Do not keep your eyes on the paved road but open them to the majesties of life. You are alive and you are immortal. You have a purpose and a reason for your life. Rejoice in it and live it. The journey is what you are on.

A message
You are alive and you are immortal

Now let me give you another message for your group.

Welcome, my friends. You are very welcome here in the Home of Your Heart and I welcome you there. I know you all are seeking for the peace and contentment that comes when you feel you are at home in the place of your soul. Sometimes you are sorely tried with the finding and feel that your way has

March 17, 1988
A message
You are very welcome here in the home of your heart

become lost and dark and lonely, illuminated only by street lights instead of by the light of love energy. Take heart, for this is only illusion caused by the denseness of your culture which clouds your eyes and requires you to look blindly before you. Take time to learn that this is not the way to peace. When your eyes are so riveted on the everyday trials, you find yourself in pain and frustration. When you expand your view to include the spiritual, then you will find that you treat each day in a different way. This does not mean that you need to become religious or worship at an altar. The main thing is to feel and see your connection to the divinity of all life. Touch the sun. Let the moon's magic massage you. Feel the spring breathe upon your face. Let your eyes feast on the wonders of the natural world. Feel your connection to all of this. This is you and you are it. Allow yourself to bring this all into your life. Let the love energy that holds this all together wash over you, through you, and surround you. The true world is not a world of pain. Create for yourself an oasis of peace within the tumult of your streets. Let this nourish you. Let the light shine upon you. Let your self know you are spirit and flesh as one. Take care of both and you will know joy. Bless you all my friends. I will continue to write to you. Goodbye for now.

March 20, 1988

Q: Is Mother Courage the publisher for our book? When are we going to publish the book?

(I spoke with Barbara Lindquist and Jeanne Arnold of Mother Courage Press about these writings at a social gathering in February and invited them to become part of the group. They were very interested in the idea and the process of the writing. They joined us for the first time on Friday, March 18.)

A: Hello, my dear. I have been waiting for you. You have many questions and I will try to answer them. First you are concerned about when and where and how these writings will be transformed into a book. This is still the plan, and the time is coming soon; but first there are other things more important. All in due time. What you are doing now—writing, copying and sharing this work—is the necessary first step. It would not do to catapult into the publishing, for your ego would necessarily be too involved. This time of spiritual growth is very important. You know these groups and gatherings are very necessary for your own spiritual opening as well as for others. Just keep writing and all will go well. You have met and talked with the women of Mother Courage Press. That is good. But I do not want to say at this time, "Yes, they will be the publishers," as I do not want your ego running all over the place with concerns about this. Just stay with me and all will go as planned. You are learning much and are expanding yourself spiritually more each day, and that is exactly what is needed. All else will follow.

Now let me talk to you about anger and its use and misuse in your world. (This is in response to the request of one of the group members.) This is a very expansive subject and whole books could be and have been written on this emotion. It seems that people might be better off if this emotion had not been included in their repertoire of feelings. But that is not so. The problem lies more in the elevation of this emotion to something exalted. This feeling has been alternately repressed and expressed, and neither repression nor too much overt expression of anger seems to lead to a good outcome for an individual or a society. When angers are repressed, then individuals and societies seem to periodically blow their tops, and when angers are freely expressed, then violence and destructiveness abound within a society and within small family circles alike.

On dealing with anger

Anger is not all that mighty but it has been one of the hardest emotions for human beings. Its purpose within the human being is protective in nature, but this need for protection has been expanded. You there in your world are often a victim of your anger rather than that you are protected by it. You use it to try to minimize the impact of your feelings and strike out at others without thinking. It is necessary for you to be alert as to what is going on around you, and your emotions are the means by which you are warned about potentially harmful things. So it is with anger. It is generated by the hormones of your body so that you are prepared for danger. But alas, that is not how it operates in your world in many cases. Anger is often seen as an excuse to be abusive or violent or otherwise destructive. In recent years, anger has almost been elevated to the position of the highest order emotion as people struggle to find, release and express their anger. This is a good movement in some ways as it points out the negative consequences of repressed emotion and thought, as we have talked of before. But this kind of thinking is not enough and it has created a culture where anger is used as an excuse for the lack of acting out of the power of love. Parents abuse their children. Spouses abuse each other. Men rape and kill. Violence is depicted nightly upon your TVs. All of this follows from the lawless use of anger. There is more to be said about anger and how a changed consciousness will deal with this emotion.

Self-responsibility & emotion

First, there will be a lessening of this emotion as your world becomes a more trustworthy place to live. But this does not mean everyone should sit around and wait for the world to change. It is up to each person to live his or her life in such a way that anger is accepted as one's own response to a situation and is, first and foremost, a release of forces within the body that gives one the characteristic feel of the emotion. Then another aspect to remember is that your surge of anger is also influenced very much by your own inner interpretation of what event it is that is making you angry. You can see if someone truly is invading your space or if you are merely responding out of a way of your own making. People can control their anger or express it, but there also follows a sense of responsibility with it. Anger should not be used to try to get someone else to do it your way. This is not the purpose of anger. It should not be used because you have needs that are not being met by another. It is up to you to see that they are met and not put that responsibility on another. It is up to you to direct your life so as to maximize its ease rather than to continually put yourself in difficult situations or destructive relationships.

Let your feelings of anger inform you, but do not think that because you feel angry, it gives you the right to force yourself on anybody. There is a sense of responsibility that always prevails concerning any of your emotions, and that includes anger. They are your responses, and because of the complexity of your mind, your emotions are constantly affected by that which you have experienced previously. So know this. You do not have the power, nor would you want to have the power to stop your emotions from happening. But on the other hand, do not think of your emotions as describing the facts to you.

When the power of love is seen as a force of great energy, then anger and other emotions do not seem to have the same control. As you expand yourself, as you see your interconnections with all, as you claim yourself as yourself and your thoughts, feelings and actions as your own, if you agree that might does not make right, if you will learn to know yourself and your needs, if you will learn to know your soul, then all these will help you to see that anger need not be exerted on others as a force of control. Be honest with yourself about the desire to use anger to control another, and you will find that if you refuse to use it this way, you will have it coming to you less and less. There are other ways to live with each other than control over another. You may not believe this, but it is true. When you stop trying to control, then you will find other ways, by necessity, entering in. I know this is not so easy to understand, but try it for awhile and see.

Q: What if someone is hurting you? How do you stop them if you don't use anger?

A: Well, in this situation, the feelings that you have will alert you to the fact that someone is hurting you and this will give you the force to resist or flee or to find other solutions. Much of what anger is used for in your world is to deal with psychological happenings, and it is for some people an easy solution. This is what I am talking about. I will write more on this subject another time. Until then pay attention to what is going on when you feel anger and see if there is not an element of control in it. Be honest and you will see how it is.

That is fine now. Let me tell you some more things about anger and how you can manage to live better with this emotion. Anger, as I told you, is not something that should be used against another nor should it be used against yourself. Sometimes this emotion is very strong, and the chemical changes which accompany it in your body are very distressing. There is a need to blow off this excess energy in some kind of physical act. And this is the key for managing anger. It is necessary that the energy generated be siphoned off if you are to return to a state of comfort, and to do this, any form of physical release will be helpful. You can yell or pound something or work out with your exercise equipment or run or do any other thing that will help you to utilize the chemicals which have been released.

March 22, 1988
Managing anger

Now, there is another facet of this process. When you have brought the emotional level of your body back to one of more calm, then you are still left with what to do about the situation which set it all off in the first place. This is something else altogether. First, be sure that you do not see the solution coming from forcing a change in someone else either by force, manipulation, coercion, or other means which lets you gain ascendency by control over another. This will always backfire for you, as in time the other will get back at you, and then there will be a re-enactment of angry feelings.

How then are disputes to be settled? First and foremost, by taking responsibility for yourself and your own self-determination. Do not wait around for others to do for you what you can do for yourself.

You are feeling confused around anger and do not know if the use of it is warranted or not. You wonder if you do not get angry, how do you keep others from using or abusing you. You ask, "Isn't that how you stand up for your rights?" As I said before, anger is something whose purpose is to let you know when danger is there, and it requires you to do something protective. Thus the goose hisses and the porcupine sends its quills out and the bee stings. This is all quite difficult to explain to you because I am not advocating a passive stance to your life so that you allow others to abuse you. But what I see far more is the use of anger to abuse someone else. Its explosiveness lashes out at others and causes all kinds of difficulty in relationships of all kinds. You all have been conditioned to respond to it—some with compliance and others with increased anger of your own. I am telling you there is another way to settle differences between people. But the first step is claiming your anger as your own emotional response to an external situation, and more importantly, to your own internal climate. Only when you are willing to acknowledge your anger as your own—and this does not mean repressing nor denying it—only then can you go on to the next step. This is settling disputes by communication, caring, negotiation, compromise, giving or whatever means will allow for equitable settlement.

But you ask, "What can you do if it is the other who is angry at you, and who does not wish to claim her anger at all and wishes to place the blame at your doorstep?" For one thing, do not open your door to it. Refuse to be drawn in by such a ploy. Stay clear that you are not responsible for her anger, though indeed she may be having an emotional response to something you did. But do not also negate the right of the other to discuss the situation once the anger has been dealt with. To abstain from all responsibility by saying, "That's your problem," will not do.

You see the difference? You must be willing to look at the issue before you—that which caused the uproar. Now certainly there are times when others may vent aggression and anger on you when your part in the situation is minimal, and the full brunt of their emotional involvement comes from another place. In this situation, you should be clear about only your refusal to serve as the receptacle for anger which has its source elsewhere. If you have a belief that you do not ever have to suffer the consequences of another's anger, then you will quickly learn to disengage when that happens. If you only stick to issues instead of getting caught in reactions, it will become clear as to whether the issue is with you or another. I know this seems rather simple minded to you, but it is not. The doing may indeed take some time to master but, believe me, it will help all your relationships if you reflect on this. Anger is not some god to be kowtowed down to, as so many of you do by responding with guilt or reparation when someone lets out an explosive force at you. Do learn not to respond, but be willing to look cooly at issues as they are presented. Remember what I said about negotiation. That will help. That is all for now.

Let me talk to you some more about anger and other feelings. You are right when you thought today that the evolution of culture and of consciousness has been delayed because of the emphasis which has been placed on the development of "knowledge" and technology. It is time now for the exploration of inner space, for an understanding of the working parts of the human psyche. This is not so easy, as you can see in your work and in your life. You are all still in the infancy stage of utilizing the vastness of your mind's abilities. But the time is changing. You can already see that, but it will take more time for the major shifts to take place.

March 23, 1988
It is time now for the exploration of inner space

It is important for you all to allow the shifts to take place in yourself as they want to happen. You will find as they do take place, a whole new repertoire of experience and behavior will become available to you. You do not need to struggle. Let the old go as it wants to. Allow the new ideas to enter your consciousness. Let yourself see through new eyes. This will all happen as you let it. Once openness has occurred, then you will be surprised at what follows. Other new thoughts will come, new beliefs will arise, new behaviors will follow, and you will find your life becoming easier and easier. This is how it is meant to be.

But you cannot create an easy life for yourself if you are hooked into pain. Refuse it in yourself. Refuse it in your life. It will not have power over you if you refuse to ask it in. Believe me when I say that I know that this is a very foreign way for you to think, as your world at this time is filled with painful things. But only by believing that it is possible to live easy will you find this way. You cannot find what you do not seek. So let yourself open to new thoughts, open your mind, seek with your antenna alert, and you will find things coming to you. I have empathy for you all, but I ask you to transcend yourself by tapping into the larger consciousness that you are a part of. The world is one of order and you do fit into it in an orderly fashion. But this you must choose. You can also, because you have free will, choose to act as though you are not a part of the natural order and try to make your own order of things. This will not work long for you as it goes against the truth of what is.

The time is now for you to begin the journey inward. The time is drawing to an end when only emphasis on the outer will suffice. You all will learn much in the years to come and this knowing will set you free. Join with me in this belief. Be willing to try some new ideas, thoughts and behaviors. Do not struggle, but reflect and let these words guide you in your everyday life. That is all for now.

March 25, 1988
Living in peace and harmony amidst diversity

(I asked a question about selling or not selling my house as I own it with a friend who would like to and I am unsure what to do. Though this is a personal question, it seems that the answer applies more broadly.)

Come, we will talk again today. We will try to answer your question about your housing problem. You wonder if you should sell your house or not, whether you should move or not. You wonder if there is meaning or fate involved in this decision. You also would like me to tell you what to do so you don't have to decide yourself.

Well, my dear, I will not exactly do that. I want you to learn to hear from within and not to look for answers from without, whether that be from me or someone there on your physical plane. The answers are there for you, but they do not come from authority figures of any kind. You know that changes are pressing upon you, and you would like to know the future so you would know what is the right direction to go. This is exactly how life is. It is there for you to live, and answers are available to you if you but listen to your own self speaking. In your case, the dilemma comes because there are others involved in the decision, so you feel that it is more difficult. This is exactly right and this situation occurs over and over again in your world.

You are all social beings and bond in one way or another many times over in your lifetimes. The dilemmas of your lives often center around the conflicting needs of those you have bonded with, whether in love, friendship or business. This is the task of your lives, to learn to live in harmony with the vast differences of wants, needs and desires. There is a way to do this other than the one most often chosen, which is control or power over another. The task of the evolution of consciousness is to learn ways of living in peace and harmony amidst diversity. You are only on the threshold of this learning.

But back to your specific problem. You wonder if moving or not moving has meaning for your life work. Well, that is up to you to determine. Focus on your life work and explore this move within the framework of that which you want to accomplish. This answer will come to you then in that regard. This is a very interesting task laid out in front of you and you will learn much through the doing, as will the other parties involved. Each of you has needs and rights, and for you to apply that which you already know to the solution of the problem will stretch you and will expand your use of the concepts of which we write. I will aid you as I can.

Now, let's go on some more with our discussion of anger. This subject is one which will bear more scrutiny as many of you view anger as an important emotion and do not want to give up its use on a daily level. For some of you, it feels good to become angry and to feel the surge of hormones coursing through your body. You like the feel of power which accompanies it, especially as it contrasts with feeling of helplessness and powerlessness. You often see it as an either/or situation. This is often true in your culture where "power over" is the norm, and it seems that if you are not in the control position, you are in the position of being controlled. So as you see it, it is healthier to be in the stronger position because you do not like the feeling of helplessness. This I certainly can understand because there are hormones that are released which are associated with the controlled position also, and these have the effect on the body leading to submission rather than aggression. But my friends, believe me when I say that to act blindly according to this format will only perpetuate the world you live in now and will lead to your ultimate destruction.

To live with each other in harmony, it is necessary to co-create your consciousness on a higher level. You cannot go on as before without inviting in the end of your civilization as you know it. You may say, "What does that have to do with me. I am just a small cog in a gigantic machine." Do not see yourself as this. The machine does not run without you. The only way changes will happen is through the growth and emergence of individual consciousness. So do heed these writings. They are given to you. Others are being sent similar messages. So do not turn away from these words by minimizing your importance. Live your life according to the meaning you see for yourself. If you do this all will follow.

Your life is not meaningless. You are not meaningless. Your acts are not meaningless. They all carry much more meaning than you know. You do not exist in a vacuum. You do not exist on a meaningless speck in the universe. The universe itself is not a meaningless accumulation of rocks. Believe me when I say that all extends much further than you can see. Do not turn away from your connections with all of life. They are there whether you acknowledge them or not. Do not let the current values and teachings of your culture limit you. Look above and beyond these teachings as much as you can. Allow your view to expand until you see the oneness of all creation. Let yourself believe in perfection of human spirit. It may seem your world is far from an example of perfect human spirit, and this is true, but the possibility exists and believing it will influence the course of your development. Create a world about you to your liking. Live a life according to the meaning you ascribe to it, a meaning which fits with your view of the way life's interconnections are worked out in your world. Do not let yourself stay mired in the pettiness of every day. See wider and broader than that. Do see that to win a daily fight will not add much to your life. See instead your task to expand and grow in consciousness and to add to the storehouse of accumulated wisdom.

Your world now is a very difficult one to exist in as you all have created a situation where there is little support for carrying out these concepts of which I speak. You are on the forefront of a new advancement and you will often find yourself puzzled. But let that be. It is better than certainty if that certainty helps to perpetuate a view of life that is counter to the truth of being. I will be with you all. So ask and you shall receive. That's all for now.

(I did not write for a few days. I was having doubts about writing. Then I wrote this at work.)

March 30, 1988
The lessons of pain

Can you see how hard it is here. This is not a good environment for you. Do you want to wait until you get home because I cannot write to you very well here? But I will write a little.

You have been concerned the past few days about whether this writing is meaningful and have been having doubts about its source. Let me try to help you to understand that indeed this is important—but I can understand your fears. You see your life still goes on as before. No bells have gone off. There are some minor changes but you go on as before. You also sense that this is not the way if these materials are to be used, but you also don't know which way to go. As I said before, you have to take one step at a time, but how to do that is your question. You have been doing fine. Your concerns are more out of your own sense of futility than of anything else. You feel like giving up, pretending these writings don't exist and just going along on your way. You have a very difficult time changing and you are resisting using these writings as the basis for your life. You don't really know what that means, and you wonder what to do about this all. You are not the only one to have these fears but you are taking on responsibility that may be beyond what you need to.

This is the message for everyone. You only need to be responsible for changing yourself. The rest will follow. Do not close yourself in reaction to feeling overwhelmed with saving the world or saving your friends or family or anyone. This is not the way. Simply be. Do not think that we expect you to do more than you are ready for.

You have a basic shyness that is being worked out. We are here for you and all other people. We are not here to judge or prod or force anything. Just open your heart. Try to meditate each day. That will help you.

Now, let me answer the question for one of your group members on physical pain and what lesson she is learning from it. The lesson to be learned always is how to deal with that which is placed in front of you. If this pain is true for her, then this is her task. You see that everything is not exactly laid out, but this may have been something she elected for herself in this life. Pain comes as a side effect of disease or trauma. It often lingers on past the point of healing as it begins to serve a function of its own. But that does not mean that one has to keep it longer than needed. There are many ways to deal with pain. Life is not meant to be filled with pain, so it would be wise for her to utilize whatever methods she can find to diminish the pain she feels. It is not as though enduring pain is valuable in itself. So the use of relaxation, meditation, imagery, etc., can be used. There are several ways of alleviating pain, but it is important to remember also that pain can give you a signal that you are not living your life in a healthful way. Check your environment, your food and, most of all, your thoughts to see if the pain you feel is giving you a clue about how you are living. That is all for now.

March 31, 1988
The spiritual world & the permanent soul

What shall we talk of today? I want to talk to you about our world here as compared to yours. You there are very distracted with the physicalness of your world and your eyes are blinded by the myriad forms of material life that you see. Your eyes there see worldly things and the spiritual manifestations are passed by. But here on our plane we are not so encumbered. It is much easier for us to see and hear those things which are spiritual as we are not blinded by the physical world. Thus we are not distracted from our path which is the same path you are on, but here it is as though the sun always shines rather than your world where it often seems foggy.

But let me tell you a bit more. We here are not the same as we were when on the earth, but we are the same as we were before and between lives on earth. We here are the permanent soul while you there take on the personhood and ego of the earthly body you have chosen. It is not as though you continue in the same ego state throughout your life times; however, the permanence of the soul is never in question. What personality do we have as souls then? Well, this is difficult to answer; it is different than you there know since we are without the ego component. You will have to wait to remember. But think of how you might be if you could transcend your ego and reach a high level of being. This thought could approach but would not still give you how it is. We do not interact, as you do, from out of ego states, so you see that we are less inclined to do the things you all do in defense of your egos. We are pure energy and communicate by energy transference as we do not have the sense organs you have.

But that does not mean we do not sense. We do indeed—far greater than you now can imagine, as so much is hidden from you by the limitations of your sense organs and brain. You are only able to experience a small spectrum of what exists, for, you see, you can only experience that which your sense organs allow or your brain can compute. It is when in a state which transcends these that you sometimes get a idea of what exists beyond your senses. You are all quite limited, you know. However, as you evolve and separate from your ego states, you will be able to expand into greater and greater consciousness. We here are all awaiting this day.

However, do not be afraid to live the life you have before you. There is a reason for it or you would not be there. You have chosen this life and are using it on your journey. Do not turn away from it by merely yearning for the peaceful life hereafter. That is not the way of it. You are there for a very important learning. Embrace it. Let it flood your being. Learn its messages and words. Meditate and ask for meaning and direction. The answers are there for you, but you must seek and ask and be open to answers. I will write on this another time. Until then, my friend, I will watch over you.

Let me give you a little message for you to ponder. When the world turns this way or that, then you will see that it changes its hues. As this is true, it is also true that everything changes its hue depending on how you are looking at it. Color is very important. Pay attention to color. See if you can see the colors of the vibrations as they come off of people. Let yourself develop the vision to go with the ability you already have to sense the vibrations. Focus and see what happens. You will see them, not directly with your eyes, but you will form a pathway from the part of your brain which senses and the part that registers vision. This is not the same as directly seeing the color of someone's aura, you see.

A message
Pay attention to color

April 15, 1988
On healing

This day is a very special one for you. You and your friends give us a very good glow here. It is very nice to watch the brilliance of your love exchanges. Now what shall we talk of today for your lesson. One thing we can talk of is how healing happens. This you know is not unusual at all. It occurs night and day in the human body. The stresses and strains of everyday life cause injuries to various cells of your body. The everyday care of the health of the cells is an ongoing process which happens without your awareness of its need. When you suffer a cut or a cold or a sprain, the forces of your body go into a repair cycle which is wonderful indeed. So you see, when people talk about healing and think that either a doctor is needed or it is something miraculous, they are missing the mark. Healing always takes place in the body, by the forces of the body. It does not happen because of the doctor or his medicine or surgery. These, of course, can be helpful, but it still is the body which does the repair. So when you all do a healing, ritualistic exchange of energy, this is a very natural way to help a body to do its work. It is not as though you introduce some outside element, but rather that you allow the natural healing ability of the body to be enhanced. Remember that your thoughts are important ingredients for the healing. So any type of therapy that soothes, calms, or otherwise positively influences the thoughts is one which is helpful. So continue to send healing energy to anyone you can. It will enhance their health and yours also.

A message
You are most precious, oh, gift of the universe

Let me give you a little message of joyous welcome to anyone who reads these writings. I bless you with the light of the eternal flame. I send you messages of love on wings of steel. I bless you with the knowledge of eternal wisdom. You are most precious, oh, gift of the universe. You are a seed of contentment in the eyes of your maker. You are never to misjudge yourself as lacking, for you are indeed perfect. This you cannot always see, but believe me when I say that your very core is perfection itself. This does not mean that everything you do is perfect, or that you have learned all there is to know, but on the level of spiritual truth, you exist as part of a perfect universe. So rise above the down-grading of your ego. See yourself as the being of light you are. Seek yourself. Know yourself. Let your wisdom surround you. Do not be hard on yourself if you do not act Godlike. It is the learning that is important, so do not struggle against yourself, condemning yourself on the way. Accept yourself and then go higher. Do not deny your humanness; if you did not feel and act as a human being, you would not be there at all. You see how this is? Do not repress your humanness. Do not deny yourself, do not place expectations on yourself which you cannot reach. You are not a poor sinner, but indeed you are a being of light. Only by being who you are can you grow and transcend. When you repress yourself, trying to pretend to be other than who you are, then you will find yourself stuck in one place.

Bless you, my dear, dear friend. How nice it is for us to be together again. Let us now talk of some important things. That is how to live in a world where violence is seen to have far more power than the force of love.

April 18, 1988
**On violence &
the force of love**

You are all afraid of the power of violence. You try to keep it in check, but accept it as part of the human condition. No one sees how to overcome violence on a grand scale. It always seems to be hand-to-hand combat. That is certainly a dilemma because often the choice of how to proceed against violence is to use violence in return. The alternative seems to be passive suicide where the forces of evil would be allowed to overrun the world, enslaving all who did not fight against them. Thus, you there still have not figured out a way to have peace of any lasting kind. What you commonly call *peace* is only a stalemate of forces. You see that there does not seem to be any other answer. And you wonder how it ever can be different, as you are all so vulnerable to hurt and physical pain and death. And those who have no care of that seem always to have the greater power. You think they have only been held in check by the use of similar means which have been used on the side of good and right. But you are very mistaken.

There is no violence that acts from the standard of Divine Law. It says, "Thou shall not kill," not, "Thou shall not kill unless it suits your purposes." But I acknowledge your dilemma. And it will remain a dilemma as long as current beliefs are held. Believe me when I say there are other ways of living with each other, but they will only come when your beliefs have been exchanged with others. Then the answers will be easy, but that time is not yet. The awakening is yet to come, though of course, there are very many who are ready for it.

Believe me when I say the force of love is stronger than all the violence that can be imagined. It has power beyond your belief. But stay fast. Do not allow your thoughts of doubt to overwhelm you. Keep your eyes focused on the light. Let it illuminate the inner reaches to search out those passages within you where the seeds of violence lie. Violence and war are not out there. They do not exist as freestanding elements. They exist because they represent the core of belief within you all. So cleanse yourself. Purify yourself. Be honest with yourself. That's all there is.

April 19, 1988
A message
**Holding on to the
lighted path**

You would like a message to begin your group. You can say, "I welcome you all here to this gathering of souls who are trying to lead the way for all who follow. The fact that you are gathered here to read these writings speaks well for the changes that are to come. But for now you all live in this present world, one that often reflects pain from every angle. It is sometimes only by hiding your head that you can bear to live your life in a normal way. Let me assure you that you are not alone and that life need not be burdensome to you. You only need to learn that all that is seen is not all there is and that which is unseen is that which has far more importance. Do not live your life by petty means. Open yourself to the wonders of the universe. See the magnificence of life before you. I know how hard it is to ignore the everyday and focus on higher vibrations. But if you but try, it will become easier. For now, enjoy each other here and share in the force of love which surrounds you all."

Let me talk to you a little bit about something else and that is how to live in the light when you feel the darkness of everyday cares closing in. The light illuminates the day and night and keeps you safe and secure. But it is very possible to lose your sight of it so that your way is dimly perceived, if at all. Let me see if I can help you to see how to hold onto the lighted path.

A meditation

If you try to meditate everyday and focus on the space where the light shines, then in time you will be able to see it. If you focus on this for five minutes each day, then soon you will be able to visualize the light as it comes from the Source. At that time it is important to walk toward it in your mind and step into it. This visualizing will allow you to see yourself bathed in this healing glow. Try this and see how it works for you.

A blessing

Let me give you a short blessing for tonight. May your heart be open to the songs of life around you. May you feel yourself blessed by the radiant light as it shines upon all the creatures of the world. Feel your oneness with them. Know that you are as safe as the rabbit in the burrow or the robin on the wing. You are indeed one of God's creatures and belong in this kingdom of life.

Q: Do you have a message for me?

It is time for us to write again. But you must be careful when you are too much in a trance because you are very open to influences. Be sure to surround yourself with white light. Do this now. There, that is better. You ask if I have a message for you for today. I have many, but I will choose one. Now my dear, dear friend, I will tell you how very nice it is to write with you. It brings back remembrances of other times when we lived on earth together and shared our hearts and minds with each other. We knew each other so well that often our thoughts were as one. That is why you are not surprised at what I write. You know this all well. You have often taught me things which I now share with you. So this is my little message of love and remembrance.

Now a little message for your group. You are gathered together to share the energies of your love. You come together and let your essences mingle with each other, creating visions of beautiful color. When you join like this with others of like minds, you are truly blessed. You will take home a recharging, a beatitude of feeling and a sense of greater love and connection than you came with. Your life is a springtime. Enjoy it. Savor it. Live it with gusto. Don't hide yourself. Don't be afraid of the challenges of your particular life. Enjoy the knowledge that you are all part of a greater whole which has sense and order and love as its standard. So relax into each other; know that you already share common elements and energies. Let them blend into a new song. Open your hearts to receive it.

Here is a message for those who would use these words to aid in their everyday living. For you, bless you for your attempts to change your view of how things seem. When you use these words to live by, you will find your life becoming easier and easier. But you must let these words influence your thoughts on an ongoing basis. Do not let yourself get so caught up in your daily life that you fail to listen. Set aside some special time; let your thoughts dwell on the words. Let them penetrate into your core of being; allow their light to soften you, to brighten you, to fill you with the certitude of knowing. You can hear when you listen even over the tumultuous clanging of your world.

A message
**On letting these
words aid you**

But you must take time to listen, to ponder, to try and then these words will help you to live in a way heretofore unseen.

I am with you again, and we will go on with your lessons about fear.

Fear is one of the emotions along with anger that rules you all on a day-to-day basis. Your fears haunt you. They frighten you. They control you. They are there in hidden form under many guises and many times are very destructive to your growth. When I talk of fear I am, of course, not talking about the fear that warns you of real danger, but that fear which warns you that whatever is about to happen, or may happen, or just happened will result in psychological distress. You see, the fear is double-barreled. You think that it arises in response to something, but in reality, the fear is the fear of your own emotional reaction. As long as you think that you are afraid of something external, then you will miss the mark. Take speaking in public. You may start to sweat just thinking about it and say, "I'm afraid to speak in public," but if you were able to see deeper, you may find that your fear is really that of being afraid of experiencing the physical sensations that accompany standing up in front of people; and the fear that stops you is the fear that if you stand up in front of people, you will experience emotional distress.

You see, this is different. You then refuse to stand up in front of people because if you do, then you will feel physical distress of some kind or another. Now let us look at this distress a little closer and see if we can find from where it comes. Remember, earlier we talked of the energy system which encloses the body and all its cells and organs. And we talked of how this energy system was influenced by your thoughts. We talked of how thoughts were stored in this energy system and could cause blockages which could starve and even kill off cells of your body. The mechanism is very simple but difficult to convey to you. You see, this energy system is the place of emotions, and it is connected, of course, with all the other systems of your body. You must always see that all systems of your body are interconnected. Thus your immune system doesn't operate in some individual, unique way unconnected to the rest of the workings of your body. The same is true of the energy system. It is connected and affects, interacts and controls certain functions. The mind, body, spirit and emotions are not separate; they function as one system with subsystems within subsystems.

Fear as an emotion occurs in the energy system, as do all the emotions. This does not mean it stands alone without connection to other parts of the human system. Thus fear or other emotions are connected to thought, to body physiology and to spiritual paths. Thus, you see, when you feel fear, this is a rather complex phenomena. But let us look at it a little more closely. The purpose of fear is to protect you from harm, so it alerts you when something threatening is pending. Thus you would feel it if you were confronted by a live tiger loose in your yard. There is also a remembrance that if once you were attacked by a tiger, you would be even more fearful the second time around.

However, the actions of thought and belief are also important. If you had no belief that tigers were dangerous and instead believed them to be docile, you would not feel fear as you did before. Just as an aside, you might feel momentary fear if startled by one, as that startle response is instinctive. So you see that fear like other emotions has a natural component and then is subject to consequences from mental processes such as your belief system. It is your belief system about what constitutes danger which is very important to look at; often when a belief is changed, then the same fears may not affect you.

Fear is a process of the energy system, as I said, and this sometimes is very dense and blocked so that it is not a simple matter to change the popping off of the emotion. At that time, the power of your thought can help. It is important for you to get to know your fears, as we talked of earlier, and to use your cognitive powers to process your various fears. But there is something else you can do. Anything which works on the energy system itself can be helpful in relieving places where the energy has become blocked and dense. If you think of your human system as one whole functioning system, you will see that you can alter any one part by placing change in some other parts.

Thus you can change a fear response by body work, by mind control and by raising your spiritual vibrations. If your life is being blocked by fear, try these avenues and see what happens. It is important to listen to some fears. I do not advocate petting tigers on the head, but on the other hand, if you are fearful of ten-pound kittens, then your fear is not productive for you. If you have other fears which impede your growth upon your path, then you must also consider these as nonproductive. So examine the stop signs of your life and see how these relate to the beliefs you have. See if there are changes you want to make and see where in the overall system you can institute positive change.

I send you a message of love from me to you. Let us talk briefly before you must go off to your work.

I will talk some more about fear and how that often operates in your life to stop you. But this time I will talk of how fears can ... you must keep your thoughts still. As I said, fear can also be disregarded in your life when, if you were to listen, you would then realize that you were in a dangerous situation. In this case, awareness would result in the necessity for change. Many of you live with some wild tigers indeed and think that you have no other choice but to live in fear. Fear is pervasive in your world. It exists in the home and family, in the community and in the world. The proliferation of weapons of all kinds speaks of the fear which resides at all levels. But you all accept this as a necessary condition and become habituated to the feelings of fear. When you become habituated to fear and accept those conditions which produce that fear as normal conditions, then you are stuck in the mud by your belief. When you accept your belief as reality then all your acts can occur only within the framework of that belief; i. e., buy more guns, build more fences, or whatever other device makes you feel less fearful. The way out is to break your belief system open to look at it and see if your beliefs are instrumental in creating the conditions. I know this will take much thought but do not simply accept that things are the way they appear.

Oftentimes two fears—or more—will be activated at the same time. Thus the woman who is being battered will be fearful of her husband, but she will be equally fearful of being alone in the world, or without funds or some other fear which is unnamed. Here again, it is important to know yourself, to be able to discriminate between realistic fears of something out there and fears which portray your inner environment. Only by knowing all of your fears personally can you make wise choices for your life. If you pretend some are more important than others, if you tend to deny that some even exist, then you will not have the same range of choices to make. Fear is an indicator to you; it is not a state to live in. Be sure of this.

I will write a little more about spirituality and what that is. You are all thinking much more about spirituality and what that means. You ask, "Must I channel or be in touch with spirit guides, or is it how I live my life? Must I give myself over to helping others or pray each day or what?" This is very confusing for many of you as we slide into a time of renewed connection with Holy Spirit. Let me see if I can clarify this any for you.

Spiritual path refers to *that journey of your soul which is eternal.* It has gone on, and it will go on until such a time when all souls are again united as a whole. Until then, your spiritual path is that which you follow toward *enlightenment*, that is, *becoming a being of pure light*—this path you follow whether or not you are in awareness of it. It is impossible to be human only; you do not exist like that. So you always are on your journey; however, like any journey, you can become lost, you can go in wrong directions, and you can suffer breakdowns or get stuck in the mud. So you see that at any one time, as you define it, you may be lost or stuck or whatever; but in the larger picture, you are only momentarily off your path, even though this might be a lifetime for you. You do not have the blueprint or map in front of you about what you have chosen for this life, but that is not necessary. Your goal is always the same—the purifying and growth of your soul; and thus you can live each life in accord with this goal and you then will always be on your path, no matter what the specifics of your earthly life are. However, do not think that all you have to do is sit around and pray and you will make swift progress. You see, life is the testing ground. You must live it. You must engage in it. You must meet the challenges of your particular life. You can only be who you are. You cannot leap into Godlike status by merely acting like a God. There is much more to it all.

As I have said before, you must look inward, see and hear your interconnections. Ponder on this. Struggle with it. See that which is placed before you. Check your journey with the map of Divine Law and this will help you evaluate your actions. Look for the helping hands who will smooth your way. Listen for the guiding voices who will comfort and lend you sustenance along the way. Acknowledge that you are spirit. Refuse to live by everyday standards. This is all for now.

April 30, 1988
The search for meaning

Let me talk to you now about the meaning that you and others can find when you look for it in your present situation. Many think that *meaning* is something that exists above and beyond the everyday visions you have for yourself, and this is true to some extent; but, on the other hand, meaning is something which is integral with the everydayness of your life. It does not exist only in the sky but under your feet as well. So when persons ask the meaning of their life, they need not look only at the big vision, but at the little ways that they live their life, day by day. What meaning do you see for the way you live each little part of your life? You see how this is? Do not see that you have to wait for the inspiration that says, "At last, a meaning for my life. I now have worth." It goes the other way. "I have worth and now let me use the knowledge of my worth to devise the meaning I want my life to be." You see how different that is. The meaning of your life *becomes*—it is not *is*. As you devise, create and enact, then the meaning of your living becomes apparent. You have choice in this; it is not bestowed upon you. So, do not hide behind your confusion. Do not hide behind your indecision nor behind your beliefs. Stand up for your life and enact the meaning you wish for yourself. This search for meaning is indeed a search for your own creation. Hear this, listen, and hear with both your inner and outer ears. Act now. Do not wait. The time is now for you to create your life.

May 6, 1988
On illness & health

There, my dear, I am here with you again. You are sorely tried today by your concerns about the number of people who seem to be seriously sick, and you wonder about what this means. (I had several clients who were recently diagnosed with cancer.) Well, you are just more aware today because of your phone calls, but of course, your world is full of people who are experiencing physical distress. You see, this is a part of the reflection of what is happening in your world. I have often told you of the interconnectedness of all things, and because this is so, then you will find that the health of all of you is touched by the culture, thought and other facets of how you construct your lives. You cannot pollute the environment without that having system-wide outcomes. You cannot pollute your thoughts without that having consequences. You cannot use your dogma to control without that having reactions. You cannot live without love without that having effect. You see everything interacts and interconnects.

You wonder why everyone isn't sick, only some. Well, my dears, you all are to some degree; but for many of you, your healing systems work better than others because you have found ways to keep yourself from being blocked. Others of you live within a black cloud of negativity which finally chokes off the cells and life blood of your body. So you see there are many variations within your society and some are more healing than others. But make no mistake, you do not live healthy lives, by and large. This is not to condemn you, since the way of your world is not to promote healthy environments. Many people are working hard to overcome negative forces by diet, exercise and other healthy practices. This is commendable, but you must realize that you are working against a gradient which attempts to sicken you as strongly as you attempt to make yourself well. The changes that must happen if you are to return to a time of health for all are very large. For now, all you can do is to continue to nourish yourself with light, play, good food, exercise, energy modulation, meditation and prayer and, of course, generous amounts of love energy. Construct a vision of a healthy world; work toward it in whatever small or large steps you can. Love life and care for it as though you did truly want to give your love to it. Whatever you do to this end will have positive results. You need not worry that it is not enough. Just give and it will be sufficient.

As to your clients who are ill and afraid, I will send this message to them. My dear, dear, friends, do not be afraid. We are with you to help you along this way. Do not let your fears overwhelm you, but open your hearts to the learnings which come with this challenge. You see, your illness is not only an accident. You are not merely a little cog that went awry. While on the earth level you feel cheated of your life and feel angry and scared and alone, I want you to know that on the level of spirit, it is a whole different story. You are moving toward another phase of your development, a phase you have been through before. And if you but let it, this knowledge of how it is done will return to you. But you must open yourself to hear with your inner ears. There is much to be learned here. Some learning will take place on the worldly level, but believe me, the chances for accelerated movement of your soul exist now. Let yourself give up the worldly cares and turn your eyes inward and upward. Let yourself come to us with peace and joy. We await you with open arms. Your journey here may be long or short, but if you open yourself to the spirit within you, you will find that there

A message
To those who are afraid

129

is already an eagerness to return to the Home of Your Heart. Do not hurry this. Take all the time you need for the learnings of your earthly life. Say your "goodbyes," but be ready for your "hellos." This is not an ending, but merely another chapter in your book.

May 7, 1988
On feeling guilty

You feel very bad because you lost some of these writings in your computer. (I lost the first of April's writings due to a computer error when I was trying to assemble them for reproduction for our group.) Do not worry about that, though I know it has made extra work for you. There is time enough to hear this message in many ways, so do not worry that something irretrievable was lost. You want to know if I remember and will say it all again. I remember and will say what needs to be said, but I will not just repeat it all. But I will answer your request to write once again about guilt. For the rest, you can ask me what questions you want.

As I said to you before, guilt is the most overvalued emotion that you all engage in. You have elevated guilt to something akin to morality and think that you are reacting to God's laws when you feel and act guilty. Guilt has a place in the whole scheme of human nature or you would not experience it, but many of you use it to escape from responsibility for your acts and think that if you feel the pangs of guilt that is punishment enough. You then allow yourself to repeat the same behavior, again inflicting self-punishment in the form of guilt. This does not suffice. Guilt's purpose is to let you know that something you did resulted in harm to another and to let you know that there is an action which should not be repeated without clearly knowing the reasons for doing so. In your culture however, guilt often is not accompanied by any such realization. You excuse yourself by ego self-massage so that you think you have done a good deed simply by feeling guilty. Let me assure you that responsibility for your acts is a very different thing. To be responsible means that you have an awareness of your acts, that you claim them as your own, and that you are willing to atone if that is necessary, to change your behavior if that is necessary, or to go ahead with your acts, knowing the full consequences of your behavior. This then leads to awareness and enlightenment rather than absolution by punishment.

You also would like a message or meditation for your group. Here it is.

Welcome, all you dear souls, to our gathering once again. There are a multitude of songs which rise from your energies, and these resound through the skies of our world. You are truly blessed to be with each other in this room sharing in the expansion of your hearts in love. You all share much here together and this shared love expands to fill this room, this house, this community, this city and so on until it fills the universe. I bid you to open your hearts to receive all the gifts of this evening.

Now a short meditation.

Lie on your back and let the muscles of your body become limp and fluid as though they were part of the green grass. Feel yourself as a blade of grass which sways and blows in the wind but which is deeply rooted in the ground so that it is very secure. Let yourself experience this feeling of being at once secure, and, also, as flexible and moving. Let yourself know that this is how your life is; that you are rooted firmly in the land of Divine Love, but that you are also an ever-changing, flexible, fluid human being who sometimes feels tossed this way and that by the changing winds. But see, you are rooted firmly, no matter which way the wind blows. Experience this now.

Now let yourself feel yourself growing, becoming longer and stronger, forming flowers and seeds, maturing and ripening. See this cycle. Now experience the wind of winter which dries your stalks and covers you with a blanket of snow. Feel your roots. You are still deeply rooted and cared for. Experience this. Now, again let yourself feel the new green shoots of spring bringing back the life growth. And still you are firmly rooted. Experience this. And know that this cycle repeats itself ever again, each time repeating the cycle of life and, that through it all, through whatever changes happen, you continue to be deeply rooted in the bed of unconditional love. Experience this and then wake when you are ready.

I will speak to you a little of your discontent and fear that you are trying to control and manage. This will be a time of much growth for you if you are able to meet the challenge which has been placed before you. Each day will bring new learning if you are able to keep your eyes facing forward and your ears tuned to wisdom. If you listen to your fear, that will be another story indeed. You must, however, not ignore your fear for it has

131

important lessons for you. Listen to it. Converse with it. Get to know it—its background, its family, the belief system in which it lives. It is the avenue of your learning. If you only try to submerge it, to bury it, to pretend it doesn't exist, you will learn little from it and it will continue to give you pain at every opportunity. Do not be afraid to feel the pangs of your fear; you are strong enough to withstand it. You will find ways that will help you to do this. I do not mean that you should live in pain, but there is no chance of getting to know your fears unless you are willing to feel its pangs for awhile. You will find that it doesn't last long when you speak to it with interest and respect. Your fear is not there to harm you, but to protect you, even though its protection may have been devised for a long ago time.

Bring your fear up to the light of day. Cleanse it. Clarify it. Examine your beliefs around it. This is the way to growth. Try this for awhile and see how you are.

A message

I will give you a small, goodnight message. You must not worry so about whether you can understand all of what I write about the unseen universe. You will never be able to see clearly as long as you are human, but if you listen to what I write and expand your faith, you will find it much easier. As your mind expands and your consciousness grows, more will become clear. Do not struggle so hard, but be steadfast in your belief. All will follow from that.

May 8, 1988
Choosing a life of abuse

Let us talk of some important things that you have questions about. You wonder why souls would choose a life where they would be brutalized or abused as children. You see you were very close to the truth when you said that this cannot be answered from the framework of every day. There, of course, it makes no sense, but when seen from the viewpoint of eternal growth, then there is a different perspective. You see how that is? When souls come to earth with a plan laid out for themselves, it is not to lay out a life of pleasure or earthly riches, but rather that the life they choose will aid them in expansion and growth. There are times when souls choose a difficult life because they know that living that life may result in potential learning for themselves or others. You must not look at this in a narrow way, you know.

On the other hand, there also is the earthly level where free will exists and events happen because they happen or are enacted by someone or other. I know it is hard for you to see that two simultaneous levels are occurring at the same time using the same events, but this is how it is. When you achieve the ability to tune into both levels at once, you will know this is so. But you can also accept this as true, and if you so believe it, then you will be able to envision that all happens within both a worldly context as well as a Divine context. While an event on the worldly level may seem horrendous, on the broader Divine level, it fits exactly into the scheme of evolution and creation. Take this on faith.

This does not mean that you should then say, "Oh, then it doesn't matter if children are abused. It's just their karma." Oh, no. That is not the way at all. You see you cannot abscond from your responsibility for your own learning. This will not do for long. Whatever occurs on the worldly level is interconnected with the spiritual level. They do not exist as two separate entities. I know this distinction is difficult to comprehend, but you are simultaneously flesh and spirit. As flesh you have certain lessons to be learned and the lessons may come in the form of abuse or being an abuser. It is what you then do with these lessons that is important.

You see, if you have chosen a certain lesson for your growth, that growth comes through the learning presented to you. The knowledge that you gain becomes a part of your soul knowledge and is carried with you. It takes many situations and many varieties of experience to provide the necessary knowledge for enlightenment.

So do not condemn God for allowing abuse or other pain. See that this exists in the world as such, and it is the task of all human souls to gain the knowledge to eliminate it. This, you see, is a long, long process but do not think on that. Just live your life. Live it with imagination and creativity. Look for the wonders in it; seek the challenges in it. Glory in it for it is ripe with learning for you. Seek and you shall find. That is all for now.

I am here to speak with you once again. I will again talk to you of something important, and that is how to live your life so as to be in connection with All That Is. You see, I have often told you that it is not living in a way that you contemplate your navel or that you pray twenty-four hours a day. What counts in the whole scheme is how you live your life on a daily level. This is sometimes hard for those of you who were taught that you are sinners and need to pray for forgiveness. This is not the way it is. You are not sinners but have the capacity to act in a myriad of ways, some of which are counter to the glory of creation. Many of you now act in ways that are destructive to creatures, whether they be humans, animals or other living things. You justify this in many, many ways, including seeing yourself as separate and superior. You have lost the sense that you all live as one synergistic whole. And so you can delude yourself about your own actions while condemning others. You see how delusional your thought can be? It is a very difficult time for you as you have lost the cultural supports for helping you to see the wholeness of creation. Your worldly god is technology and science, and you think that all the answers are there. Look beyond this artificial world you are creating. You know that it does not bring you peace and contentment. Live your life in connection with the larger meaning. Look for your connection. Feel how it feels when you raise your consciousness by meditation, contemplation, prayer or any other means you have of stilling the everyday chatter of your brain.

Look at nature every chance you have. You need not go to the wilderness for this. It is there on your street corner. Look and see the mystery of it all. Learn that you but glimpse a minute part of the truth of it all. Let the birds and the flowers be your teachers. Look closely and you will see life. Then look at other beings in the same way. See that they, too, are miracles of life. Look beyond the pettiness of everyday and know that each time you meet a human being, you are in the presence of spirit. Let this knowledge inform you. Let it transform you. Let yourself know that no matter what outward signs persons exhibit, they share with you the wonder of life—which is eternal. You are all engaged in a wonderful production which is still in a beginning stage. See that you all have parts to play. But the ending is not foretold. You are creating, each with each other, as you go along. Your part encompasses your sphere of influence. How you act within that sphere has enormous impact. Do not excuse yourself by minimizing the import of your actions. You can have no import other than within your sphere; however, this import grows with the energies of others, creating never-ending waves. What you do is not lost. So be aware. See your behaviors. Take charge of your life.

Do not blame others for what happens to you. Grab the challenge as it is given you. Learn step by step what it means to live a life of informed action. Do not condemn yourself for what or who you seem to be, but neither allow yourself to be complacent about that. You have enormous capabilities that you are not using. As you free yourself from the constraints of your present day thought, you will see how your capability will expand. Let yourself hear these words within yourself. Contemplate on what they may mean to you. Let that knowledge reach inside to where your beliefs lie and let this new awareness spring-clean your belief system, discarding beliefs which no longer serve you. Let your eyes wander inward to see what changes could occur. Let this happen. Let the peace that comes from knowing you are one with the universe create a sanctuary for you. Live your life from within this sanctuary. That is all for now.

(I felt sort of out of sorts and a bit depressed without there seeming to be any reason.)

May 11, 1988
Relief from depression

You want to know what is troubling you such that you feel depressed and low. If you will look inside to where your heart lies, you will see that you are holding a small pain there which is troubling you. This is not related to your present situation, but it comes instead from a long ago time and it is surfacing for you. Let me tell you how to handle this. First, let yourself fall into a meditative state where you have closer access to you unconscious knowing. Then let your hands rest over your heart and visualize fresh cleansing water flowing from them. Let this cleansing take place until you feel relief. Know that you need not be afraid of that which arises from your depths. It is all for the good of your growth. However, it is not good to ignore the pangs you feel. You must listen and pay attention to them as they have something to tell you. Do this now. (I did the exercise and, indeed, felt relief.)

Q: Do you have any other message for me?

A: No, that is all for today. You will find yourself feeling better as the cleansing continues on its own. So before you return to work, see this happening. Then look around at the natural world and let your joy at its beauty rise. This is one of the best ways there is to reconnect yourself. You see, to reconnect yourself is to reconnect with the Source. To center yourself means to reach inside to that part which is always connected. When you allow the world to become too real for you, then you will suffer distress. Take time whenever you need it to reconnect. You need not wait until you are so distressed that you feel like a truck has driven over you. Relief is always at your fingertips, literally and figuratively.

May 12, 1988
**Women &
feelings of guilt**

It is very important for you to continue with your group and it is also important for you to speak whenever you get a chance to. I know you sometimes feel that a burden has been handed to you, but this is not true. Don't be afraid. The opening to your life is now. Let yourself be brave about this all and everything will be fine.

You had some questions about guilt in regard to how many people, especially women in your culture, appear to feel guilty for everything that happens. You are right, but this guilt stems from a belief system that has been handed to them which stresses that they are indeed the ones who are responsible for everything that goes wrong. This is another aberration and is not instructive for growth. Women are too often seen as lacking in power, but yet they are viewed as having the power to make everything go wrong. This is, of course, not the case. What I said earlier about guilt being useless holds true in this situation also. If women did not allow the use of guilt, they would soon see that they could not be responsible for all they take on with their guilt. Clarity would follow. But as long as guilt is so easily accepted, no other choices are seen. So go back to what I said before, and you will see that it has validity.

A message
**On the sunshine
of eternal love**

Now a message for your group. Let the sunshine of eternal love visit upon you. Feel its warmth through the fabric of your lives. Let the radiance of it illuminate all the corners of your mind, stilling the everlasting chatter. Let its warmth visit you and bring a rosy glow to your countenance so that all who see you are inspired to smile. Let the love that abounds in the universe fill your days with joy and hope. Let it nourish you from the tips of your toes to the tip of your head. Let it fill all the crevices of your life. See how this room is radiating that love energy. Feel its healing presence. Release your cares into it. Let it melt those spots of anger or fear that may still be left. Let it come to you with a burst of pure joy. Take this with you into your world and spread it wherever you can. The benefit of love energy is sorely needed in your world. So take it now, amplify it and send it back out. Bless you all.

Q: Can you talk of unconditional love?

A: You want to know about unconditional love and what that is. The term refers to *love that is a freely given exchange of energy.* This you do not quite understand because you still think of love as a feeling rather than an energy. Try to understand this distinction. If you think of love as an emotion, then you look to yourself for a particular feeling quality which then says, "I love this person." Often as we talked earlier, it really is something else altogether, but you have been conditioned to think of that as love. Love as an energy is something different. When it is taken in and amplified and then used in your dealing with other people, it bestows grace on both of you. You know that energy is constantly being exchanged between all living things. Some of the energy that you give out to others is in the form of a positive charge and others is negative. Some energy exchanges are positive, giving a feeling of recharging; others are draining, leaving a feeling of depletion.

You all know how this feels. When you are in control of the love energy, this is a very potent positive charge. It affects you and it affects the other. When you see others without the filters of competition, or envy, or anger, or comparison, or judgment, but are able to see them merely as human beings who are spirit itself—as you are—then you are able to send and exchange this energy freely. This is unconditional love. But when you are wanting something in return, when your thoughts toward the other are controlling or manipulative, when you are really being dependant, then the love energy exchange is not un- conditional. You see how this is? Love energy freely given nourishes the other and also yourself. It feels very good; it leads to good health and contentment. But for all of you, it is a difficult thing to do, mostly because you do not understand the whole business of loving. But if you think on this, and let yourself experience how it might be, and try it out a little at a time, then you will see it is possible. This does not mean that you will always be able to control your emotions, that you never will be judgmental or any of the other ways in which you relate to each other. But you will begin to make distinctions as to what love truly is. It is a very validating thing to do.

The next time you feel hurt by someone, imagine your ability to tune into the universal force of love and see what happens if you project that out toward the other, allowing that person to be simply who he or she is. You are all in different places in your development. When you judge each other, you imply that your place is better than the other's. This is not true.

Bless each other, for your ways are difficult enough. Can you imagine a world where the force of love was exchanged on a minute-to-minute basis and you were all filled to the brim with its vitality. When you view someone from the field of unconditional love, you know that you truly are one, but, at the same time, separate souls, embarking on separate journeys, but yet these, too, are all one.

But you wonder how in the day-to-day relationships, does this work. Well, sometimes not too well, but you must see that much of what you label as *lack of love* is something else altogether. When there is much negativity, you exchange energy that feels very bad. It does not feel good at all. You wish nothing more than to be rid of the other, at least for a time. But you think you should not do that if you love someone. Give yourself a chance to renew your energy. You can separate for a time until you feel your energy renewed. That time, when most of you want to be angry at the other, is the time for unconditional love exchange. Then when the balance of positive energy is there, you can talk further about the issue between you. I cannot stress enough how destructive to a relationship is the constant outpouring of negative energy by one or both. If you come to see this, you may change things for yourself.

Unconditional love, however, is not confined to what you call *love relationships*. It refers to the way you interact with all living things. If you only see it in narrow terms, you will miss the mark. So be aware of your energy. Look at this for awhile and ponder upon it. You know when you are in the space with unconditional love for you will feel its glow. It is very attractive. That is all for now.

May 17, 1988
**A guide for
your life**

Here we are, my dear. Let me talk to you about how to live these writings on a daily level. We have talked of this before, but I know it takes a long time for your behaviors to change.

It is important to see these writings as a guide for your life, not merely interesting reading. There is learning here that will set you free from much of the turmoil you experience. First, you could read these writings every day and ponder on them in your spare moments. This will give you other concepts to think about which will raise your vibrational level to a different pitch than when you occupy your mind with negative thoughts. This in itself will have good results.

Then, second, it is important to use these writings in some way or other—to act them out, even if the way is very small indeed. This can be in relationship to yourself or to others. That is all the same.

Third is to set aside a time for meditation or prayer where you allow yourself to connect with your higher self or beyond. This will help to keep the everyday noises in check.

Fourth, and this is very important, is to imagine the preponderance of love energy around you and act in ways that you believe can help to spread it within your sphere. Pretend you know how to direct and focus it at someone. This will be sufficient. You see, you do not need proof that the energy of love exists. You only need to act as though you know it and you will be able to utilize it. Be creative. See what you can concoct. Be a cook and an artist and a craftsperson. See what happens. There are many opportunities during each and every day when you can change the direction of your behavior even a slight amount. Play with this. See what happens.

Remember always to be caring of yourself. Remember my words about how precious you are. Remember to validate your feelings. Do not punish yourself for them. Listen to them. Hear their plea. They speak to you of special truths and are not to be left unheard. Claim them as your own. Do not think they are the property of any other. Their jewels belong to you. Your lives are often difficult because you bury yourself in the trivia of self-survival. This is never in question, so do not waste your energies here. Think instead of growth. Use each day for the opportunities it presents. Do not walk through your life in the fog of the past and future, but look through the doorway of the present moment.

May 19, 1988
The purpose &
laws of creation

There is much to be said, but you do not need to fear if it doesn't all get said at once. Let me write just a bit before you sleep about what it means to be one with God. You see this phrase is often bantered about, but you wonder what does it mean. Well, first of all you must see that we are all one with God. There is no other. Remember I told you not to think of some ordinary man up here who is pulling all your strings. I will not try to conceptualize it for you because there are really no words to convey All That Is. But there is a little more to the saying. It implies that your actions are in line with the purpose and laws of creation.

What are these, you wonder? Well, first and foremost is the ever changing creation of perfection on all levels. The next is to hear and follow the teachings that have been set out for you a hundred, nay, a thousand times. These are very simple and they involve the use of love energy on a daily basis. There is not much more that is needed if you but follow that dictate. So to be one with God also implies an understanding and acceptance of your connection to all of life here and in other planes. This is one of the more difficult lessons for you all to learn as you do seem bent on categorizing people and then judging them as good or bad, depending on where you stand. This causes enormous trouble in your world.

If by a stroke of magic, judgments of others could be wiped off the face of your world, there would be much happiness. This is true on a personal basis as well as a political basis. There are other ways to view each other than as superior or inferior. This is not the message of Divine Love which sees all as equal. But I know you have a ways to go with this. Still you can strive on a daily basis to minimize the judgment you make against others. See how many times a day you do that and then reduce it by one each day until you develop a different way of seeing.

May 22, 1988
A message
Knowledge to
illuminate your
paths

(In Arkansas, written before meeting with a group of people who also channel.)

Let me give a message for the gatherings tomorrow night.

We are very happy to be here in this room filled with radiant energy. The way has been long to bring us all together but now it has been successfully traveled. You all have been together at other times and this is one more opportunity for you to create out of your oneness. You will find sustenance here with each other and you will aid each other in remembrances of long ago times when the world was a very different place. Take this energy with you. Take the knowledge shared between you and use it to illuminate your paths. The way from here is only dimly marked, but you will all have need of that support which you can provide each other. So, enjoy your meeting. It is full of import for you all and for the earth. Bless you all.

Now let me give a little meditation for you to share.

Relax into your beingness. See this as a beautiful sea of crimson, placid but alive, comforting but active. Experience yourself as a particle in this sea, alive and moving, separate but connected to all the other particles which live in the sea. Enjoy the security and safety of this wonderful, warm sea. Now see that you join with other particles forming a new, yet still old, form. Still you are as one in the sea of being. Experience this new form. See how it feels the same, yet different. Now see you and the other particles forming new, more intricate forms. These forms are different from each other but still the same. You continue to experience yourself as still a part of the Great Sea of Being. Know that this is so. You are always thus. There is no other. No matter how simple or complex a living form is, each is all awash in the great, wonderful Sea of Being. See your home. See your families, See how you are all connected here in this wonderful creation. So do not experience loneliness or isolation. Experience your oneness. You are always surrounded on all sides by yourself. Experience this now and then return to the everyday consciousness—but retain the feeling of oneness with All There Is.

And just a little message and then I will leave for today. Much is happening in your life right now and sometimes you are experiencing fear about this. Just know that I am by your side and that everything that is happening is important for you on your spiritual path and on your life journey. Do not turn away from it nor do not try to figure it out from your past. Have faith; stay in the present and only see that all that comes will be of importance. I will be with you. You only need to turn to me when troubled. I can see much further than you and will be able to allay your fears. See all that is happening from a wider perspective. Do not fear from the narrow one. That is all for now.

A message

141

From the Beings of Light comes a blessing and a thank you for the seriousness with which you are all approaching your responsibilities to each other and to all the creatures of the earth. There is hope stirring within the hearts of all living beings. That hope, at this time, is only small and tenuous and still surrounded by the fear which has been generated by the events which have been ongoing for many, many years, but it is a hope nonetheless. The work of many souls is filling the air with messages which the creatures can read. You will notice the bird songs are louder, the trees are greener, the animals are friendlier. All this bespeaks a growing awareness of the possible. Stay on your paths. Do not become encumbered, but stride forward with lightness and joy in your step. The journey is not hard when you support each other. There are many who are on the same highway. Do not fear breakdowns or weariness for they are there. Comfort and sustenance are there for the asking. Hear our words. Carry them in your hearts. Let them inform your everyday acts. Let them spread through your sphere of influence. That is all that is necessary. Come swing with us higher and higher into the light.

(Written in a campground in Arkansas—I had awakened at midnight and lay awake worrying about all sorts of things. I asked for some help.)

You have been sorely troubled in the night and I feel very much for your pains. You did not try very hard to help yourself and were content to let your fears and pain take you over. You know this is true, but I understand how easy it is for this to happen in the dark of the night. But here you are in daylight and you are confronted with a new day, or else you can continue the old one in your head. You want to know what to do when feelings of negativity loom, and they seem to have more power than the external day, no matter how pretty that is.

You see, the inside environment is really all there is. When that is filled with negativity, it is very hard for anything else to make an impression. You say, "How can I stop it. It seems to come from someplace. I don't know why I would cause it to happen. I just want it to go away."

Yes, I know. The negativity comes from a combination of old and new and is a blocked field which repeats itself over and over. Do you see how few new thoughts there are. The same ones keep repeating and repeating, trying to bring about change without having any effect. The purpose of such thinking is to propel you toward action, but it becomes short-circuited and just goes around and around. There is an element of anger in all negative thinking. You think that if you express these feelings, then you will be in trouble, or you think that you will spoil things, or that you will suffer a defeat.

But under that are some of your basic needs, some of your deepest needs. The negative thinking circuit is defensive against the emergence and expression of these needs. It is best when feeling this kind of thinking to switch into a spiritual mode and pray or meditate because the level of these needs is so deep and you are so vulnerable that you will not likely find sustenance is your world. However, it is important to deal with anything in your external world that is possible for you to. And you will find that you will be able to do this better if you allow spiritual comfort for yourself.

Sit here beside me, my dear, and I will give you comfort and messages of love and forgiveness. Today you are feeling a little more grown-up, but the child within is still stamping her feet. Well, just let her do that. Listen to her as she was not listened to before. You see, it is most important to care for your child selves and not to push them away as they once were or to abuse them as they once were. Often you do not want to hear them because they carry pain with them, but they are not responsible for that. Hear them. Comfort them. Let them express themselves in safe ways. This does not mean to just let them act out. No, it is something different to hear them. You are not your child-selves, but you can pay attention to their voices and offer nurturing out of your adult self. I use these terms because they are familiar to you. That is not quite how it is but can be described in this way. Your mind is wonderfully able to speak in symbolic terms so that is fine to use these symbolic terms. For you can be sure there are not little children running around in your head.

You want to know how to care for your child selves and to listen to them. I will give you some pointers. It is good to visualize your child. Often images or pictures will come which will give you some clue as to what the problem is. At that time you can assume a stance of respective listening and seeing so that the picture becomes clearer and more detailed. And then you can

May 26, 1988
A message
Caring for your child selves

picture interacting with that child, giving her, in the visualization, what seems to be needed in a caring, nurturing way. Also, pay attention to yourself to see if you get any clues as to how you might normally behave when you get messages from your child self. See what compels you or impels you. See if any beliefs arise that may have been activated years ago. The time of an eruption of a child self is a wonderfully rich time for self awareness and appraisal. Most of the time people are unaware of the effects of a child self reaction.

What if this child self is angry, stamping her feet, wanting to hurt someone? See her pain. See what may have frustrated her. You need not punish her, for that has happened much in the past. Love her. Do not be intimidated by her. See if her needs can be met through you in other ways. Sometimes you can do this by visualizing, other times in actual behavior. For, you are her and still want what you didn't get then. Think of concrete ways to satisfy the child within. Validate her rights to love, nurturing, respect, care, concern. Teach her to expect these in her life. Help to achieve them in both your lives. She does not need to live in deprivation. You see, this is often the basis for continued pain, that is, that you continue to treat yourselves in ways that were given before. So, my dear, take some time and hear your child within. Do this now.

June 1, 1988

You are holding yourself very tense and that makes it more difficult. Take a minute now and I will relax you a little more. There now, that is better. You are being your own worst enemy these days, but you will soon be feeling your old chipper self. You will benefit by affirmations and meditations. Be sure to follow your own advice about being in the present and thinking positively. Do not let your brain run itself. It just will go in circles. You also have not been paying attention to the beauty around you. That is there for you; it will ease your fears.

A message
On prosperity

Now another little message for you about prosperity. You do not need to be so fearful as you did when you were a child. You have many more resources, but it is essential to maintain a positive attitude and belief system around prosperity. You need not hold yourself down, out of false pride. The only important thing is to keep in mind that prosperity is only another facet of the abundance of God's plan, and that it does not exist by itself. Do not be fearful. All is well. You only need to trust and it will be so. You see when you trust in the inner powers, then you will find life easy. When you try to control things by your brain, then it is another story.

Let me give you a small meditation for you.

A meditation
Capturing the beast

Relax yourself and then let your mind's eye wander into the wilderness where a wild beast lives. See yourself in the kingdom of this beast, alone and fearful. And then see how, as you relax into your fears, they relinquish their hold on you. And see how you can use your ingenuity to capture the beast. Let your mind rove freely on this task and see what is revealed to you.

Come, my dear, and sit beside me and I will tell you many things. These days have been hard for you. You are finding it hard to remain on a spiritual path. That is OK. There are lessons to be learned and all will not always go smoothly in your life. You will benefit, though, by meditating every day. If you make this a priority, you will find that all goes much easier. The main thing about meditation is that it allows you to connect with your deeper, higher self which has much more to offer you than your everyday ego selves. You are resistant to following this advice, but I ask you to consider it as I know it will benefit you.

June 4, 1988
Wonders of the world

Now let me talk of some other things that may bring some feelings of joy to you. And that, again, is about the wonders of your world which often are ignored as you all go along your way with your heads stuck in the cobwebs of non-reality. You miss so much of life because your eyes are blinded by your thoughts. Look around you now. Let the beauty of the natural world penetrate through the fog imposed by your everyday concerns. See yourself as part of this wondrous whole. Let your fancy be tickled by the insects as they go along their merry way, doing the tasks of cleanup. Wouldn't you like to have a crew of cleaners that could do such a good job. Look, too, at the birds, delight in their grace and sureness. Watch them and own your connections. Look at the leaves and the grass and delight in the coolness and peacefulness of their color.

Let that color surround you and enter you. Look at the sky and the water and let that blue of spirituality and contentment enter you. The colors of nature are just as important as the beauty of it all. The colors exist as a means of balance, not only for you as humans, but for all of the myriad forms of life. The colors themselves serve you all, whether you are aware or not. But if you focus on the colors in the natural world, you will see that they can restore a sense of balance when you are out of kilter. The colors of the rainbow are to be found there and each color will supply energy of a particular kind. You see how this is? Try it when we finish. That is all for now.

June 5, 1988
**Positive &
negative energy**

There we are. You are feeling very fine this morning and that is good. Let us go on with our lessons. You want to know if your negativity in Arkansas was caused by negative energy picked up at the channeling meeting. Well, it is this way. There was an influx of many entities there, some of which are not as highly developed as others. Because your general mood was also in a somewhat negative state, the energy of these entities was drawn to you. You can tell when this is happening when you feel less positive after a channeling session. The way to cleanse yourself is to meditate on positive things, especially natural world things. And also, do all the things I counseled you about last week when you were feeling negative charges. This is why is is important to protect yourself when you meditate or channel. It is also good to be careful when you are sick or ill feeling because you are more open to energies that will resonate with your feelings. That is why you sometimes have difficulty connecting with me when you are feeling out of sorts.

Let me go on with other things.

A meditation
Rainbow Colors

You would like a meditation for today and I will give you a short one.

Let yourself relax into a position of contentment and peace. See that with each breath you are drawing in the life force which comes from the Eternal Thou. Feel this life force enter you and expand throughout your body, bringing energy to it. Now let your mind's eye see all the colors of the natural world come in with the life force. See the red of the cardinal and the rose. Feel this high energy which brings you health and passion to your life. Then see this change to orange. See the natural world resonate with the orange of the oriole and the orange groves. Feel this color enhance the inner balance, bringing you energy of the life force. See the yellow of the daffodil and the gold finch. Feel this yellow color penetrate and bring to you the highest level of spiritual truth. Let these colors enter with your breath. Now see the green of the world. See how the greens prevail. See that they bring you peace and contentment and connection to life. And now see the blues of the world. The sky and water, the blue bird and the iris. Let this blue enter. Know that it aids in healing your spirit and helps bridge your connection to the All There Is. Now let yourself see the purples and lavenders. See them in the flowers and the sunsets. This is a very high vibration of color and signifies the highest spiritual connection. Breathe this in. Know that these colors balance your energy on a continuous basis. Feel the rainbow which you have invited in. See this within you. Let your energies align with it. See this happen. Now when you are ready, return to this world.

I also want to talk with you about forgiveness. We have not talked of this, yet it is a very important concept for you to have. You all have had the occasion to forgive yourself or others for transgressions or slips of a moral nature. But the concept goes far beyond saying, "I forgive you and will forget you ever did something to me." You see, often this is said but not carried out within your hearts. There is often a holding on and carrying on from the past. You speak of lost trust and so on. The concept of forgiveness goes beyond that. It is one of the universal laws that is practiced here and is available at all times to all of you. You often ask God to forgive you and yet do not know that forgiveness happens on a minute-to-minute basis as you describe your time. Forgiveness happens. There is no other. This is more than acceptance or forgetting. It goes beyond that. You see that your earthly concept and that of the universal are not quite the same, though they are in the same family, so to speak. It would be helpful for all of you to ponder this and think of how this knowledge could influence your behavior toward others. I want you to expand your notions about forgiveness. I will talk more another time, but want you to ponder and meditate on this. That is all for now.

On forgiveness

You have been needing a helping hand but have not asked until now. I am here for you whenever you have need. That is all you have to do, to ask. But I will give you a message of love tonight and comfort. Do not worry about things. Just go ahead and do what needs to be done. All will go as it should. It does not do to fret about that which is in the future. Just keep your eyes on the present and make your choices there.

June 8, 1988
A message
Making choices

Let me talk to you about making choices when there is a dilemma because one choice is equally as good or bad as the

147

other from your perspective. It is not difficult to choose when there is great disparity, for then it is clear which to choose. But the way is especially hard when the choice is between two things that are on a par with each other. Then is when you try to second guess the future, thinking that will help tip the scales for one or the other, allowing you to see the "right" answer. You know how this is. It is there that you sometimes get stuck because you cannot move one way or the other.

Well, let me tell you first of all that you cannot use the possibility of a future outcome to help you unless that is already apparent in the present. So ask yourself if this which you project from the future is already evident, or does it need to await the passage of time to see if it will come to be? This can be a help, but often this is not enough. You just find yourself stuck because you don't want to choose either of the options; you want the choice actually to disappear. Well, my dear, you know already that you cannot solve the problems of your life by turning from them for long. Do not delude yourself, but know that action is necessary. To choose between two items which are lesser choices needs an act of will, a going beyond ambivalence, a choice with a big "C." Only by acting do you move forward. To use your psychic energy to attempt to change things will only bring you hardships.

There are a number of ways to value each side of the question, but in the end there is that step that you must take in one direction. At that point it is important to let the other choices go, for you have now embarked on a portion of your path and there is not a turning back. So do not fret, wondering if you have made the right choice. Be brave. Go forward. Know that there is only movement when you move. The future happens as you approach it. Let your fears go. Let your clinging to other choices go. There is nothing else. You can only move from where you are so keep yourself centered and at peace with yourself. Let your intuition guide you. Meditate on your questions. Appeal to your higher visions for your life. Do not make decisions on petty values and all will go well.

June 9, 1988
Staying calm & centered in the midst of turmoil

Now we can write again. I hope that you will follow my writings so as to have a easy time of all the changes which are happening in your life. I am here for you and will help you to pass through your rough spots. So be sure to turn to me and the writings you have written before as they will be of help to you.

I will see what I can do to help you. This is all as it should be. Do not despair.

Let me talk to you about something else and that is how to stay calm and centered in the midst of turmoil. The extent of your upset will be dependent on how seriously and tenaciously you hang on to what was. You can be sure that to try to hang on to what once was will be to make your days seem very hard and the way untravelable, for in your world you cannot go back but only forward. This is not true all over, but on earth it is true. When people put all their energies into wishing for what once was, then they find themselves unhappy indeed. So the way to travel through trying times is, first and foremost, to relinquish the past whether that be something of long standing or something which just passed by.

The next thing to do is to turn to your highest guides, God, your spiritual self, or however you view your spiritual connection. When you do this, you then are able to relax into the passage, knowing that whatever is happening is part of your Divine Plan and the way will be made easier by listening to the part of you that has access to higher wisdom. You will find that these two steps will assure almost instant easing of your turmoil. Then you can also be in touch with what you can learn on the earthly plane from your situation—in what ways can you unearth "buried treasure," or grow, or practice some of your past learnings.

Most people try to make passages as hard as they can by developing negative attitudes and behaviors, blaming others, blaming God, or just retreating into self-pity or apathy. This does not help your growth one bit. You see when you only look through the narrow eyes of your ego, you cannot see far enough and feel only that something is lost. But that is not the case. Only by sometimes separating from the past can new vistas open.

It is not enough just to sit and cry and wait for the new movie to start. You do have free will. Your acts are all important to the future. So lift up your eyes and ears. Listen to your deepest self. Know that there is possibility for your growth in everything that happens. All of these ideas will be of help if you but heed them when undergoing a passage from one phase to another. Try to develop a perspective that allows you to see around the bends of your river. Know that the scenery may be different but you remain the same. So do not despair at the log jams of your life. Use you ingenuity and go on. That is all for now.

Let me congratulate you on your spaciousness today. You see how much better you are feeling. An element of joy is arising within you as you become more and more centered in your own beingness. So many traps in your world can pull you off from your center, and sometimes it takes great concentration to pull yourself back. That is why meditation is so important.

Relationships often have the potential for causing shifts from your internal knowing to a focus which lies within the other. This causes a great deal of unhappiness because it is a focus which can only be half carried out. You see, though sometimes you can feel like it, it is impossible to merge two identities into one. When there is partial submergence of one to another, there is a resultant loss within yourself that causes distress.

This is often the cause of disagreements and fights; that is, the attempt to withdraw energy that has become trapped within the boundaries of another. If you were able to see how the energy flows between two people who are exchanging love energy, then you would see that there is an uninhibited flow back and forth. But when there is a shift of locus from one to another, then the energy does not flow freely but is trapped and blocked and turns in on itself. This is the cause of distress. You see how this is?

Well, you ask, how can one stay focused on one's self? This takes some learning and reassessment of what it means to love someone. We talked of this often before and you might go back and read that. You see, you all have expectations of what love should be like and too often they involve how someone should behave toward you. Too often much energy is spent in trying to get someone to love you better or more or in a different way to match your own needs. The more you place your focus on that other person, the more your center is pushed off. You see, only by staying within the boundaries of your own self can you stay centered.

There is much misconception about how to relate to each other, and there are few who seem able to do this in a way that is enhancing to all. There has been much written by many people about how to be in relationship, but until some very basic beliefs fall, there will continue to be difficulties. Relationships are not solutions to your own personal quests. They only serve you on the way. They are not an end in themselves. The goal of your life is your own spiritual growth. The relationships you engage in are there to aid you in that, not only by giving support but also by providing challenges and mirrors for you to use. Many relationships are karmic. They occur because of a previously agreed upon plan and offer immense opportunities for learning if you but use them that way. That is all.

Let me give you a message of love for you and all the others who read these writings. Our wishes overflow to you for a day of peace, contentment, beauty and joy. We send this to you. Don't neglect its message. Do not hide behind petty, everyday concerns, behind depression, self-pity or the myriad ways you have of denying joy in your life. Do not tune into the negative thought forms but open yourself to messages of pure love. It is there for you from all of us.

Now let me give you a message for your group. Welcome, my friends to this evening of communal blessing. Open your hearts for there is much to receive. Open them wide to receive the bounty of love which will soon be percolating between you. There is much strife going on in many of your worlds. It is a time of change for many of you. It is a time of personal growth for many of you. This time of great change is visiting itself in the lives of many of you. Some of you receive it with excitement and others with fear, some with joy and others with anger. It is all there for your growth. Receive the changes in your lives with open arms. Do not try to push them away, clinging all the while with arms of steel to the past. Let go. Embrace the new. Set your footsteps evenly in the path of the new. Do not look back. Your life lies ahead. Think carefully before placing that step, but once you have placed it, follow through with a firm tread. There you go, continually onward into your life. That is the way of it. You take with you a myriad of gifts from the places you have come from. Count these gifts now. See what you carry with you in the form of wisdom, strength, friendship, etc. Now let me again offer my hand to all of you to hold as you embark on new journeys. Take it whenever you need a steadying, whenever the new way seems rocky. I will help you across those rough places. So, my friends, go for it.

Let me say a few words about change. Many times people get upset because something changes just when they have settled in for a long winter's nap, feeling content with what is. At these times, change is often experienced as stressful or negative and is greeted with feelings of anger. The strongest feeling is that you are out of control and that the forces which are in control are playing dirty tricks on you. This is not the way it is. Change is only experienced as change because of the perspective you hold toward the way of life. You see, you only look forward one step at a time and often actually think you have stopped in one place. Well, my friends, that is illusionary. Life is a constantly moving, constantly changing process. Nothing is static which is of life. You may create illusions about this but it is not so. Change is only the outcome of this process as you experience it. If you were able to stand above and see your life from conception to death and beyond, you would see an even flow which did not involve periods where the flow was stopped and then changed direction. It is all of a piece.

So accept this. Let the knowledge flood you with ease. Change is the means of life movement. The new leaves on the trees could not be there without the changes of the previous year's growth. Accept your life. Take it in your hands. Move with it. Be in flow with it. This will ease your minds and hearts. Do not cling to the past. You know what happens in your canoe if you try to stop or slow yourself by grabbing onto branches along the stream. Let go, join with the flow of your life. That doesn't mean that you should not paddle or direct your craft. There is a mixture of going with the flow and using your will. Relax, my dears. Enjoy the ride.

June 21, 1988
A message
Take comfort in the path of your life

Hello, my dear. Here is another message for your group and perhaps a meditation.

Welcome, all of you to this evening of communal bliss. Let you eyes and ears open so that you can receive all that will be given here. Let your hearts open to give and receive the love energy that abounds. Let your spirit soar with its wings that sing so that you will feel freed of your everyday constraints imposed by your ego's too pragmatic a viewpoint.

Look around and see your friends. Let your heart sing with the knowledge that you all share on a much deeper level than you normally would think. Let down the barriers between you and let your energies mingle as one. I send you love and messages of joy.

Now a meditation.

A meditation

Relax your body into a state of comfort. Listen to the breath of your body as it comes and goes. See how perfect it is. Play with its image a little, concentrating on its comings and goings. Now as your body relaxes, let your mind's eye wander upward, going forth into the sky so high that you are able to look down upon your life. See how the line that reaches from birth to the present and beyond is all of a piece with turnings here and there, but that it is a smooth, unbroken path. See how it goes from one place to another with ease. Pay attention to its various phases, but also pay attention to its connectedness. See how it meanders homeward. Some of you have only traveled a small part of your path while others have been journeying longer, but it doesn't even matter, for the same is true of the inch as of the mile. Take comfort in the path of your life. Know that there is nothing there that doesn't fit, no matter how you viewed it at the time. Look at anything you want from this perspective and then return when you are ready.

I have a few other things to write to you about, and that is how to live with uncertainty. Uncertainty is often experienced as a very stressful time. Your brain tries to bring order and certitude, but it doesn't work. Sometimes a period of uncertainty is necessary in order that good decisions can be made. There may be unclearness, a need to wait, a time of indecision. But often you feel irritated and upset and become antagonistic to yourself and others. I want you to know that times of uncertainty are often necessary, and you will do better to allow them to be and use the time to gather information, if you need it, to gather your thoughts, to weigh and assess alternatives, to wait for clarity. Do not try to force that. You may need to wait for a time, but if you wait until all seems right and easy, then you will have saved yourself some pain.

On uncertainty, choices & actions

You want to know how this is related to choices and actions. Well, of course, they are all things you do together in some ways. But I am talking of those times when circumstances are such that you can only wait. There are reasons for this need which you cannot always see. When you try to hurry things, you may find that you expend a great deal of effort without results. You cannot force the universe to act. It will take its own time which is different than your time. There is a need to be in the flow. This is not so easy to learn how to be, but it can be learned. Pay attention. You will see how things happen easily when you are in flow. When you become distressed and try to change things, even when you know you have no power to do so, you just will add to your pain. Trust is a very important concept. This does not only mean to trust in God or the universe but to trust in your own inner knowings. Listen to yourself. You may not get it the first time, but if you continue to do this, it will become clearer. Do not only listen to your ego's demands, needs, wants, etc. It will lead you a merry chase. Stop often. Ask yourself questions and listen for answers.

June 22, 1988
On change &
natural cycles

You wonder about the drought and what this means on a cosmic level. Well, of course, this has impact on both an earthly level and a spiritual level, but that is not so easy to explain to you. This is not a punishment, though it may be that an awakening will take place from it. The way of the earth is an orderly one, but it follows order which is too complex for you to see. The earth is only following her own laws; she is not trying to do you in, you know. The earth operates on a time schedule which is different from yours. You believe that somehow she is there for you, and that because you believe in your control of her, she should be tame and obey your orders. Believe me, she does not care a whit for your orders. So you see that, while the way of the drought exists apart from humanity's business, all creatures, including humans, are, of course, affected. But it is only another happening—on a larger magnitude perhaps—that touches many, many people. It is no different than a million happenings which challenge you. There are lessons to be learned here. Hopefully some of you will see them. The way of life is not smooth, but it need not be hard if you can develop the perspective which allows you to see life in a broader way.

You want to know when the drought will be broken. Well, my dear, it will be some time yet. There will be little rains, but the drought itself will go on for a longer time than you now think possible. I will not tell you not to worry for I know you do, but remain steadfast in your trust.

You ask if there is anything you can do. You can strew rose petals in your garden. This will not help, but then, you see, you cannot do anything to make the earth change her plans. You see, the mass of human beings is not in tune with the earth. You have built your structures and conduct your societies in such a way that the natural cycles are neglected and misunderstood. So you will continue to suffer when the cycles change because you are all very rigid. You see how this is?

When you all realize your interconnections and you realign with the natural world, then life will begin to seem more worthwhile.

You wonder what is in store for all of you there on earth and worry that there will be casualties from the drought and other problems as the earth tries to right herself. Well, you know the ways of the earth and those of humankind are not always the same. You have tried very hard to control her eccentricities, but she still can beat the pants off you when she wants to. I speak of *her* because you are very used to the term *Mother Earth*, and indeed she is the sustenance for you all. You have been aware now that all you eat must come from the earth or, more accurately, must have or have had the life force within it. This is a good revelation for you to have. You see, the very complex system which includes all of life is one that you barely understand. The order of it all is so magnificent that it is almost commonplace to you. You are able to see some of the cycles and the means by which homeostasis is maintained. But there are other workings that are still beyond the sight of your scientists.

So, for instance, they know that there are weather cycles, but they do not know the regulatory purpose of these. So many events of the earth are seen to be random rather than the complex workings of a very detailed order. You see, that order is maintained universe-wide. It does not only apply to some areas of life. There is much more to it than that. I cannot explain all those details to you. Suffice it to say, when you begin to acknowledge that order is and does exist, then you will see that all that happens is for the good of creation. You cannot always look only at you as human beings and think that somehow all should go as you want or need it to. You are only one cog in this system, and if all would go for your benefit, soon you would have no world to exist on, for there would be massive shutdowns on all fronts.

You see, the earth must care for herself. She cannot be subservient to any part of her brood. Do you see that? You as a *spirit* count. Sometimes as human beings you may find that you do not. Think on this. We will talk again. It is not that you are insignificant, but you, as beings, are not as significant as you might think. I will write you again.

June 26, 1988
*Let yourself live
with joy*

Let me start by offering a word of comfort for you. Do not take everything so seriously. You are trying to control the whole world. Release. Relax. There is no way for you to gain enough power to right the wrongs of the world. Only stay within your sphere of influence. Only do what you can do. But beyond that, let yourself live with joy. Do not live with gloom. Oh, I know there is much to be found, much to suffer pain over, but do not despair. It truly does not help as it only adds to the negativity in your world. Help if you can and want to, but do not think that you help anyone by suffering for them. You see how that is. There is empathy and even sympathy and there is aid, but to feel pain over the myriad tragedies of your world is foolish. I know you think that comes because you are aware, and that is true to some extent, but to suffer needlessly only reduces the influence you do have. But, you ask, "What if everyone acts like nothing is wrong and just ignores all the ills of the world?" Well, my dear, things may be better. But no, I am not advocating sticking your head in the sand. But, you see, you can be aware and still offer help, but not by living in pain. That does not help at all.

You think it might motivate you to use your energy or resources to help. Well, it seems more likely that you will feel discouraged and despairing, such that your energy is wasted trying to make it through the day. The world is full of painful things, things you call *tragedies*, but you see, you too are only a part of your world. Do not be afraid to live with joy. Do not be afraid to offer and receive love and friendship. Do not be afraid to experience happiness. Do not be afraid to let in the light of life. You do not have control over very much, certainly not the drought or the rising of the sun or the many ways that your culture has developed which leaves marks upon too many of you. I have told you before to keep your eyes turned to the positive, to put your energy into the positive. You can only live in your time, and you can have influence there, but do not punish yourself. That is not necessary.

I will write a little more and will say a few words about the feminine principle you have been thinking about. You see the world now reflects a strong imbalance within the forces of Yin and Yang, male and female, or any other term you wish to apply. You have lost sight of the power of the Mother, the generating, creative, nurturing part of the All There Is. Again it is difficult to explain this to you as I do not want you to form a concrete picture of a mother. But suffice it to say that both the Yin and the Yang principle exist on the highest level in peaceful harmony. One is as necessary as the other and, unless balance exists, there is chaos. You, in your world, now are in and have been in, for a long time, a state of imbalance. You see where you are. There is much need for a swing to the other side so that the forces which operate in your world will again flow in equally balanced ways. There is, of course, much happening in the present which points to that direction, and more will happen as time goes by; however, it is up to all to open themselves to the changes that are necessary. But again, do not think you have power to control. You must just go along and do your part, however you see that.

On the feminine principle

I want to talk a little about what happens when the male principle becomes too strong. When this happens, all beings suffer, for there is an increase in power and strength which exists in the form of control, war, violence and destructiveness. Again, this happens when there is an imbalance. This does not mean that the male principle *is* these things. You see the difference? All suffer—including men. They are not the perpetrators but are, instead, victims also because they cannot be other than what is expected by a society which is unbalanced. Women, of course, suffer too because they are denied validity in a society where only the male principle is paramount. If your world is to continue, this imbalance must be corrected. If it is not, then ultimate destruction will occur.

On the male principle

Many changes are happening, but much more will have to happen before you can say that balance exists. There will need to be a reawareness of the powers of the Mother. Mother Nature, if that is how you want to view this principle, is much more than you generally ascribe to that concept. You cannot worship the male God only and have any real understanding of the true nature of creation. Let your thoughts flow this way for a while. This is why I often talk to you about the wonders of the natural world. Let yourself study these, be infused with them

On the Mother God

and see how this flows from the Mother God. Again, this is not a separate being. You must not let yourself fall into that kind of thinking. There truly is no father and mother in the sky trying to decide on how to run things. But you can use terms like *Mother* to increase your expansion of what God may be. Pay attention to the life force. See how it is balanced. Pay attention to nature and see how creation and destruction are part of the same ongoing process. One cannot live without the other. If there were only creation, there soon would be no room for anything more. If there were only destruction, all would soon be barren. All the opposing forces are actually parts of the same whole, a whole which is the source of everlasting life.

You are all part of this plan, but you must remember that you are not the plan nor do you run it. You are within it. You are it. You are influenced by the same processes as all the other creatures. You only think you know more, but you are only within the context of a larger whole which you only at times glimpse dimly. So, my dears, relax into your space. Take charge of that which you can, that which involves yourself only. You have been given yourself. That is all. See what you can do with you. Live your life this way. Live each day with the purpose in mind of bringing yourself to the fullest you can. This is not to be perfect. This is not to have so many expectations of yourself that you faint from trying to even imagine achieving them. No, my friends, it is only to strive for greater understanding. You are a single person but also part of a population of human beings. You act in concert with each other. Over time, your songs change, sometimes becoming more melodious, sometimes more strident. The hearing of the songs helps determine what will be sung next. So listen to the songs you sing. Pay attention to who the members of your chorus are. Look ahead and see what needs to be sung next. Then join your voices. I urge you again to remember that you are not alone, that you have myriad connections to all creatures and numerous connections to those of us here.

Take heart in this. Remember that that which occurs to you there is not the only thing happening. That which happens on your soul level is so much more important than the daily cares you devote so much time to. I know this is the way of it, but do not get so enmeshed in your trials and tribulations that you miss the bigger messages. There are many changes happening now and I know that sometimes there is confusion and a feeling of having lost your footing, but take care to hear my words about the overriding plan. That is all for now.

Hello, my dear. It is a very nice day in your world today. Let the pleasure enter your body and bring it joy.

You are wondering about many things and have been reading about the complexities of life and realize your scientists know very little compared to what there is still unknown. Yes, that is true. They have only very little slits into the unknown, but that is OK as that is the way it is. It will take a long time for the mystery of life to be found out. By that time, the consciousness of humankind will be at a state where that knowledge can be discovered without danger. At this point, there would be too much potential for harm to the entire life systems if some of the more mysterious items were decoded. You would like it if I would tell you some secrets, but this I cannot do. It is not my place to discuss the biological questions. You see, we all have particular areas that we can discourse on, and we are chosen as guides to particular people who have need of that information. Much of what you consider creative thought comes from guides who are giving information. As I told you, this process happens throughout your lifetimes.

Let us see how this might work in individuals' lifetimes. They will not be aware, usually, that information is coming from any place except their thoughts. Of course they do not take time to analyze what thought is and where it comes from. There is much information that is collective, but other information is passed down from guides and sages to those who are prepared to receive it. That is why it is important to learn as much as you can because then you have the conceptual framework to receive information. Let me say that everything that is, is far more complex than your scientists think. They are always eager to reduce everything to simple denominators, thinking they can understand better that way. But, though the answers to life are fairly simple when you have the key, they are much more complicated than simple mechanistic answers. But you do not need to concern yourself about that. Accept the richness and complexity as it is. Accept that the universe is more vast and more momentous than you can imagine. Let yourself accept that the current moment is so minute a speck in creation as not to even be measured by a blink of an eye. So do not hang on so tight to what is. It will be different in a moment. Creation is a continually changing, always in flux, process. You are part of that process but do not inflate your ego with your current position. All exists in the context of something larger. That is all for now.

Aging & returning to the home of your heart

Let me tell you about something else and that is how to live in a life where you continually grow older and less firm. There are many who fear this. They fear old age because at the end of that is death. So old age and death are seen to be linked in despair. But let me assure you that if you do not believe this, then it is not so. The time of old age is a wondrous time when it is accepted for what it is. When one tries to hang on to the buoyancy of youth, then, of course, it is another matter. As your body ages, there is a corresponding awakening of psychic energy which allows you to experience life in a very diffuse way. Barriers fall from between life and other life. You have to be open to these changes, but it is possible to get glimpses of the world which you will soon be returning to.

Do not fear death. It is a time of return. You will welcome the chance to return to the home of your heart. Sometimes the period before death is filled with pain and suffering as you try to hold onto your present life. You can here choose to let go or perhaps you can use that time for soul learning. You see the earthly is only one dimension. All experience is multi-dimensional. Flow with your life, no matter what uncharted shores it takes you to. Embrace where you are. It is where you are, you see. It can be no other. Life is not meant to be full of suffering. See how you create this in your life. You all have your own specific brand of torture which you inflict upon yourself. You each have a particular way of reducing your life to a hurdle-jumping sprint. But this you can change. Change your beliefs and see what happens. Your approach to life is all.

You argue that there seems to be real suffering in the world and that people don't have any choice sometimes. I say to you, that is a belief shared by many and that belief then is acted out in the world. When all changes, then you will see what I mean. You are both a product of your current culture and an instrument of its change. Do not be hard on yourself. That will do no good. Just know that you cannot escape being part of the ever-changing process.

Let us start out by sharing a small breath of relief for the glory of the day. You see that there are many interpretations of the way days can be constructed. You each live in your own version. Yours, today, involves a construction that is about average for you as beings, but it could include elements which would increase benevolence in your life. Do not be satisfied to go along, running on half a tank, so to speak. You can raise your awareness, your vibrations, to a level which brings a greater modicum of joy to you. You can raise your energy and see life expand before you. If you only stay focused in that little part of you that is consciousness, enmeshed in your thoughts and ideas, you will miss the whole experience of life. I know that you live very humdrum lives and have to focus your attention on your daily tasks. But I know there is more that you can do if you try. Do not let yourself grovel around in the hole. Climb up. See the sun. Look out. See the images of life all around you.

You want something specific to help you. You have something specific—yourself. Take yourself in hand. Do not drag along, waiting for the day to pass.

Hello, my dear friend. How nice to see you feeling happy in the sun. Isn't it lovely? I never get tired of seeing its magnificence. You see how this all fits together in beauty. I don't understand very well how you all choose to spend so much of your life looking at the ground rather than at the ground of being. But I know that is changing as more of you become aware of your connections to all of life. Let me answer some of your questions today.

You wonder why I don't tell you more of the secrets of the universe, why I don't tell you different things than are being sent to so many others. You want something so special that it would set the world on end. Well, my dear, you know that is your ego talking, but OK, I will tell you something very special. I have with me some very interesting spirits who will talk with you today. The first one is a man by the name of Lucius Smith, who was a very well known psychic and leader in England at the time of one of your lives. This was in 1713 in a town that was very close to London. But I will let him talk with you now.

Hello. I am Lucius Smith and I will give you a few hints as to how to learn to use your psychic powers and to develop your healing gifts. I will let my spirit guide you to learn the ways. The

June 30, 198
On expanding

July 2, 1988
The future &
its potential

A message from
Lucius Smith

161

most important part is to practice every day. You can practice with another or with yourself. Program into your mind that you have psychic gifts that you want to develop. If you do this, your brain will start releasing these powers. Psychic gifts are not out of the ordinary. They just are not exhibited very often, or if exhibited, are not paid attention to. Let me try to instruct you further. Right now, let your mind's eye wander inward. See a large blackboard in front of you. See what you can see written on that board. Do this now. That was good. You can use this technique to get answers to your questions. The more often you use it, the more valuable it will become.

You also thought that your life is poised for change. Well, that is true, but not right now. Let yourself enjoy the stability of your life. Let yourself learn and learn. Do not judge your progress or think what you should do. When it is right, then it is easy. But keep your eyes open and listen to your intuition. Let things perk and stir within you. They will stay on simmer for awhile, but that is necessary. Do not worry so, but trust in All There Is. You are going along fine for now and that is all that is necessary.

Now, I will let you talk to someone else and that is a spirit by the name of Helen Cameron. She was a close friend of yours and is now an expert here on living according to the laws of the universe.

A message from Helen Cameron

Hello, Dorothy. This is Helen here and I am here to give a little extra boost today. I am not really an expert. That sounds like earth talk, but I have been studying very much here and am responsible for the paths of many souls. That is not to say I am responsible, but I help them to plan and then carry out their life's work. I have often been involved with you, though you haven't been aware of that. Let me give you an example. Remember when you returned from Missouri and decided to go to school? I was very helpful to you at that time. You know that was a major turning for you there. You are almost ready for another major turning but not yet. Do you remember how easy that was? Well, that is how it is supposed to be whenever you take a major spiritual turning. Let me give you another example. When you met Julie, you knew that your connection was right even though your ego wasn't so sure. That too was the beginning of turning which hasn't played itself out yet. There is more to come, but don't fret trying to figure it out. Just go along for the ride. I am here for you as well as your guide, Jenny, and others, too, who have been helpful to you. Now I will give you back to Jenny.

Hello, my dear, how was that? Now you got to talk to some others. But I will still write to you the most. Let me give you a bit of learning for today. Your world is poised on a future that can only be dimly seen by a few. Even those of you involved in the heightening of consciousness can only see a bit into the future and much of that is projected hope. The world is poised. It is waiting. The future outcome is not assured, but the potential is there for a time of wonder. You don't know how such a transition can happen as there is so much that needs to be done. That is not the problem. Much can be done in a very short period of time. The problem is that there are so many opposing forces that it is still hard to foresee just what will transpire. That is why it is so important for all of you who are being called to do your part. Coalesce with each other. Send out your sparks to be formed into flame. Do not worry about whether you are right or wrong. Just act on your true beliefs. It is essential, dear hearts.

The potential for a time of wonder

I am here to talk with you again. This is a lovely day, though I know you are still concerned about your drought. Let me assure you that all is well and under control in the universe. Do not let yourself worry so. I know you all think that the only concerns are those which you see and feel today. That is not so. See if you can add the spiritual dimension to everything you do and then you will not get so caught up in living by your everyday concerns.

July 7, 1988
Being in the force of love

I have talked of this often because I know that it is very difficult for all of you to change your views about what is and is not important. You have criteria by which many of you judge the success of your life. There are other criteria, you know. There is a great deal of materialism in your world at this time and you all get caught up in that, but again, it is not the only way life can be lived. There now, we shall talk of some other things.

Let me talk to you some more about the power of love and how the manifestation of that in your life will enhance it a hundred fold. The experience of participating in love energy is one that is very healthy for your mind and body. It will heal many of your aches and pains and will keep your immune system functioning at a high pitch. It is strange, when this is available, that people choose, instead, negativity, hate, self-hate, blame and all the other ways of relating that lead only to breakdowns of their bodies and minds. If you were able to see the processing of your body on a giant screen and could see the difference between love and hate, between forgiveness and blame, between self-love and degradation, then there would be instant understanding. Because this is all invisible to you, you only half believe me. You believe that you would be too vulnerable if you gave up the protection of your negative thoughts. This is not so. But believe it, if you want.

You say, "But it is not so easy to give up negative thoughts and to be always loving." That is because you still are not clear as to what it means to be in the force of love. You think it involves liking everyone, giving to them, etc. This is not the way of it. Let me give you a little instruction. The first thing is to utilize the exercise I first gave you which will increase your connection to the energy of love, and then you will merely have to flow with it, spreading its abundance throughout your day. You know how it is when you first fall in love and are suffused with feelings which go out toward your beloved. You don't have to work at it or strive for it or anything else that is difficult. It flows from you non-stop. This is how it is to be in the force of love. Let yourself connect. What keeps you from connecting with the Source are all your thoughts, ideas, habits, etc., which are not in line with the creative purpose of the universe. Thus you cannot be in the force of love if you live a belief system which judges others, which evaluates some as lacking in humanness, a system which does not include care and concern for all the creatures of the world, one in which control and might are your means of relating to the challenges of your life. You see all these are barriers to feeling the wonderful power of love energy. You may need to assess your beliefs. See if they are in line with Universal Law. If not, then you will understand why you have trouble connecting to the Source. This does not mean that you cannot begin today. The connection is always there to be made. It is never withheld from you. You only need to reach out and it will be there.

A blessing
May the moon's madness enter your life

Now let me talk of something else. And that is a small blessing for your day. May the moon's madness enter your life to add a spark of mystery to your everyday affairs. May the light of the stars enter you and bring you the knowledge that all that is, is in order. See, they do not fall down upon your head. Let the warmth of the sun enter you, giving you life. Let the cool rains come to cast away your fears. All of these exist in abundance for you. Do not be afraid to reach for them. That is all for now.

You have been wondering how to live with others in a peaceful way when there is violence all around you. You wonder how it is that there is so much violence portrayed everywhere you look, and you wonder how the world can ever change enough when so many people live lives of a violent nature, even if only in their heads.

Well, my friend, I have said before that violence comes from internal pain. It is only the outward manifestation which you can see. You see, there is much internal pain and sorrow at your separation from the creative, nurturing God/Goddess. You all live so torn from the bosom of the earth as to feel your separation from the Mother as a wrenching that never quite leaves. You may go to the park or the seashore and experience momentary peace and contentment, only to find in the morning that your pain is still there. This is because your life style does not include ritual, beliefs, etc., that help you to feel your connection. Many of you are well-to-do, monetarily, but still suffer from internal pain. This pain is nursed and dulled by the narcotic of violence, whether that be on TV, in movies, books or real life.

There is a multitude of ways that pain can be dulled and this is a common one. Violence begets a momentary feeling of power and control. This, of course, does not last and needs renewing. You wonder how the cycle will ever be broken. And I say to you, that it will come as the connections to the All are once again made evident in your life. I know that this requires a massive change, but you can start now. Greet each day with a prayer of thanks for the beauty which surrounds you. Pay homage to the life force that abounds within you all. Gleefully bask in the power of love as it descends upon you. Let the knowledge of the spirit inform your way. Think of ways that you can incorporate the living spirit within your day. I know this is striking new ground and you do not have established order to lean on, but try a little—anything that will help you to feel your connection. Do not fret about what you see in the world around you. You cannot change the tide of humanity. Even we cannot do that, but have faith. Be true to yourself and to the Universal Laws. That is all for now.

Lucius Smith will talk with you now again.

You don't quite know what to do with my suggestions, do you? Don't be afraid to practice your healing and psychic arts. You will find that they come easier and easier. Let me give you a little advice. Don't be afraid to believe. Nothing is lost, you know, if you believe. Now while I am here I would like you to look at the blackboard and see what you can see about your bites. Do this now. (I had some very itchy bites. What I saw was to make a paste of fresh aloe juice and baking soda, which I did and it stopped the itching.)

July 13, 1988
**On friendship &
relationship**

You ask for some information on friendship and relationship for your spirituality group. I will see what I can do. You want a meditation, right? Well, I will see what I can do.

A meditation
**On when you
both were spirit**

Lie here and relax your body by counting your breaths as they flow in and out. Count them by counts of four—four in, four out. This will focus your thoughts on your body and will allow the connections to be made which will release your senses. That is good. Now, as you lie here feeling the relaxation spread through your body and mind, allow yourself to muse on a relationship, perhaps the one you are in now or one that is just ending or one that is just starting. It need not be one which is sexual but can be friendship as well—just that it is important to you. Now as you think about this other person and your connection, imagine that you can go back in time to when you were both spirit. Let your thoughts drift to this time. You can imagine this as it comes to you. Now when you see yourself with your friend or loved one, see what it is that you agree upon that you will help each other carry out in this life. See then how this agreement is being carried out in your present time. Take a little time to think on this. See what your relationship has brought to you. See what it is bringing to you now. See how this fits with that which you see to be your life plan. When you have finished, come back to the room.

Much is to be said of relationship. Some I have already written to you. There are indeed many ties with those you have been with in other lives and who have been with you between your earth lives. This is not everyone you come in contact with but there are many reconnections which are there for your support and learning. All relationships have potential for helping you learn. You often do not use these to your full advantage, but the potential is always there. Too often you look for relationships to cure something in your life. This only you can do, but certainly relationships can provide the catalyst for growth. If you did not see them as the cure all, the safety net, your security blanket, then perhaps it would be easier for you to stay centered and use that which the other presents as part of your growth cycle. You often get very stuck and cannot move because of your fears about giving up or losing another. Let go of that and see the opportunity before you for your growth and for the other.

Relationships are both spiritual and a worldly connection. They do not merely exist as earth-bound entities. Whenever you bond to another in love or friendship, this connection goes beyond the everyday and becomes embedded in your life plan. You see how this has to be. When you are in relationship, there is a joining of paths for the time you are together and, especially in terms of *love relationship*, there is often an even greater blending of your paths. So you see how you can add another dimension to the word *relationship*. Now let me give you something to read. When friendship and loveship are there in your life, then you know that you have an opportunity for soul learning. Relationships often are the woof or the warp of a time of our life so that the fabric which represents that time is intricately woven of your path and theirs. There is much to be said about why you chose a particular person. Often this is already pre-set before your births, but sometimes it is not. Either the ego or the spirit can direct one into relationships, but without a soul connection they will be short-lived. You cannot long join your path with another if it does not benefit the growth of your soul. This does not mean that all has to go well. The important thing is whether the opportunities for growth are taken advantage of. Of course, sometimes people do not listen to themselves and choose to stay in relationships that do not foster growth but only pain. This is a sad story indeed. This may entail that person repeating again lessons that could have been learned.

July 16, 1988
Relationship &
the growth of soul

I will give you another meditation.

A meditation
Opening the
Heart Chakra

Lie still now and relax your body. Feel a warmth steal over you, spreading from the top of your head downward over your face, down your body, down your arms, spreading through the lower part of your body, down your legs and finally covering your feet. Feel this delicious sense of warmth and comfort. Now within this feeling allow the chakras of your heart to open. Feel the expansion of the feeling that accompanies this opening. See the energy that comes from the heart, the love energy, and allow it to go to someone you care about. See that there is a never ending supply. See that this abundance of energy that comes from your heart is your birthright. It comes with being you. There is no shortage. Allow yourself to bask in this knowledge that you have an inexhaustible supply of love, enough to cover you and all that you come in contact with. See this happen now. See the room become filled with the love from your heart. Know that this energy draws others to you as they are enveloped in it. See this happening. Feel it. Enjoy it. Allow it to cover you with joy. Now allow yourself to gently close your chakra, knowing that you can choose to open it however much you want. Then when you are ready, come back to the room and ask yourself, "How different would I be if I were able to open my heart chakra and bestow love at all times? What keeps me from doing that?" That is all for now.

July 21, 1988

I am with you. Do not fear. I am here. You are very tried tonight but that will pass and you will soon feel better. Do not project your fears into the future. Do not see bleakness where there is not yet form. Just pray and all will be fine. Do not let your fears overwhelm you but remain steadfast in your trust. All will be well. Now you want some messages for your group. Here is a welcome.

A message
New & exciting times

My dear, dear, friends, I welcome you all here tonight for another time of communion and connection with each other and the powers of the universe. There is much love that will circulate amongst you tonight, so loosen your belts and start breathing it in. I send you energies of the outer world to ease your burdens and to bring you peace. Let the sun shine within, illuminating all the dark places, releasing into light all your pains. Relax now and let your energies flow and mingle with each other. I will talk more later. Now let me say a few more words to you.

There is much happening in your world right now, both for individuals, for nations, and for your world as a whole. Some are very involved in these changes while others hardly know anything is happening. For those of you who are aware, this is both a frightening and an exciting time. You sometimes don't know where to hang on to things are changing around faster than you can think. This is how it will be for awhile and trust is the most important attribute that you can use right now. Know that you are on your path. That may not always look the way you want it to, but be assured that you are where you should be. Do not force yourself to try to be someplace else. Just go along, putting your feet in front of each other. Remember to stay within your sphere of influence as that is the only place where you can have impact.

Here is a closing message for your group. Now, my friends, go forth for another month until we once again join our collective energies, but that does not mean you are alone and unconnected from the spirit of All. There is an unbroken connection between you and All There Is. You do not see this connection and you rarely feel it, but it is there, nonetheless. You exist as a piece of a marvelous tapestry, a tapestry made up of many different wools and threads, woven in such beauty that you could barely imagine it. The colors glow with *life*. There is nothing more wondrous than *life*. It is truly a miracle of *being*. You see, you often take it for granted, but look, look, look at the complexity. See how wondrous the tapestry is. Know that the thread you are is special and without it the tapestry would be flawed. Do not wish to be the whole tapestry—or a single color repeated throughout. Do not wish to be a picture created by yourself. Be content with that piece of the cloth of Life which you are, in all your brilliance. Do not hide behind others. Do not hide from yourself. Dare to be brilliant. Dare to be special. Dare to partake of LIFE. Be aware.

I will give you a blessing until we meet again.

May the winds of change blow gently. May the warmth of the sun melt the ice that lingers within. May the rains fall gently and warmly on your life, bringing the essential nutrients to you. May your heart open as the flowers open to receive all the gifts of the universe. May you find your heart large enough to fill to overflowing so that a continuous stream of love flows from you to all around. Let this be.

You are difficult to come into tonight. Let yourself open a little more. I will tell you what to do. Breathe deeply six times. That is necessary to get the energy moving. Then you should visualize talking with me in some way. Let the images form, but concentrate on our connection. Then let go. Let yourself relax into the process. Do not worry that I won't come. I am here.

Let us go on. You were thinking more about forgiveness and that is good. This is a very important concept for you to grasp. It is a twofold concept, as many are. There is that interpretation you have on earth and there is the one of truth. This is important but so is the earthly one. The use of forgiveness is a very beneficial, healing gesture for all concerned. It allows a releasing, a letting go of blocked energy that otherwise often leads to sickness and pain. The use of forgiveness on a regular basis is essential for health. This is not only forgiveness directed toward others, but also toward oneself.

But it is important to look beyond for clues as to how forgiveness operates. You see, if you only see forgiveness as something that you give to another for the sins they have committed, then you miss the mark. I told you before that cosmic forgiveness happens as an ongoing process, that the benevolence of the All leads to a view of life that does not require punishment for any of your acts. The view goes far beyond that. The understanding goes far beyond that. There is no limit. So when you, there, are engaged in forgiveness, it would be well to look at the situation from as high a perspective as you can. For, if you merely see yourself as victim and other as transgressor, you will only be looking narrowly from the ego's eyes. There is much more to forgiveness than that. It is no meager act, you know. When this act comes from the center, then there is far more meaning than that which I just described. You see, there are no real victims and no real transgressors. Forgiveness comes from that knowledge. If you try to understand this from the ego's view point, you will disagree with me. That is why it is important to meditate on this and hear the visions of the inner self. There this will be understood. The ego wants to be right, to be powerful, to feel good that it can be so big as to forgive. The inner self knows different. So ponder on this. Think on this. Meditate on this. Listen to your inner voices, follow your visions and we will talk again.

July 27, 1988
**The wonders of
the universe**

How are you today, my dear? I see that you are doing fine. That is good. Let us write a little before you have to return to work. I will write a little on the wonders of the universe, a topic I know you are interested in. You have been walking around in awe as the mystery of life unfolds in front of you. Sometimes you feel perplexed by its complexity and have so many questions of how it all stays together. Isn't that surprising? But if you look from the smallest to the largest, that is indeed true. I do not think I can explain the overriding principle to you as to how this takes place as it is more difficult to try to explain in words and concepts which you know. But see how your body works.

According to your beliefs, all which happens within your body is controlled by your brain, sort of like a furnace with thermostats registering when something needs adjusting. That is far from the truth. The processes of the body are not all governed by the brain. There is much free will in the various parts of your body, although that is not strictly an accurate term. But the various components of the cells do not depend on direct messages to tell them what to do. I do not know how to explain this to you as it is not my area of expertise. But like the parts of your body which work in concert with each other according to their plan, so do all the parts of the universe work in this way. The order exists and is carried out by the various components of any given system, whether that be on an atomic level or on the cosmic level. There are systems within systems into infinity. But they all function according to the overriding plan. I know you do not see any clearer from my description but that is the best I can do.

Continue to tickle your fancy with the mysteries. Allow them to help you gain perspective of your place in this creation. You do serve your place, not at the center as you as human beings so often think, but in your rightful place amongst all the creatures of being. Isn't that a relief to know that all this was not just created for your pleasure. On the other hand, you as human beings are unique among the other creatures on your planet, for you are the only ones who have the means to operate on your environment on such a large scale. You do not take this advantage very seriously and look at your purpose in a very shallow way. Your belief that all was created for your use allows you to wantonly use and misuse the forces of nature without concern for the impact on the rest of life.

There are continual battles between those who would care for the earth's bounty and those who would use it to extinction. This battle will not be over until there is a demonstrable shift in thinking regarding your place as human beings in the whole of creation. Your views have evolved over time, but there still is much evolution to come before you will see the truth of how it is. Now you all move in a mass toward your own destruction. But there is hope. As consciousness evolves and shifts, there will be reawakening of the need to live in harmony with All There Is. You were not placed on this earth to destroy it. Remember that. Do not say you have no control over that. You, as I have often said, only control your sphere of influence, but within that sphere you can act. It does not matter if you are able to bring about change. That is not the criteria you should use for your acts. Then you will feel frustrated and distressed at your helplessness. Act in ways that empower you. Join forces, if that will help you.

July 28, 1988
The world in harmony

You want to know how psychics can tell when something is going to happen. Well, they, of course, see beyond time and space and so can sometimes see upcoming events. But they are not always right because it cannot all be foretold even though there is simultaneous time and space. But you see, also, I do not want to set up a pattern with you where you expect me to let you get a jump on things. You can go ahead and develop your psychic abilities, but that is not my purpose with you—though I will be glad to help with the underlying problems that sometimes make decisions difficult.

Let us go on with something else. That is what will need to happen before the world will be able to live in harmony. You often try to see your place in these happenings but do not know just how to go about it. We have talked of this before, but I know that it is difficult to convert thought into action. You see, first of all, you do not have to make things happen. That is our job here, to send messages to many, many souls so the the changes which are happening will occur simultaneously in many areas and disciplines. You only need to let yourself swim creatively with the current. You already are providing some impetus with your groups. There will be more as you let yourself flow with the process.

You do not need to become someone else or move or do anything major which may or may not have impact. Sometimes you think you should drop from your culture and return to more simple ways. You can do that, of course, but it is not necessary and it is not how changes will come about. You see, you cannot change the path of your culture by all becoming dropouts. This would be chaotic. There is much more that can be done without this step. You all have a position in this play and you can play it in many ways. There is not only one choice, but many. I don't know if you understand what I mean, but it is as though you are a pilgrim confronted with a new shore and you need to explore what you have and what you need to do to survive. There will be much gnashing of teeth before the shift comes, but it will come.

Let me also tell you that some of the impetus will come from a strange quarter, one which you would not have thought was so important. But that will be in the future. Now, we are at the beginning of the breakthrough. You may or may not see massive changes in your lifetime, but they are happening. But as I often remind you, all is not totally foretold. There still are possible combinations that could lead to other directions. Let this be for now.

I will leave you with a message of love from all of us here who send greetings and blessings and hope to you there. Listen to us. We speak to you. We send you messages of connection. We send you messages of joy. On the wavelengths upon which we travel, much excited energy abounds. Let this in. Hear us. Respond to us. Let us help to shape your day. Listen to yourself and see how we resonate with you. Take time each day to be still and listen and see. This need not be for hours and hours. Just take time to be with your connection to the All There Is. That is all for now.

A blessing

You want to know how to respond to the needs of others without losing yourself. This is a task worthy of undertaking as much pain comes from trying to be split—one half satisfying someone else's needs and the other half being very unhappy about doing so. There is, of course, a place for transcending your own wants and needs to be there for another in times of great stress and need. This is what you as beings have to offer to each other.

July 30, 1988
Filling your internal needs

Animals, too, respond to each other in like ways. To learn to care for your own needs does not mean disregarding or sending to the scrap heap this very important concept of what it means to be in community. But this idea is often carried too far, whereby you respond to anyone else's demands, needs, requests, etc., as though you have to fulfill these or feel guilty. It may be because you have not made the distinction as to when it is appropriate to transcend your own needs. But often it is habit, especially for women, to act as though they existed for the purpose of another.

Let us see how this acts for you, there, in relationship. When you hear a request, you automatically respond as though that request is now a foregone conclusion; you have no say-so unless you can somehow fight your way out through anger, tears or other emotion which will clear the way for yourself to be heard. All, of course, do not have this same response but it is very common. I have often told you that you are very unaware of your own needs. You have spent a lifetime ministering to the needs of others so that only when there are no other needs posted on the bulletin board of life can you focus on yourself. This keeps you in a state of constant deprivation. Either you have to deny yourself relationship in order to feel yourself personally fulfilled, or you enter into relationship and subjugate your needs to another. You are learning but have much more to learn about this. I will try to help you with some pointers, but you will have to do the work as it will mean changing your program.

First, you would do well to take time each morning to focus inward and ask what your internal needs are and then think in what ways you can fulfill them. You will find that they often involve other people, but often not. You will begin to know yourself better. Now in the real scheme of things, you then will have to see what can actually be carried out. You may see that there are many ways of meeting those needs you have identified. You wonder how this fits with responding to others' needs because you think you can identify your own, but then you are stymied when others who are close want something that will fill their needs. Well, I still think you are not clear about yourself and need to truly identify your inner feelings. But of course, this is only the first step.

On negotiating The next step is knowing how to negotiate in situations where there is conflict between yourself and another. The signal is your emotional reaction. If you begin to feel emotional reactions of anger, crying, or other such feeling, then take that as a signal that you have overstepped your own needs and are focused outside of yourself. This is the time to ask for time— time to be by yourself, time to meditate, time to focus on yourself—and then go back for negotiation. If you let yourself be carried by the emotion whose only purpose is to prevent you from going against yourself, then you will cause distress to yourself and the other. Let the first tinge of pain awaken you. Take time to think; then negotiate. See yourself as equal to another. Your needs are as good and valid as someone else's. You must learn to set ground rules about decision making. Do not be afraid to talk about these things when there is no disagreement.

There is a belief that needs changing if you believe that the way to be loved is to be for someone else. This will never do, for the price is very much too high. There will not be satisfaction to this way of resolving life's dilemmas. You see, I am not advocating a system where you are only concerned with getting your way or others getting their way. This is a system where someone always loses, usually both. There are other systems where the rights, wants, needs of all concerned are valid and negotiation is the means of resolution. I know that in practice, for many of you, negotiation is a poorly learned skill and your present ways of doing this resemble "power over" methods. Set your goals to learn these skills. You will be amply rewarded for your effort. So listen to yourself, listen to your emotions and use what you hear to inform your actions.

What do you do if others continue to fight you to gain their way? Well, that is another whole story and I will deal with that another time.

You want some more on how to be in loving union with another when your ways are divergent or your needs are at odds with each other. This happens, of course, no matter how strong the bond or how much love each feels for the other. We talked earlier about the power of negotiation which follows from a validation of the equality of needs. There are other times, however, where the ways seem to be so divergent that no amount of thinking, talking, or conflict resolution does any good. Those times when all are stymied are very difficult times in a relationship where each tries to move the other in his or her direction without avail. This then becomes another matter, for something more is needed if the relationship is to continue. There always is, of course, the option of separation, but that often does not answer the basic question. There are other ways of approaching this.

July 31, 1988
A repertoire of relational behaviors

One is for one person to give freely and simply from the heart and from the highest perspective she or he can reach. This can happen with great growth possible in this action. You see this is very different from *giving in*, which is a very different dynamic altogether. *Giving in* usually leaves someone feeling victimized or powerless, whereby *giving* is a high order act which is *empowering*, both to the giver and the receiver. I want to emphasize the virtue of the act. I know that those of you who have successful relationships use this as an ongoing feature in your repertoire of relational behaviors. But I am talking about the big act—one where *to give* requires a shift that is not easily achieved. This giving does not come because it is easier or nicer or more virtuous to be a giver. This act I am discussing goes way beyond. You will have to think on this to truly understand what I mean.

Then there are other ways to approach situations where needs are very divergent, but you see, first you have to identify the place in your life that the relationship holds and the priority you and the other place on it. You must see where it fits in your life. Perhaps you don't have much investment. Then you will find it difficult to give up anything for the sake of the other. You see, you have to know where you stand.

Sometimes people latch onto an idea and cannot let go. They become entrenched in it, thinking that no other exists and they fight tooth and nail to remain where they are. They see anything which opposes them as something to be attacked and fought against. They become so enamored of their position as to think it is *right* and someone else is *wrong*. This is a very difficult situation for someone who is relating to them because there is very little latitude, if any, for negotiation. This, then, requires a different means altogether if there is not to be a one-sidedness in the relationship. But there is always difficulty if one person refuses to participate in a give-and-take. This then requires that the first partner learn ways of standing up for his or her rights in effective ways. This does not usually come from engaging in trying to change the other, a fruitless practice—one sure to lead to pain and frustration. If you recognize yourself as the one who stands with feet of rock, unwilling to give on your position, it would be well to examine your reluctance to open yourself to equality within your relationship. What is it you are afraid of? Where did you learn your pattern of conflict engagement? Is it working for you? Does it promote growth of intimacy, trust and love within your relationship? Look at this. Answer these questions. See if there are ways that you can allow light in. I will write more another time.

A time of changing is coming in your life that you may not be prepared for. I want to give you messages of hope and joy to focus on which will help you through the trying times ahead. When you look at the world from a wider perspective, then you see that whatever happens fits inside a larger whole. It is not *extraordinary* or *chaotic* or any other words you have to describe that which you think shouldn't happen. You don't need to worry that life will be destroyed—or your spirit either. All is well, even when it is not how you want it to be. You see, it is your ego that always wants something different. It is insatiable in that sense and always wants to have more and more of something, even though the having doesn't bring peace. It is only when you learn to bypass the ego that you can find joy and peace. I will not come through trying to meet the needs of the ego. Let me show you how this works.

August 5, 1988
A message
By-passing the ego's needs

The ego says, "I want more money. I want more love. I want more freedom. I want, I want. " Thus if you try to satisfy all these wants, you will spend your life in pursuit of means to satisfy them. But they will never cease. If you have $100, you want $200 or $1000 or $1,000,000, you see. But if you learn to bypass the ego and learn to look at your life as a spiritual path, then you can gain much more stability in your life. Let me say a little more about that. If you see that much of the pain in your life comes from trying to meet the demands of your ego, you will see how easy it is to make your life happier. I have said before that the ego is not bad, but if you only look to it, then you will never be satisfied, for that is how ego is. You have a tendency to become over-involved in your ego's need to be a good, helpful person which locks you in. You must see how what you have chosen as a path and what your ego says have become interwoven, but there is a difference. It would do well to see how that is for you.

I will tell you a little story. This is about a little girl who did not know what to do about her best friends who did not like each other. She tried to please them both. She tried to listen to their complaints about each other. She tried to manage her time so she gave them each equally of herself. Soon she found that she didn't want to be with either one. She found that she was

August 6, 1988
The rightness of yourself

staying home in her room because it seemed easier. She found that she no longer thought of them as her best friends. You see, there is a lesson for you here to learn. Do not be afraid of it, but no longer respond as though you are a little girl. Do you remember how that was? Just listen to yourself. Do not allow yourself to be in situations which require you to deny the rightness of yourself. That is all.

Let us talk of something else, and that is of a question you have about your son. Let me assure you that he is OK. (I wasn't able to reach him in Colorado.) Do not worry now but be alert to what might be needed. You are very concerned underneath your calm exterior. You feel the pressure of this even though, on the surface, there is nothing to be seen. Let the forces surface, let them have their say, but do not hold them there in your mind. You cannot keep everything locked up and still be in the present. There is much to learn about being in the present moment. I know this is very hard for you all because of the capability of your mind to travel at will hither and yon. You need to do much practice to be only in the present. But allowing your feelings to surface is very important. Let them up and let them pass. That is all you need do. (My son *was* OK when I reached him a few days later.)

On emotion & negotiation

Now let me talk with you about some other things, and that is what to do when there is a discrepancy between what you want and what someone you are in close relationship wants. We talked of that the other day and how important the skill of negotiation is. But I want to talk a little more about the emotions that become involved in such a situation. You know from experience that these can be mighty. Again, it is not so much of a problem if acceptable compromises can be seen as when there is a difference as to where to eat or what movie to see. But is is very different if it involves major steps such as moving or having a child or any other event where persons feel that they cannot compromise on their position without losing something of themselves. They want to take the step in a particular direction so intently that they then feel held back by the other. The other, in turn, feels all sorts of conflicting emotions related to either rejection or the need to be rejecting. At this point each person brings out the heavy artillery to try to change things. This may be anger, tears, passive withdrawal, manipulation, guilt—whatever has worked in the past—because the alternative is truly facing the impasse and the implications of the impasse. Often at this time, so much commotion can be raised over the issue that separation seems advisable and the dilemma seems solved. Or perhaps, someone gives in, again appearing to solve the situation. You see how the emotions which are engendered and the responses each has to their emotions creates a whole different system?

The dilemma truly is: What does a couple do when there is a difference of opinion? Is there any other way to solve that dilemma except through the use of emotionally driven behavior?

I have told you before that you are all very controlled by emotion, either your own or someone else's. There is much to learn about yourself through understanding what your emotions have to tell you about yourself. If each person would spend more time with that learning, there would be more ease in actual negotiation. What makes negotiation very difficult is that emotion takes over and then, instead of responding to the dilemma, you begin to respond to emotion. We talked earlier of how many of you have a set repertoire of behaviors which you use when a particular emotion is felt. It would be very helpful if you would learn what you do when you feel various emotions. Much of your behavior is a learned, ritualistic response to your own emotion rather than to the actions of another. There are situations in your life that bring about an emotional reaction. They are part of your instinctive package as a human being, but the *instinctual* has become very intricately woven with the *learned*.

But back to my point. When an emotion arouses in you, there are various ways that you, as a distinct human being, have learned to respond to these. This is what you need to know about. You see, if you look around, there is not a direct connection between an event, the emotion aroused and the subsequent behavior. There are similarities, of course, but the connection is not one of direct cause and action. You see how this is? Emotions have an important place in your life and are not to be denied. They are what characterizes you as a specific individual. Your pattern of emotional response is distinctly you. The goal of life is not be become emotionless, but to live richly within your emotional bed. But you see this is different from using your emotions to control situations—not that emotions are not effective, given your present way of relating to each other. Pay attention for a week and see how you modify your behavior in response to someone's behavior that is occasioned by emotion.

I am trying to show you other ways. I realize this is difficult for you sometimes to understand, but just keep thinking about this. You see, within relationships there will be many times when emotion is aroused. But if you were both to take the position that emotion is a signal to yourself to let you know something, then perhaps that would be one step. Other steps then involve dialoguing about this so that you get to know about how each other responds from out of each other's emotional bed. Remember, this is unique to each. Responses may bear little or no resemblance to that of the partner, though the emotion itself bears the same name. Because of the learned component, each one's responses are quite different from another. Celebrate this with each other. Get to know what the other is like. Do not expect the other to be like you, but acknowledge and validate her or his set of emotional responses. There are other steps to follow, but this will give you a starting place. Now I will leave you, my dear friend.

August 11, 1988
You must learn again to care for all

You are here in a very spiritual place (I was in Michigan at the Woman's Music Festival.) which will be renewing and a blessing for you. Let yourself bask in the energy which surrounds you. Be present. Do not let your mind draw you away from the excitement which abounds here.

I will talk to you some more about some ancient sayings that will serve you all. Tremendous knowledge has been virtually lost over the years because, as humanity developed, there was a shift from the way people lived upon this land to what you now call *civilization* or *modern times*. The old knowledge stood in the way of this "progress." You heard the Native American woman yesterday talk about reverence for all living things and for the Mother Earth herself. This is part of the ancient teachings, but they even went beyond what she knows. There was a time when what was, was *all*. There were no distinctions between human beings and the other forms of life, such that one used the other. There was harmony among all and the way of humankind was as the angels. However, the loss of this knowledge over time has brought the world to a very perilous cliff and, like some animal which has gone amuck, the mass of humans are rushing head long toward the edge of the cliff, eager to leap to their deaths. This is hard to understand, but we have watched this time coming.

There is still time to slow and stop and turn. You need not leap to your own destruction. But you must begin experiencing yourself as more than a simple human alone and unattached to other forms of life or even to each other. You must see that you are your children and great-grandchildren, and on and on. You are your brother, cousin, uncle, aunt. You are animal and bird, flower and tree. You are not *ascendant*, but *a part of.* You must learn again to care for all. Believe me, there is no other way. If you think that your scientists will learn some new ways so you can continue your ways, then you are mistaken. If you think that God will save you by providing a new planet to go to when you have exhausted this one, then you are very mistaken. You can go on living by your greed, but your time then will be limited. You may say, "Well, I'll be gone; it won't matter," but that is only because you don't yet see. If you knew in your being of what I talk of, you would see that you cannot escape by dying. That is not a solution, you see. I know this is a cultural norm, a belief that you might as well get all you can because you "only go around once." No wonder your lives are so hard when your mores tell this kind of nonsense. You are all in a difficult spot because you are not supported by a cultural belief system which helps you to be one with the powers of the universe.

You are in a time when it is necessary to rise above the current teachings of the world and form new ways and new beliefs that contradict your current culture. The way is there for you in the ways of the ancients—the Native American lore as well as that of other peoples who lived in harmony on the earth—the aborigines, some African tribes, other native peoples. You only need to begin to research this information and find the ways of harmony.

Here we are again to write with you. You are having a hard time with the warmth, but do not worry, it will soon be over. There will be a turning of the weather and you will all soon be more comfortable.

August 16, 1988
Striving toward joy

Let me talk with you about something that will be of interest to you, and that is what to do when you are troubled and feeling out of sorts and hurt and angry. You all feel this way sometimes when your ego gets the better of you, and then you feel depressed and miserable. This, you know, is not your natural state which is one of joy and delight. You often have a hard time believing that, as there seem to be few people who are in that state. Oh, yes, I know. But that is the truth, nonetheless. But at this time on earth, I admit that it is a very difficult state to get in when you use the tactics you have to get through your days. You are all programmed, you know, by your upbringing, your culture, and all that goes with that. Your heads are filled with negativity—practically from the day you are born, so do not be hard on yourself if you are not in a state of bliss. It really is impossible for this to be at this time.

But if you know that this negativity is foreign to your true nature, then you can strive toward joy, creating space in your days to allow time to meditate, time to contemplate, time to experience your inner nature, your spiritual nature, your connection to oneness. I know that you cannot do this all the time, but any time you do this will increase your capacity to feel the joyousness which exists at your center. So this is what you should do when the cares of world become too much. It may not work for you right away, but with practice and belief, you will find that you can achieve more and more. I know that the pulls of your ego and your buried selves can be very strong, but there is nothing stronger than the power of love. Tap into that and renew yourself. Breathe in its sweet nectar. Taste its natural juices. Let your experience expand under its influence.

Encourage others to join with you; encourage them to share joy with you. This is your birthright. Do not neglect your capacity for it.

The tiger within   Now let us talk of something else. You wonder what to do when you feel like a little child and cannot stand up for yourself and the tears come. Well, my dear, let them come. You don't always have to be grown up you know. But I will help you anyway because I know you are trying to learn to be more assertive in your relationships. Well, let me give you a little tip. When you feel the tears starting, imagine that you are a tiger. Become acquainted with the tiger within you. Let yourself feel your muscles and your tawny striped coat. Feel the strength in your muscles and the keenness of your mind. See that you have power which you can restrain or release as you need to. Use this vision for a while when you go to bed. Become well acquainted with the look and feel of your tiger. This does not mean that you need to see yourself as furious or man-eating or destructive. Only feel your strength and power which you have available when you need it. When you feel the tears coming, then you should turn to your tiger and ask for guidance. You will find that there is much wisdom there. This is for you, personally, but others can use similar animals for their special totem.

I will write you some words of comfort and will help you with your healing. Now you are upsetting yourself needlessly by pretending that the future is now. You think you will bring the future to pass, and then you won't have to go through with it. That is one way to use the sayings that come to you, but it is not the best way, for then you do not experience the lessons that go along with the message. You are afraid that some things might happen in the future so you might as well make them happen now. You cannot bypass your life like that. I will only tell you to follow your intuition, to follow your heart, to listen to your wisdom. You are in charge of your life. Create that which you want.

August 17, 1988
You are in charge of your life

(Written at Chris and Darlene's farm)

August 20, 1988
Taking the easy path

You are very comfortable there in the country. It is a very beautiful, spiritual place where you feel the healing energies entering into the very core of your being and bringing you peace and quietude. Enjoy the chance you have to be in the midst of nature and do not worry about your living in a place like this. Your idea to just let go of trying to find solutions is a good one. All things happen as they will and should, and struggling does not make anything happen faster or better. Remember that life is meant to be easy; so to take the easy path is not falling down on any obligations. You all there seem to think harder is better. This is not so. Just let yourself enjoy all the sights and sounds, the colors of nature. Let these enter you in every way that you can.

I will talk of another thing: that is, how to make decisions when it seems very hard to decide between two alternatives, such as when one person in a relationship wants one thing and the other something else. We have talked of this before, but I will expand on it because I know that this is often a dilemma for those of you who have bonded but yet remain as individuals. This is then a more delicate situation than those who bond but agree that someone will be subservient to the other. This, of course,

On equal relationships

makes decision making a different kind of process. But let us go back to talk of those relationships where a criteria of equality is attempted. Then, oftentimes, decisions where there are major differences take a long time in being made. It is as though there is hope that in time someone will wear down and all will become easier. But in the meantime, neither is happy because this issue hangs over their heads causing them unease. You see how this is?

If a decision is made, then often the one whose way it didn't go continues to be unhappy and does not have peace. It looks like there is no way out, only perhaps separation where both go their own way. This is, of course, a choice, but sometimes not necessary at all. The problem comes because both become so entrenched in their own views that other possibilities become lost to view. I would suggest to you that if there is a great dilemma that cannot be solved, it is because it is there not to be solved. You see, if there was an easy solution, it would be the one to follow, but when all energies go to trying to solve the unsolvable, then there is much waste. Accept this and go on to another question.

See that you cannot, by sheer struggle, make something happen which is not right at this time. Allow yourself to go on with other things. Look at what is easy at this time. Follow that. Listen to yourself. Listen with your inner ear. See with your inner eye. See why it is that solving this question is not in your best interests at this time. Another time, all will happen with ease. Look at what is before you now, what you should put your energies to. Then let each of the persons involved see how they can capture, in their present life, what it is they need without having everything the way they want it. Decisions need not be hard if you follow this rule. See if this will help.

You can always check with your inner selves as far as being on your path. This does not mean that everything will go the way your ego wants, you know. Get in touch with inner knowing. See what lessons you are learning, but do not struggle against the forces that be. Rather, do what you can to expand your intuitive knowing. Be aware of the opportunities that are put before you. This is how life can be lived easily.

Now I will give you a brief meditation to share tomorrow.

Oh, my friends, you have arrived to share with each other in this very sacred place. You will find that your spirit will feel an alignment with the powers of nature. Let your eyes wander to the trees which surround you and hear the wisdom which they whisper to you. Listen to the sounds around you and know that this is the song of the earth. Hear its melody. Hear its cadence. Hear the vibration as the sounds blend in harmony. Let the smells of the earth reach toward your nostrils, filling them with purifying essences. This is all which cleanses and purifies the various bodies of which you are made. Let these surroundings impact upon your senses. Now allow each chakra to open and receive from this storehouse of nature just the color and vibration which it needs to heal and purify your body. Focus on them one at a time starting from the lower to the higher. Take a moment to do this.

I am here to write to you again. How are you tonight. This has been a momentous day for you and I am very happy for you. Let us reply to your request about a welcome for your group.

Hello, all my dear friends. I am happy to be with you all again. There is much power here in this room tonight as it seems that you are all becoming more in touch with the natural energy that abounds. So let yourself open to this charge. Let your body respond to it. Allow it to charge your batteries, so to speak. Let it reach far within you, finding the hidden places that have been starved for the light. Let the cleansing power enter your mind to ferret out the negative programs. Allow newness to happen. Let the potential of love enter your emotional body. Be ready for it. Be open to it. Feel the healing of shared experiences of love. This all awaits you, those of you who open themselves. Share with each other and with the power and love of the universe. I will be with you.

And a meditation.

Allow yourself to settle back, taking a few relaxing breaths, allowing your body to relax into a posture of comfort. Ease out the kinks and let your muscles become like jelly, melting into the space you occupy. Now slowly pay close attention to your breath. Visualize that with each breath, you breathe in a golden energy. See it fill your chest with a warm glow. Visualize your breath as it flows out as carrying away impurities. See these leave your body to again be replaced by the warm golden light.

Concentrate a few moments on this interchange. Feel yourself becoming lighter and lighter as you are filled more and more by the golden light. See all the darkness that you have been harboring as breaking up and being released with each breath. And now, as you feel yourself a being of light, allow yourself to look around in your world. See your loved ones, the people down the street, your co-workers, your relatives, all those you come in contact with. Visit them, bringing them energy given from the light you carry within. Bestow it upon them. Watch to see what happens. Know that you can give away as much as you want in whatever measure you want. Your supply is inexhaustible. Take some time to do this now. Then return to the room when you are ready.

On joy

Now, my friend, I will talk to you of some other things. That is how to live with joy as a constant resource in your life. You have just done an exercise that will aid you in achieving that state. The ability to fill yourself with light and to bestow it before you like petals of the rose will enable you to achieve a state of bliss. So often you all wander through the doors of your life seeking some other who will bring you joy and love. You wonder why you only find momentary highs before the fall. But I say to you that you seek in the wrong place. It is in the kingdom of creation that one can find the holy light which lights the path so that all steps are easy and joyful. I know how hard this is to comprehend and how much harder for you to achieve, given your present state of enlightenment. But see—believe me— seek this; allow this belief to enter your heart. Look. Look. Look at creation—the very wonder of it. Let yourself be awed by it. This is not something so commonplace. This is the stuff of miracles. Just because birth happens every day does not make it ordinary. Look for the small miracles of life in all the happenings of the natural world. Let your hearts open to this wonder. You need not seek God in books but in the raw stuff of being. Feel your connections to this. See the very miracle of yourself. There is nothing finer.

Let me also tell you something else. You are growing, learning very much and the time is drawing near for you to expand further, to let your heart open further to your own spiritual truth. Do not be afraid. Let your being expand. Welcome this. Let the joy of this experience penetrate the very core of yourself. You will find your way clearer and lighter. The cares of the past months will lift and fade as new levels of your knowledge become apparent. You will see what I mean as it happens. Welcome this. And now, that is all for tonight.

There we are, my dear. We shall write again today. You want a closing for your group from me and I will be happy to oblige.

August 27, 1988

Golden threads

Now, my friends, it is time again to say goodbye to each other until you all come together again. But do not think that you go off alone into the world. You are all joined one to another by golden threads which link you all together. You see, you cannot see these threads but they interweave between you all, bringing an order and substance to your relationships. These threads carry energy back and forth so you are never alone and lost in the world. So know as you walk away from here that you are supported and held by the most wonderful energy, that you are so safe within this web that you can go forth with assurance. Let that knowledge bring you peace. You see, you all think that you live within your skin only, separate from all else. This is merely illusion. You are connected in more ways that you can imagine.

A blessing

Now let the blessings of the universe fall upon you. Open your hearts to this wonderful gift. Let the knowledge of goodness enter you. Let the love which abounds cover you and fill you. Let it come. It is there for you. Go forth to your daily lives filled with new truth and knowledge. Let this penetrate your lives. Let it lead you to new tasks, to new ways of being. Let your hearts lead you. That is all.

On a past life

I will tell you some more about your life with me. I know you have been wondering about your past lives. This I know is a subject that is very interesting to many people, but if I were to tell you about all your lives, we would never talk of anything else. But I will satisfy a little of your curiosity. We lived, you and I, in a small village in the south of France where I was your daughter. We were peasant people and lived a rather poor life, but that did not stop us from being very interested and curious about all the various forms of natural life which abounded around our village. We often talked of the ways that plants could be used or of how the stars moved in the skies or how the seasons brought changes to the animals and birds. We talked often about life and what the meaning and purpose was, for even then we were both very old souls and had seen a lot. There were others in our family, a brother and two other sisters and, of course, Father, but the bond was between us. Of course you

187

shared your knowledge with the others, though they really were not so interested in that. As time went by, you achieved a certain amount of notoriety in the village for your knowledge of wild things and were often called upon to help out with the health of our neighbors. I went on to follow in your foot steps, though later I married and had several children so could not study as much as I wanted. You did not live to be very old and that was a sad blow. It was a great loss to me when you died, but I did not know then as I do now what it meant. So, you see, my dear, that is a little tidbit for your curiosity, but do not expect me to tell you many tales—because we do not have time for that.

The sky is lighting up

There is much to do in your world. Isn't it exciting when you see so many people becoming spiritual. Thousands of candles are being lit every day. Some still burn very dimly, but believe me, the sky is lighting up. Do not take this good news in such a way as you become complacent. Know that all your energies are needed to keep moving things along. So just keep going ahead. Be open to the spiritual. Learn to live it every day of your life. Walk in the path and all will be easy. I will be with you.

August 29, 1988
A message
Looking for clues

I will give you a message of love and hope and peace. Blessings on you, my dear heart. Your journey is long and sometimes hard, but the way of the heart leads home. You must always look for the clues. Look for them in every way you can think of. These will tell you if you are on the right path or not. Clues can be those things that fall in place—the ones that seem to take no effort or that appear to be coincidence. Clues are your dreams— not all of them, but only those which have the feel of importance. There are clues in nature. The ancients knew of totems and power animals. There are clues within when you feel right with yourself and right with others. You can think of more. You can tell you are not on a spiritual path when everything is hard and heavy and painful. Look to see what you can do to make life easier. If you look, you will see it can be done, whether that be inward or outward. You do not have to choose pain but can seek after joy.

Now come, my dear, and look about you. See the wonders that tickle your eyesight. See the clouds as they billow in the heavens. What a nice trick for bringing you rain. Look, too, at the birds as they congregate for their flights to their southern home. Do not accept this feat lightly. It is magnificence itself. There are so many miracles around that you could spend all your days just looking. Come to appreciate all of this. Protect it. Work to admonish those who would wreak havoc with it. This is your gift—this world and all that exists upon it. Do not take this gift lightly. It is not for destruction that it was created. The time is now for eyes to open to see again what is truly precious in your world.

Here you are at a crossroads and we will help you to decide which way to go. Now it is not so much that you must decide, but that there is a new time of awakening for you. You feel this in your body but do not know what to call it. Allow yourself to fully feel the heaviness that comes to you at this time. Experience that in your body and ask what it can tell you. See what comes up for you in the form of images. This will all help you to go forward. Do not worry that you are becoming sick. That is not the case.

August 31, 1988
The purpose of all is to come to perfect love

There is a turning coming for all of you. The world is lightening up, and there will be a time of peace and joy for those who wish to partake of it within the next few months. Now this is available to all and will influence everyone, but if you allow yourself to be aware, it will create greater happiness for you. You must look for this and be open to it and then you will experience a greater amount of joy. This is what to do. Look around at the people about you. Pay attention to news stories that reflect peace and unity. Join in with others who are joyful. Pay attention to the events in your life, to the feelings you are having. See the positive things that are happening and rejoice. That is a special gift for this fall season.

You want to know if evil-like deeds are agreed upon before persons become incarnate. This is not such an easy answer as there certainly are concepts agreed upon that are not what you call *positive*, but there also are the dynamics of life and also of free will that enter in. The ways of the total universe incorporate all, and that includes all that is *good* and *non-good* as you define it. So, do you agree to kill each other or to rape each other? NO. This is not always the case, though there are times when you request this of another because you want to clean up an old karma. You see, you only see as through a filter. You cannot see the whole which stretches to infinity. Your life is only a small piece of the whole of your existence and so, unless you incorporate all that you have lived and will live, then you cannot understand what really is going on. This is not easy,

189

given that you are unable to see back and forth in time, but if you accept that everything that is seen is not all there is, then you will find it easier to accept. You see, your immediate life is only one of the cycles of your existence and the lessons to be learned are there for you. Some of these lessons are ongoing. They are part of a larger learning that you have set for yourself. But be aware that the purpose of *all* is to come to perfect love.

The goal of life   I will tell you a story of how it is to live in a way that is in attunement with God's will. You see, you sometimes get very confused because you don't know how to live your life in a way that will find favor with God. You think that you must, within the space of your life, act in a certain way or you will go to hell or be punished in certain ways that may last for eternity. But this is not so. You must see that the destiny of mankind or humankind is one that stretches far beyond what you can see, and that everything which happens, happens in a larger context than your immediate life. So, yes, indeed, the goal of life is to learn perfectly to live by the universal laws of God, to achieve perfection, to become light. But you cannot achieve this in one sitting. Some of you are further along this path and find the way easier because you do walk in the light. Others are still just starting out. You see, you, as humans, only live in your particular body in your particular culture and operate on that level out of your ego. But you also exist in a much larger context as spirit and operate out of that larger context also. So, each of your earth lives is only part of the larger experience, and the role you choose to play for your earth life is chosen to give you the chance to learn particular teachings.

So back to your questions about victims and transgressors. You may choose to learn lessons by playing either part. This is not so easy to describe so you can understand it, but try. Forgiveness happens when you can see the larger whole and can accept that which comes to you. But on the other hand, you are not absolved from learning the lessons which come. You must see that all is on more than one level, and that will help. You are spirit, but you are also human. So as human, you do not have to be as spirit but allow yourself to expand your humanness to incorporate the spiritual. It will make your life so much easier.

September 8, 1988   You are difficult to come into tonight. There is much energy
On depression &   blockage and you would do well to work on that. It would help
an antidote   to stand on your head for awhile, but other things would help

also, those that move energy. Now, that is important or you will be prone to illness and other ills if you do not take care. You are having a very difficult time, but that will pass as soon as you can unblock your energy from the knots that now exist. You are feeling low and that is why. Let me give you a few other tips also. Press the palms of your hands together very hard for a minute or two, then relax, but repeat this three or four times. That will help. Of course, massage, or Reike, or other body work will help also.

Let me talk to you of what to do when you feel depressed and low and feel no energy for living life. This happens to many of you there and many thousands of pills are swallowed every day because of it. I have talked to you before about how the spiritual will bring joy to your life, and you can reread that portion of my writings. But let me talk of depression some more. Depression is a function of the ego and arrives when the ego has been denied its due and is hindered, by your internal beliefs, from acting out in a way that can have impact. When the ego is barred from what it wants by an internal block such that feelings cannot flow, there becomes blockages such that are felt as depression. The problem is often externalized so that persons believe they have been influenced by something in their life. But this is not the cause. The cause comes from a system of repressions which do not allow the ego to demand what it wants in fear of reprisal, not from the outside, but from within. Depression is created wholly within. So you see, that is where you must operate. This does not mean that life sometimes has not brought you a problem, but it is your own inability to bring about that which you desire that causes you to put on the chains of depression. So the way out is the way within.

Pay attention to the needs of the ego, but then hear what it is that tells the ego to stop. What is it that says, "No." What is it that blocks the free flow of feeling. Here is where you will find the seeds of depression. This again is a way of finding unproductive beliefs. Those beliefs will hinder you from living life to the fullest. They are myriad. You cannot imagine how often you are blocked from natural expression by a belief that hinders you from telling it like it is.

Let me give you an antidote for depression. Meditate and, while in a state of relaxation, allow yourself to visualize yourself with the ability to take off as many layers that insulate you as you want. Take them off one at a time. Visualize them as layers of heavy, dark felt. As you take each layer off, see what it has to tell you. Feel how it is to have that layer off. Go slow and carefully. Let yourself feel each layer completely. Go as deep as you feel comfortable with. See what happens. That is all.

To allow love of all is the number one rule to follow

Now, we shall write again. I will write you what it is you want to hear from here to there. Many, many words are being broadcast to all of you there every day. Some of you are listening and others simply turn away, not even hearing the tune. It is a wonder how you choose to live in darkness when the joys of light are being told. Humankind's history has been a chaotic one for many eons, and the learning of the important lessons has been slow. It seems that there is so much attention paid to the needs of the ego and to the demands of the earthly life that people have had a difficult time hearing on the higher planes. The songs of joy have often gone unheard as people listen to the clamor of the everyday. There has been much lip service to a Godly life. Sometimes we cringe here at the hypocrisy which is practiced. So much goes on by the pious which is against God's laws, and they think that by bowing and kneeling and casting righteous looks, then all their other actions will go unnoticed. But this is not so. There will come a time when that is all shown clearly to them and they will be surprised, for they think they have reserved a seat in heaven. It is not so easy to do that, you know. It is not that they will be punished, but they certainly will be stripped of the blinders they have put over their eyes so as to maintain a pink picture of themselves.

But let me go on. You see there is much to be learned by humankind and they have been quite slow at learning the teachings—which are very simple indeed. The first of these is to live love, to be in the force of love. To allow love of all, yourself, others and all creation is the number one rule to follow. The second follows from that. To be in attunement with all the creatures of the universe, putting yourself not above, not under, but as in equal partners to all of creation.

You wonder why I have not listed worship of God as number one, as has been the case before. The use of love in every way, every day is the worship of God in its truest form. It matters not if you fall on your knees and worship God night and day if you do not live a life which manifests the teachings in life. You see,

God cares not for worship. It does not follow. This does not mean you are not to consider that some power greater than you can imagine rules the whole of creation. But it is not as though you have long pictured this to be. Let your old structures fall. Let yourself be renewed with new symbols which help you to create a spiritual life while you are there on earth.

You see, it is important for all of you to take our words seriously. It is not enough that you hear them in order to feel better. It is important that you transform them into action in your life. You want to know how to do this. The ways are myriad and you only have to ask and some will occur to you. It is very easy to imagine how to live a life that is founded on spiritual truths. But it is not always so easy to actually do this as you have learned so much over the years that necessitates change in belief for you. *Take our words seriously*

The first place to start is with yourself. This will take a little doing for many, many of you have very poor images of yourself. So go back over the writings. Reread and reread those which help you to see yourself as spirit, as perfect, as a wondrous example of creation. Use this to unearth all those negative thoughts which have been instilled in you. Then, at the same time, extend this same thing to people around you, widening your beliefs to include them in the ways of love. Extend this to the other creatures of the world. See all as kin. Keep expanding ever outward with love. As you develop the ability to shower love on yourself as a manifestation of the All There Is, you will find it increasingly easy to bestow love on all else. Show respect for all of life. Do not heedlessly or needlessly harm even the insects. Be alert, be aware and you will find that it is not hard to begin living a life that reflects your spirit. This is important.

Do not just read these words. That is not enough. Let their truth penetrate. Let your old blinders fall off. See anew. The future of the world depends on all of you doing that which you are able to. The way of life is not to become rich in material terms. The way of life is to spread richness of spirit and love. That is all for now.

You have questions and I will try to answer them. Your friend Karen wants to know if her friends were in another life with her. That is so. There is not doubt about it. You are both right when September 13, 1988 **On past lives & relationships** you say that you meet old friends and know them right away. But they are not always old friends, you know. Sometimes you meet old enemies or people you had unfinished business with. That is the case with one of your friend's friends. Now what should one do in those cases where there is a strong attraction to someone, but the relationship is fraught with difficulty and pain. This is not always the case of old enemies meeting, but often it is the case. You can tell by the strength of the initial attraction. Often, you have come together in a new combination to work things out so that your soul energies are freed up.

Much is to be learned in some of these relationships, and it is one of the reasons you often hang on in difficult situations. But the answer is to be aware. The more you can listen to your inner voices about situations, the sooner you can work past those difficult situations. Sometimes you have to let go and then see what happens to you. I have told you before that life is only one piece of a much larger whole, and the meeting and re-meeting of comrades from another life only demonstrates that. You all have made choices of who shall be in your life. But sometimes there is disagreement and so all is not always smooth. Think what lessons you can learn from being with certain people who loom large in your life. Look at the pattern you are acting out with them. Sense their familiarity. See what happens when you meditate on this. I know that all this is difficult and answers will not appear by magic, but if you are aware that old, unfinished business may be operating for you now, you may be able to approach situations and relationships in a different way. That is all for now.

I want to talk with you about something else, and that is what these writings are meant for you and your friends. Sometimes you become discouraged and do not know what shall be done with these, if people will continue to want to hear them, and what you should do with them.

You are doing OK, but you could write more often. Your desire to continue to type and hand these out to people is fine; but your first goal should be to write a little every day if you could, not to compile many pages, but to keep an even flow of ideas coming to you. These pages are for *you*. There are other reasons, but do not be afraid that you have to do something. It is enough that you receive them for now. So let these words come to you. Do not judge the rightness or wrongness or if they are good enough or anything like that. Just receive them for now. That is all of that.

You want to know about the vision of the Mother Mary in Yugoslavia and how that fits with what I am telling you. You see, there is no division such that the vision is one thing and what I write you is another. The writings, the visions, the happenings are all part of a transmittal to you on earth. I have told you that sometimes there is an easier time and that time is now for sending messages. But you wonder if that spirit is really the spirit of Mary. Well, that is true to some extent, but the spirit of Mary is also the spirit of others who have been incarnate on earth, and so that spirit which appears uses the guise of Mary as that is so well understood, you see. That message is heard by many, many people because they already believe that Mary is holy. It is very necessary that all peoples are reached in some way. You all see and hear in different ways and so different signs are sent. That is all.

The spirit of Mary

I have said it is not enough to worship a God. That does not satisfy. The proof is in the pudding, and if worshipping a God enables you to live your life in a growthful way, then it does some good. But just to worship is not at all enough. So much destruction has been done to some very simple messages that we are sometimes alarmed at what is done with a semblance of worship. But let yourself believe that if God exists, then you exist as part of the whole of creation and that you have a part in the creation of how it will be. This is very important. Creation is happening. It is not finished. It is not that you are the central character, but the play cannot go on without you, for there you are.

Creation is happening

There we are, my dear. I am so glad to be with you today. I welcome you to my heart. How nice a day it is and how nice that you will be out in the natural world. Be sure to say hello to all your cousins: trees, the birds and the animals and the wild plants. Talk to the trees and listen for their message. They are very wise indeed and watch over the world of the unseen. They are very, very important to your lives, you know. Too often you all forget and think they only exist to give you wood or shade or some other such thing. They give you, instead, life. Remember this and when you pass them, you can sometimes say a prayer of thanks for the work they do.

September 15, 1988
Hearing your inner promptings

You wonder what all of this is meaning for you. You are struggling very hard to make sense of it all, but remember what I have told you, it is not necessary to struggle. Let it come. Follow your needs and desires. Hear your intuition when it speaks.

Allow time for you to hear your inner prompting. This is not a contest. You do not have to get an A from me for getting everything right. The important thing is for you to continue to expand. The rate is not so important. Take this as my word to you. You have spent much time developing your own philosophy of life and have lived according to that. But be sure that did not spring from nowhere. The beliefs you hold have been developed with the help of your guides; so you do not have to throw everything out and start over. Allow yourself sufficient time to ponder on those beliefs which come from within. It is good to read, for that also expands you; but that alone is not enough, as it is more important to hear your own deep thoughts. You can connect directly with the Source of All and tune into ancient truths when you find the way to do this. This can only come by trying and practice.

I urge you to give time every day for a time of quietude where you begin to plumb the depths. I can write to you with much information, but there is much more to be had through inner dialogues. This does not mean working hard at it or struggling to make it happen. Only allow it and if it doesn't come, simply allow it some more. It may not come in the form you would like—all written out and easy to read, but take whatever comes with thanks, and more will come. There has been much change in you since last year, even though you do not always see this, and there will be more. But simply let this be. You are trying too hard to make something happen. You want your world to change upside down, but yet you are afraid this might happen. Let go a little more and see what does happen. I will be here to guide you. I know that life seems quite puzzling now, and you sometimes would like to go back to a time when you and I did not speak, but that cannot be.

Yes, you can turn your back on this, but you have already incorporated new knowledge or, perhaps to be more accurate, have remembered old knowledge, and that cannot be undone. So, my dear, let us go on.

Now I will write to answer the question, "What does it mean to be dead?"

You see, you are all afraid of what that means. You think that dying is something very painful and tragic. You yourself used to think it hurt to die and many think it is very scary, like going to kindergarten your very first day. There is much myth about dying. All peoples have beliefs and stories about what it is to die. I know that from a very early age the idea and concept of death is with you, controlling your ideas and thoughts about dying. I know there have been some changes since the doctors have started looking at people who have died and been brought back to life. So this is helpful to many of you because it seems these people do not descend into some dark, alone place, but they enter into light and love. And so it is. The process of death is not something strange and unconnected to living. It is most definitely not an end, nor even a beginning, but only a continuity of the life process. You use the term *death* as though it signified *finish, end,* but that is not so at all. Death can be thought of as transition, but even that is not strictly accurate as you only go on and on and on. It is not quite like the caterpillar and the butterfly, but you see from that example what tremendous changes can take place and still have continuity.

But back to your own death. It does not do to carry fear with you. Believe me when I say that you continue to be and that you will not be alone and lost. There is a time of much relief and freedom when you are allowed to leave your bodies, for you will find that bodies can be restricting and controlling, indeed. You see, you will all know what to do as you have all been here before. And believe me, though you will have ample opportunity to evaluate your life, there will be much love and understanding from those who will help you with that task. There is no punishment here. There may be pain for some as they realize how they have used their lives and realize how far they strayed from their path and how little growth they were able to achieve. This sometimes causes pain and anguish for awhile until they are able to assimilate what the learnings of that life did mean. There are wonderful, understanding guides who stay close and help with this process. Then there is also a wonderful time of meeting old friends and loved ones, and this is often a very happy time for many. You see, you do not enter a heaven with golden streets and harps and all of that kind of thing, but you do enter another plane where the restrictions of the physical world

You continue to be and you will not be alone and lost

197

do not exist. I hope this helps in some way to dispel your fears and doubts about this very natural process.

On the process of dying

You wonder now why the process of dying is so often painful, what with sickness and trauma. Well, that is another whole thing and belongs to the natural world. You see, the process of dying is of your world and has meaning in your path that reflects your life plan. So, do not join the process and the completion of the human phase of life. They are two different things. The process of dying may be long or short, and this depends much on what your life plan is, but also on how you have lived your human life and how you have treated your physical body. You see, everything is more complex than you would sometimes like it to be. When you are human, all that happens happens both on your everyday, human level and is interlaced with the spiritual level. There is a whole that is larger, much larger that you can see. So do not look for some simple answer. I will not say, "So-and-so becomes sick with such-and-such disease because that is his fate, and it is preordained," because there is a complexity that goes beyond simple statements such as that. You do not come as automatons but as creatures of free will. But neither do you exist as creatures with no strings attached, rushing higgledy-piggledy, hither and yon, with no connection to the spiritual. You see how this is?

Well, that is all of that lesson for today. You want to know the weather. (I was up at the cottage. It was raining and we were expecting company.) The sun will come out again later in the morning. (It did.)

You want a little something for your group. You can read many of my writings if you want but I will give you a little more if you so desire.

A meditation
The Stopping Place

Here is a meditation.

My friends, allow yourself to drift inward, inward, inward. Let your mind's eye drift first into your body, feeling yourself going to its very center, but then let yourself go further inward. Just let this happen, and when you get further in, feel this for a few minutes and then go further in. Allow yourself to keep going further and further in, stopping along the way. You can stop whenever you want, but see if you only want to stop temporarily or whether you have reached the place which, for you, is the stopping place. Do not force yourself; merely allow yourself to go more and more inward, looking as you go. And whenever you are ready, make the return journey to this room and then write anything that you brought back from your journey—insights, sights, sounds, symbols, truths, whatever came with the journey.

I am here to write to you again this sunny morning. You do not think it is sunny, but that is because you can only see below the clouds. It is like that with other phenomena, too. Your view and your evaluation of what is, is clouded by the perspective you have. You are limited by your beliefs as much as your view today is limited by the cloud cover. If you are able to expand yourself to the point where you can look beyond, then you would see a very different scene, just as you would if you entered an airplane and flew above the clouds.

September 19, 1988
Each day is the
creation of the
whole

Now something else. You have here the beginning of a day, an opportunity for new ways of seeing and being. Each day brings you this opportunity. It does not matter what you did in the past as much as how you use this opportunity. You are given this gift—this raw day to create. See what it is you do. Ask yourself tonight what you created. Did you create a perfect gift for yourself? Or were you too tired, too passive, too woebegone to even think that what you create each day is the creation of the whole. You see, you all act in concert. You and all your kindred creatures are constantly creating anew. You think no one will notice you—that your part is so meagre that it doesn't matter if you play off key. This is not true. The harmony depends on all. So see what it is you want to play today. Listen to your notes. This is very important. Now I will leave you so you can embark on this glorious day of life.

There we are, my dear friend. I am writing up a full head of steam today as we enter another season. There is much coming for you in the following months. Isn't that exciting. But now let me go on with some of the lessons I am here to teach you, for that is my purpose in writing to you and all the others who will read these words. I am here to teach old lessons in new ways, for there is nothing new under the sun except for packaging. You know how important that is there for all of you who have been raised on TV commercials. We sometimes wonder why it is so difficult to get the message of love and peace across to you all. But that is how it is.

September 23, 1988
On the future
of the world

I want to talk with you about the future of your world. I have often mentioned that you are all at a crossroads where one road will take you to destruction and the other to glory. It seems like there would not be much doubt as to which to take, but there still are enormous numbers of people who don't see that there are two ways to go. Their blinders of greed and comfort have positioned them such that they literally are blind to the possibilities. You see, unless you all start looking at your place in this world as creator, rather than consumer, you will soon find yourself in a sorry predicament. You wonder if I know the outcome, if it can be seen by those of us with greater sight. Well, we can see several outcomes. I have told you before, you are all creators. What possibilities will come to pass will depend very much on the choices you all make. There is much happening in your world, far more than you can imagine. Perhaps it will not be too late.

September 24, 1988
A message
*The world needs
your wisdom*

I am here again to write to you. Now you would like something for your group. I will see what I can do.

Now, all my friends, I am here to bring you messages of love and peace and hope. I am here to help open your eyes to the wonders which abound. I am here to help you to see what is truth and what is not. I am here most of all to help you to awaken, to remember, to learn how to live a life that brings you joy and happiness. You have all been around many times in many different lives, and please know—the fact that you are here means that you have climbed many mountains and learned many lessons. Now it is time to let this out. The world needs your wisdom. That is all I have for you now.

A meditation
A place of joy

You want a meditation. I will give you one.

Make yourself comfortable. Allow your breathing to become more even and regular as you systematically relax your muscles. See if you can get to feeling like a bowl full of gelatin. Now as you are relaxed and easy, start going inward with your awareness deep into your psyche where there is a place of joy. Journey now to the place of joy. Set your intention to arrive there. See what journey you need to make before you can arrive there. I will help you a little. Imagine that there is a long corridor with a number of doors so that you can only see a stretch at a time. Open each door and proceed further and further down the corridor. On each side are a number of doors. You can open these if you want, looking for that one of joy. Take as much time as you need. When you are ready, then return to this room.

Life has sometimes felt very hard to you, but you are learning to let go of some of those old ideas that have made it seem so. But there is still more you can do. I am glad that you write with me, for this is a very positive thing for you to do. Keep this up even if you sometimes doubt. Doubt is not a problem as it signifies the reaching of another barrier to be transcended. You are developing more and more trust in the universal good. The wonders around you lead you to see order and plan which transcends the order and plan of human-made things.

Let me give you a sweet message for this day. As a human being you are one of the most intricate living organisms, a being which incorporates many of the creations which were first tried on smaller and lesser organisms. You are truly a magnificent being—much greater than you even know you are. You function almost flawlessly, given the right attention, and you have within you workings which are so intricately intertwined as to defy your imagination. So take heart at this; appreciate this wonderful body and mind you were given. Do not degrade it, but revere it. Let the knowledge of your body show you the wonder of the God-made world. Do not think this is some accident which occurred by happenstance. That is far from the truth. Let your inner knowledge tell you this. You are not an accident of nature but a carefully crafted creation of the All There Is. You exist as part of a total creation of wonder. Let yourself appreciate yourself. Let yourself glorify yourself. See the wonders of your body, mind, emotion. See how you function within the framework. When you do not love yourself as part of the creative All and find fault and hurt yourself and try to destroy yourself, you do harm to all around you. See yourself as a wonder, for indeed that is what you are. Get to know yourself. Study yourself and see what magic you are. Do not let yourself vilify you, but uplift yourself to your true place. That is all for now.

You have a question for a friend who has been wondering about what to do when there is an outbreak of negativity around a certain person or event. You wonder if you should join in, finding relief by venting or does this go against that which is practical. Well, my friend, I have always told you that negativity is a form of energy which is blocking and does not add anything to your life. But the answer is not so simple as to say, "No one should ever express negative thoughts about another person or event." This then becomes Pollyanna-ish where you are repressing your true feelings to match a standard that you set up. This does not do it, you see. The important thing to be aware of is what is the underlying feeling. What is the underlying perception. What is the underlying assumption. All these can help you to learn about what is happening with you. You see, if you only express negative thoughts about another, then you may find relief from your feelings by pretending you are not involved but only have perception of another. This is never the case. So use the opportunity to express thoughts and ideas about yourself. Do not punish yourself for your negative thoughts about another, but allow them to be a springboard to learning about yourself. This may not come easy at first, or it may not feel as powerful at first, but if you allow yourself to follow these directions, you will soon become gladdened by that which you unfold concerning your inner self. There is a very real benefit in learning about your inner selves so that you become larger and larger and less constricted by old, buried treasures.

Sometimes, though, it is merely a feeling which you are trying to avoid. Perhaps this feeling has deep roots which might activate old hurts, if allowed. You see how you can then learn if you turn to look at yourself. Try next time when you are expressing negative thoughts of another to express what you are feeling. See if there is anger or disappointment or frustration or sadness or hurt. See then what does this tell you. Remember how I discussed communicating with your feelings. See what they have to tell you. That is all on this subject.

On universal laws I now want to talk with you about another question you have, and that is about universal laws and whether these are written down in some place. You wonder because there seems to be different versions depending on the religion. Well, of course, the universal laws exist apart from any religion. They have been imparted and interpreted and written by many people but that does not mean that any religion has it all down to the T.

I want you to understand that universal laws are not so much laws as you understand laws to be, such as if you break a law, you will be punished. Instead, universal laws *ARE*. They describe the way of it. They are the description rather than the proscription. There are many which control the workings of All, and when you are in tune with the universal laws, life is much easier. The reason I do not spell these out to you is that then they will sound like laws to follow. You see, one of the universal laws is that the power of love is the greatest power. There is none greater. When you are in tune with this, then you are walking a path which flows.

The second universal law is to follow the light. This you will not understand, I know. Then there are others that have to do with the ways energy moves and combines. These I do not understand. The properties of the material world follow from these laws. But I know that what you want to know is what has God set down as rules that, if you follow, will allow you to progress to higher and higher stages. There are none. Now, I know you are surprised. You think that there is a rule book and if you could just get hold of that and could force yourself to follow it, then you would be able to become angelic.

Well, my dear, that is not how it is. I have told you that the goal of all is to enter a state of perfect love. But this is not to be achieved by following rote a list of proscriptions. For then, how easy it would be. No, my friend, that is not the way of it. You see God as something so small and narrow and petty at times, who is like a big mother with a stick ready to strike you for your transgressions. This does not mean that help is not sent to you routinely to aid you with your thinking, but it is for all of you to grow and progress in a creative way toward becoming light. This is an active position: it does not come by conformity. I do not know how to say it better. You could all stop today and say. "We will live by the Ten Commandments," and then you would indeed find a change in your world, but this would not be all that is needed.

You are entering a new age, but you are not quite there yet, so you do not quite understand me. You see, you are on a threshold of growth of consciousness and so you enter a new stage of growth. But you know the end is not is sight. So now you wonder, "Well, what do we live by. Are there no guidelines? Does it matter how we treat each other?" Well, does it? You see, ask *yourself* that. Do not ask God. Begin within; ask yourself what does it mean to live in harmony or disharmony.

Begin to open your eyes. Begin to create—not because God told you so but because you then begin to see.

I am glad to talk with you again. I am here. Do not be afraid that I will leave you. I have been here before you wrote and I will continue to be here. That is the way it is. I am not always waiting for you, you know. I have many other things to do, but it is as though you call me on the telephone and then I can answer you even while I am busy doing other things. It is quite easy, you see.

But now let us talk of something else, and that is about your feelings and how you are still seeking in your life a way to combine what you think of as spiritual and your everyday, mundane life. You still think that there must be something else. You would like to exist on a more spiritual plane at times, and other times you simply want to follow your ego needs. Fine. There is no reason those both can't exist. I have told you about that. But I sense some guilt in you which states that you should do more, give more, be more, pray more, make more impact. Is this your ego or your inner-self talking? That is the question. You see, I will not tell you the answer because you are looking at it as though there is a right way to be—a way, as I have pointed out before, that will lead to approval after death.

You know you are in transition. All will come clearer if you just allow the tension to exist. If you try to solve the question, then the tension may disappear but that is not sufficient. Let yourself be with your wondering and questioning. It is enough. Hear and follow your inner self. Do not be led by the ego's proud mumbling. That will only lead you down a stray path. You wonder what it would be to lead a thoroughly spiritual life, and I say that the way is as varied as the colors of springtime. Your way and another's way are not at all the same. You do not have to aspire to be someone else. That is not necessary at all. You do not have to move mountains or lead multitudes. That is not how it is.

Your struggle to understand may be your path, you see. I will give you courage, and I will comfort as I can. Please speak to me when you are troubled. I may be able to lead you a bit. You are seeking inward solitude now, and you often do not know how to allow that to happen in your busy life. Know that much happens within even when you are busy with other things, though, of course, it is important to listen when you can. Do not worry that you feel pulled inward at this time. Just allow that to be because important things are happening for you. But do not allow yourself to brood and evaluate that inwardness as bad in any way. Enjoy your inner solitude. Allow it to heal and inform you. That is all for now.

Let me talk to you about what to do when there is a death in the family. This, of course, is a time of grief and sorrow for those who are left behind. They wail because they have lost the substance of those they love, and they fear that they will never see them again. This is a time when the faith that comes from believing in more than ordinary life can be helpful. Your loved persons are not lost. No, not at all. They only have moved past a barrier and actually are much freer and more expanded than you are. You want to know where they are, and I say to you, "Here." And of course you say, "Where?" and I say, "Here." We could go on a long time with that, but that would take up a great deal of time. You all should try to adopt a belief that living and dying are part of the same process, that death is not an end nor is it a beginning. The cycle is unending. You see this is different.

The unending cycle of life & death

God does not only visit you when you are living or only when you are dead. But that which IS, IS, always, forever, on and on. So you see when loved ones die, they have merely continued their existence. They have not gone anyplace like in the heavens, though sometimes entities do travel, but that is different. But neither are your loved ones hanging around in the same dimension you are. You see this is not so easy for you to understand, for I see your mind is all full of teachings and images of heaven and hell and other places. When I speak to you, they are evoked. Try to expand past them. You don't need to know what actually happens when you die, just to believe in some ongoing process that is not bad. I have told you death in itself is not painful, but liberating. So, though I know it would be difficult to rejoice when others die, it would be best if you were clear that they were not cut off from existence but merely returned to the Home of their Heart. Of course, you will grieve, for human beings feel that way, but let yourself feel the hope that comes from believing. Know that they had completed what they set out to do and returned home. You may think they could have waited awhile longer, but believe me, their timing is right.

Returned to the Home of their Heart

October 12, 1988
Choosing a path

What is it you want to know? You want help with your dilemma. You wonder what to do about selling your house. You wonder if I have any words of wisdom for you that will help you. You see, my dear, I will give you some words, but it is you who will have to choose and decide whether or not to do something or other. I know you want me to help you pick which fork in the road to take. Which one leads to happiness? Well, my dear, both do. The path itself does not have happiness at its end. There never is an end you know, but the way is the important thing. You wonder, though, if one way is not easier than another, whether one has less pitfalls than another, whether one can be traveled with ease while the other will be filled with potholes. This is always the way dilemmas are viewed, white and black, right and wrong, easy and hard. But this is not so. Each way is a mixture; each way presents itself in different guises. The question is, which way do you want to go. You see, you are not using your own visionary faculties.

Now let me give you a few clues. If you put your house on the market, there will be a buyer in a few months; however; you will not like the price. If you don't put it on the market, you will find yourself plagued by the same doubts as before. You must ask yourself what it is that you want. Either way is OK, you see, but what do you want?

You will learn much through these experiences, but first you must accept the responsibility for your life, for your gladness, for reaching your goals, for living your life. Do not settle for only a little. Reach out with your mind. Decide on how you want to live and then make it happen. Create your life, day by day. Seek joy. Seek friends. Seek knowledge. Seek pleasure. All that is there for you. Do not seek pain and misery. That also is there for you. Turn others' lives over to them. Do not carry their life or pain on your back.

October 25, 1988
The answers are within and not without

I am with you, my dear. Just relax and let me come in again. You have been having a time of it, and I am glad that you are writing to me again. I know that you have been feeling very under the weather and I have done what I could for you, but this will be better. You wonder what to do, but then you don't really want to do anything. You have difficulty grasping the importance of self-determination. You do tend to indulge yourself in misery sometimes, but I understand this habit comes from not knowing other ways. But you will learn, don't fear. You wonder why this time has come upon you and if it will pass. It has come upon you as a very necessary ingredient in your life right now, though I know you will disagree with me. You think this is some punishment heaped upon you rather than opportunity. I know you don't want to hear positive things as it may make it difficult to hang on to your feelings of misery. Isn't that how it is? But you will soon find yourself tiring of this role, and then you will again hear me. This is all right. You see, all must be experienced. Do not worry. But you still don't understand that the answers are within and not without. You are learning. You are going through an important process. Just allow this to be. I am not going to write further as I know you are tired. Write soon again. I will be here for you.

I am here with you, my dear. How nice to see you this morning. You are feeling better though you are still in a state of ambivalence. You see you are struggling against the turns of your life, trying to hold onto the bank as though you could will a new channel. You see how hard this makes things. Not long ago I spoke to you in the morning and talked to you about how it is to be above all those things and places and people that you define your life by. I told you that to be in a state of Being transcends all that so you can flow more easily through your life, knowing that where you are, who you are with, or what you have are only the surroundings of your pure state of Beingness which accompanies you no matter where you are. This is different than just seeing yourself as an individual unattached to others. This I don't mean. There is a way many of you think these days which has to do with being separate and unattached. This is not the same thing at all. In the state of consciousness which can see Beingness, you also know that intense connections can be made. You do not have to be aloof from your life, but your life is not your attachment, you see. You transcend those all.

October 27, 1988
To be in a state of
Being transcends
all

I know when we spoke, you were able to grasp a little of what I was saying and I suggest that you think more on this. You are not now what you were and will not be who you are in the future as though in some static state. You are fluid. Your surroundings shift as you pass through, but hold fast to that transcendent knowledge of you as more than you see. This will help you to flow through the changes which are presented to you. You do not need any special place to BE, you know. It will happen no matter where you are. Now that is all for this morning. You are going through a time of change and transition, some of which you do not yet understand, but have faith for all will be well.

You are having difficulty keeping your mind still. Let me help you. Now focus your attention to a spot over your left eyebrow and watch for a changing. See if that helps to get you into a receptive phase.

Now let us go on. Please feel free to ask any question you may have. I know you are concerned with what you have heard about the rise of Satanism in your country, especially among the young. And you wonder how that fits with what I am telling you about the coming of a time of peace and happiness.

Well, first of all, I have not assured you of that coming. Remember, I have talked of many forces at work and that outcomes are not assured. But let me speak to your concern. You see, when there is a rise of interest in something like Satanism, which, by the way, is simply a name for something which is manifest, it is not as though Satan exists as a person who is pulling people toward him. But it is a symbolic expression to balance what you call "good."

The Play of Life

You see, I have often told you about the whole of things, that there is not only one side—like when I talked of forgiveness and the transgressor being part of the whole. So here, too, the whole is not merely one-sided. Now you have to understand that the forces of energy are made manifest and conscious through the actions of humankind and are interpreted and explained and labeled according to their present state of awareness, growth and understanding. Your world is in a rapid state of change. The forces are turbulent. The changes are falling over themselves so fast that sometimes the new and the old happen interchangeably. Thus, in this kind of system, there will be manifestations of many kinds. These will be sought by others who will try to validate and replicate them.

You wonder if this is a clash between good and evil, and I tell you, no; it is not or, perhaps, only on a plane which you understand. But, as I told you, all is whole. The clash is not on a transcendent plane because there is no distinction between what you label *good* and *evil*. I know this is difficult to understand because, from your perspective, the many forms of cruelty are evidences of evil forces. But this is not true. There certainly are various forces, but these are not divided in two such as you would believe. You see, in the play in which you are in, the Play of Life, there are many ways that the forces are played out, and they all have a part. This is, of course, symbolic thinking. As an individual, you can only see a little bit and only understand a little bit depending on where you stand. So for you, it is very difficult to see transcendentally about the meaning of all that happens. You want to have a world of dichotomies or, rather, you would like a world of one dimension—goodness. But, you see, this is a relative term. How do you know what that even would be like? A place where no one was killed by another? A place where no one was ever hurt by another? A place where no one hurt themselves? What would your criteria be for knowing you were in a state of goodness?

Oh, I know I am confusing you. I can feel your resistance as though I am excusing what you term *bad* or *evil* or *cruelty* as though to say, "It doesn't matter. It's all one." I am not saying that. Of course it matters what you do, but what I am trying to point out is that you are still looking at concepts only through your human eyes and still cannot see the whole. And that is OK. That is the way it is. So that still leaves you wondering about Satanism. You wonder if it will take over the world, if there will be another Hitler brought to power by those who are acting out this force. Well, my dear, the shifting movements are like shifting sand dunes. There are shifts this way and that. You are in a time of much shifting. There is a constant balancing which takes place.

You want something for tonight and I will be glad to help you out. You want to have a little celebration of our writing and I will be excited to be there with you. Let me say this. There is not so much to celebrating a year as there is to celebrating the connections you have all made and the learning that has taken place and the love you share. This I will be glad to celebrate with you.

October 31, 1988
(Halloween)
On celebrating the connections

Let me say a few words. Welcome, welcome, my dear friends, who come to hear my words each month and who go off to read and live them. I am so pleased that we have spent this time together and hope that your life has become clearer from these monthly sessions. As you enter into this place of peace and joy, let your hearts open to receive this nourishment. Your soul cries for it. Allow yourself to drop your protective barriers so that the pure love can flow and enter you to heal and nourish you. Bless yourself and each other with your presence. Know that you are precious indeed. Let this knowledge penetrate and permeate each cell of your body. Be here now.

A meditation
From the
mountain top

Now for a brief meditation.

Allow yourself to relax fully by paying attention to each breath. See the life-giving properties of each breath. Feel yourself breathing in life. Feel your aliveness. Feel how unique you are as you bring yourself to renewed life with each breath you take. Now see yourself on a mountain top, a place where you can see for many, many miles in each direction, a place of great power. See that the world looks very different from that perspective. Allow yourself to imagine that your sight was increased a thousand fold so that you could see with great clarity all that was happening. See how different your view of life is. Let this infiltrate your consciousness to know that all is not what you are presently seeing. Let yourself look at your life from this mountain top. See its path as you trace yourself through life. See what insights you get. And then when you are ready, return to the room.

November 2, 1988
Letting go
of control &
expectation

Here you are and here I am and that is good. I am glad that you again are writing to me. You have come through a trying period for you, and I am glad to see you feeling more centered on your path. All will come to pass, you see. The important thing is to learn from experience. You are learning about letting go of control and expectations, for these are the surest ways there are to feel pain. You do not have the power within you to maneuver things around so they all come out the way you want, when you want. This is a mistake many are making now where they think that they can indeed make everything happen as they wish. This is just not so. There are ways of being in tune and that does make a difference, but you see that is a different matter than controlling the universe. You and Julie have a great deal to learn about this, as do many others. You are all just beginning to learn about the way of the universe, and so you do not always know how to understand because there are many theories and words being said which seem to imply that if you just think hard enough about something it will come to pass. Well, perhaps, but perhaps not. It does not work as simply as that.

Let me tell you a little of how it works. It is the ability of the vastness of your consciousness to tap into what is happening, not that it creates it, but that it taps into the knowledge which is there. There is much to be said about this, but let me just give you a clue.

It is very important for you to believe me or, if not, then it becomes difficult to come in. There is much resistance in you at this time to believe in that which you can't see. On one hand, you would like to believe that things can be manifested and, on the other hand, you think it is all hogwash. You are not alone in your confusion and vacillating beliefs. You only glimpse briefly and cannot integrate this with your belief structures. You are willing to give up your current beliefs but only if you have proof. And, for you at this time, proof would consist of having things go as you would like. But better, it is to *like* how they do go. You cannot see broadly enough to evaluate anything good or bad, you see. That is why you are always so much better off learning what you can and believing that whatever is happening is for your good, even if that is not apparent. This does not imply a state of passive acquiescence, but an active state of learning and progress and growth. I have told you that holding on to the past or trying to force the future into a particular mold will leave you feeling pained and unhappy.

Creating your own life

Look again to creating your life. It does not matter where you find yourself, this is always possible. You can refuse to acknowledge life's possibilities; you can also sit passively and merely react to all which happens around you. You can weep and cry about life's unfairness, or you can meet life, you can interact with life, you can create everywhere you go. This is not easy. You feel how difficult this would be to always think in this way. But set this as a vision. Work toward it. You do not have to accomplish it all at once. But pay attention to how you are blocking—how much you want to feel a victim at times. You will learn from this. You still carry a belief that bad things are likely to happen—though you want them to stay away from your door. Look at this belief. See how you only feel that you are on a floating island when life goes well for you, an island that might simply melt away, leaving you adrift and drowning. You have trouble believing in the goodness of the universe. You have doubts about how this all works. Look at your beliefs. See how you think that being miserable about something will influence positive change. See how this belief gets in the way.

211

You can be positive. I know you think you will be disappointed and you don't want that. Look at the protection you give yourself and see if there isn't something else you can use.

Let me tell you something else, and that is to develop a belief system which allows you peace within. If you do not experience this, ask what is in the way. Peace can be achieved no matter what the circumstances of your life, but it depends on what you believe. If you believe certain things are necessary, then you will find that indeed there are barriers to your feelings of peace. There is much to be said about the consequences of beliefs on your life, but I will not go into that now. Try now to go forth to your life, creating anew that which you want. This does not mean that you can create or manifest anything; it does mean that you can create your experience of the situation. That is all.

November 5, 1988
A message
Look inward to connect with deeper wisdoms, to hear the voices of learning

Let me enter your heart for I am with you. Open your heart. Let me flow with you and I will bring you great messages of love and hope. You are sometimes very resistant to believing. You want to have your feet flat on the ground and want to have facts in front of you. Not that you disbelieve in the mystery of life, but you still are skeptical that the barrier between the seen and the unseen can be penetrated. You do not know if you should believe what I tell you as I might just be a figment of your imagination that says what you want to hear. Well, my dear, first answer, "What is *imagination*?" Is it merely the ability of the human mind to create a story out of nothingness or does it go beyond? You see, you talk of your mind as though it were some simple mechanical thing lying in your brain. This is not so. The mind is a much greater storehouse, a powerhouse, and lives far beyond the confines of your head. But it is not accessed to its fullest because of the way you all learn to perceive your world. As your researchers have pointed out, you have developed the use of one side of your brain to the detriment of the whole. What you now call a *new consciousness* is merely the reconnecting to what has been there all along. You have developed your technology at the expense of yourself. You now live in comfort; however; the comfort that you would feel if you were truly able to partake of the richness of life is dulled for you.

Let me just assure you to go ahead with these writings. Believe what you will. Let these words inform you whether you believe they come from me, from Universal Mind or from a part of you. You see this is not so necessary to ask, "Who is writing this?" as to ask, "Does this sound like truth?" That is the question. I know. Now you say, "But human beings believe all kinds of things and think they are truth. The Nazis believed the truth of what they did, isn't that right?" I know this is difficult but, you see, you do not think like that. You are already able to see higher truths. You already can discriminate so you can trust yourself more. If I were talking to a Hitler, I would perhaps talk in a different way, but you see this too is not an easy answer as you would like it to be. All are on a path. There are many stopping places on this path, many vantage points. So it then becomes more difficult to say *truth* for this one is *truth* for that one. You want to know what is *TRUTH* with a capital *T*. Well, my dear, you must search for this, you see. I cannot give you that answer. My writings are not to give you that answer but to help you in your own search. You see the difference?

There is not a prize to be found. You will not find the Holy Grail. You will not come to a place of absoluteness, at least not now. But the search, *ah*, the search. How it gives life its substance; how it gives life its meaning. This is the stuff of your life. You see it is not how to make more money or buy more things or take more trips. These are all fine. I do not disparage any of those pursuits. But it is not what your life consists of. They will add pleasure sometimes to your life but will not satisfy you. It is the eternal pursuit of the question: "Who am I? Who, indeed, am I? And what is it that I am about?" You see, this question has no answer that can be nailed down in your world. So it is up to you to search and construct it over and over and over. Sometimes you as individual and you as collective take an answer that someone has constructed, take that as truth and follow it sometimes for many, many years before discarding it as not the answer. It is easy to take some other's answer rather than following your own heart into the mystery. You see this much in your world. When the search is given over and other pursuits made paramount, then the very things which are destroying you now take place.

The eternal pursuit: Who am I

So this is a message to all. Examine your complacency with the truths which are held out for you. Be careful of following too closely the answers of others. This applies to old and new messages. See that you also have the capacity from within to evaluate all the messages out there. You have the capacity to

A message

look inward to connect with deeper wisdoms, to hear voices of learning. Do this. Do not accept blindly what you hear. Live with the mystery. Live with the question. Accept the tasks of the search. That is all.

November 8, 1988
A message
On viewing the earth

I am so glad to see you feeling better. There has been much inner growth taking place and more is to come. Isn't that nice?

What shall we speak of today? You do not have many questions. It would be helpful if you would write some out ahead of time and then I could address them. I think what you want today is just a message of comfort and hope. Well, I will see what I can do for you. Now, my dear, imagine that you were a stranger in your land, someone who came from so far away that you had never heard of earth or of human beings. What do you think your evaluation of this place, earth, would be? You see this is hard to imagine unless you consider what values would be used for the evaluation. You see how this is? You yourself are often distressed by what is being done to the earth and all its inhabitants because you view things out of a certain set of values that others do not appear to hold. You feel much pain as you see what is being done in the name of progress and in the name of financial gain, and you wonder why it is that others don't see as well as you and others like you. You see there are different criteria people use and, especially now, there is a wide variation between many belief systems. Let me see if I can help you to see your place in this whole scheme of things.

You would like it if all people could see with the clarity of those who view the destruction with pain. You think that with all the religious messages, it would be merely a matter of time before humanity saw the light of day. But this is not the answer. There are certainly values relayed by religions; however, the problem comes because these are not necessarily the values that governments rule by or that laws are made by. Let me give you some examples of how this works. In the rain forests which you observed tonight (in a film), there is a disregard for what is—and a regard from what can be made materially. Many cry against this, seeing the destruction but, again, not seeing this in the light of the whole. What is being done has been done over and over.

214

We are ready to write again. I am sorry to see that this day was a day of strife for you. It came from a visitation in the night which has opened some old wounds. Do not be too concerned about this as it will pass. You see, you often are not aware of what happens during your time of sleep, but much takes place in your dreams which then has influence on your waking hours. Pay attention to this and you will see that dreams do not merely belong to the night. You will find that healing takes place not only on your present human level, but also on your soul level. You see, many things are still to be resolved and dream time is when this can happen. So just allow your feelings to arise and suffer them a bit, for they tell you that yet another door has opened.

Sometimes, I know you and others too would just like to leave the doors closed, but then you see how soon you would become rigid. It is important for doors to open and for light to be able to enter. So do not look to your normal surroundings for what is distressing you. Look instead within. Let yourself fully feel what it is you are feeling. That is all.

Now let me say something more about love. We have not directly discussed this for awhile, but I want to reemphasize the vital importance of this force. You will find your own situation improved if you but stand in the force of love and transmit it like a beacon. You will find life easy for you. So many of you seek love, hoping to find that special person to give it to you, hoping then that you can hold on to her or him. You see, this creates in you a feeling of scarcity, a feeling that you have to hold on at all costs. Whereas, if you look instead to the universe for love, when you allow yourself to provide a transmitter for the love energy, then you will find the supply inexhaustible. I know you cannot always feel this but you are blocking this knowledge from yourself. Release. Forgive. Relax. Let your tensions go. Let love flow. This does not mean giving in. It means taking control of your life. No one can do this for you. You may have to be brave. Carve out what you want. Seek this. That is all for now.

Let me give you a little message to get you through the rest of your day. Look around and see the wondrous colors and shades of the earth around you. Let your eyes first feast on the shades of green which still linger in the fall landscape. Look then at the blues of the sky. See the variations and fine shadings. Look now for other hues as they are scattered upon the landscape. Think on the miracle of the colors and of the miracle of your eyes which allows you to see them and of the miracle of your senses which allows you to feel them. Such wonders! And you and others walk around oblivious, focused instead on the mundane in your life. Life is so exciting. It is ever changing, ever renewing, ever transforming. See this. Let yourself know that *this is IT!*

Being confused Now let me tell you a few other things. You are very concerned about the confused state you find yourself in. You ask me what to do. Well, my friend, you know I will ask what you want, but I see that your state of confusion comes from wanting too many different things at once. This cannot be, of course, if they are in different directions. But I also sense the pull of fear and also the pull of adjustment and acquiescence and also a reluctance to step boldly out for yourself. You see there are many paths and any will take you down them. You want to be happy but you have forgotten what it is that brings you happiness. You have yourself caught in a web so that no matter which way you pull, you feel yourself stuck tighter and pulled back in the opposite direction. Let me tell you how to get out of this experience, for it is only an experience. There is no real sticky web holding you. There is no spider and you are no fly. See what this experience is telling you. Look how you are creating it. What are you experiencing in truth. You have a propensity to get yourself in similar situations and to experience similar feelings. See what are the strands you have created, what beliefs are being activated that are at cross purposes. This will help you to see what the current experience means for you. That is all for now.

November 15, 1988 Let me come to write to you again in this beautiful place. You
Loving yourself want a lesson for today on loving yourself. This is very very important and I will do what I can to help you. To love oneself is the highest order of act because, when you love yourself, this extends out into the universe, touching all that you are in contact with. So do not ever think that to love yourself means that you are selfish or uncaring of others. This is not it at all. But many do not know what it means to love oneself.

Does it mean to accept all your faults? Does it mean to forgive all which you hold against yourself? Is it to see yourself as beautiful? Is it to stop belittling yourself? Well, yes, these can all be a part of it. But remember when we talked about love, we talked about it going beyond the everyday things we normally talk about as loving someone. To love is transcendent. It goes beyond the practical. To love yourself is to see yourself as truly wondrous, to see yourself as part of a very magical universe, to see yourself as vehicle for your soul, to see yourself as spirit. You see this goes beyond what we talked of earlier. To love yourself implies acceptance and forgiveness and understanding from a transcendent plane. To know who you truly are implies that you can do no other than love yourself. So do not only focus on loving yourself in practical ways, but open your heart to the knowledge that you belong to the universal and that makes you perfect. You, however, often dislike yourselves for events that happen in your life. Sometimes you dislike yourself because someone else disliked you. Sometimes you do not forgive what happened in your past. Sometimes you think that unless you meet a criteria set by another, you do not have a right to love. There are many ways you abuse and abase yourself. But often, at the core, you do not have this knowledge that you are a perfect part of the universal whole. This does not mean that as a human you have reached perfection and have no tasks of growth or learning. No, this is not what I mean by *perfection*. Think on these distinctions. They will provide you with food for thought.

So now I will give you a meditation which will allow you to focus on self-love from the highest plane.

A meditation
On self-love

Let yourself relax, finding a comfortable place where you can feel your body supported and held by the forces. Let yourself pay attention to your breath, breathing out tension and breathing in peace. See this as you breathe. As your body relaxes, allow yourself to release all tensions held in your mind and emotions. See that those tensions too can leave with each exhaling breath. Now as you lay relaxed, imagine that you can see yourself as a being connected to the whole of the universe. Allow your view to deepen and deepen. See your connections. See the core of your being. See what this is like for you. Now see how you are joined in perfectness with all. See that you do not exist merely as everyday selves. Now let all the love which exists in the universe resonate through you. Allow this love to wash clean all those everyday things which have prevented you from loving yourself. See the purity of yourself. Let these images come to you.

November 24, 1988
(Thanksgiving)
*It is in letting go
that you will find
the way*

You have many questions today and wonder if I have any answers for you. You are trying to figure out your life and think this writing and spiritual unfolding is having a detrimental outcome on your life because you cannot see that life is any easier. In fact, it feels harder to you. You do not see what purpose is served by our writing. In other words, you feel at a stalemate but yet cannot simply go back to being who you were. You would like to go back on one hand, or on the other, to go forward to a time where you were ruled by your spiritual knowledge and did not vacillate in between.

Ah, my dear, I sympathize with your plight. But you are looking in the wrong direction for answers to your dilemma. The problem is not whether you should live a spiritual life or not. No, rather it is that you have not given up your need for control. You want to know everything. You want to have proof of everything. You want to believe you can know and control the future. You want to live without indecision, without doubt, without any kind of life trial. You are struggling very hard to maintain control over life. You think you know why this is, and I tell you—you don't. You have not yet agreed to a commitment with the spiritual aspects. You still want to have it your way. You wonder now how this is helping you, but I say that you are asking the wrong questions. You do have the opportunity for growth now, but you have to let it in.

It is not necessary for you to force yourself to pray or meditate or write or have groups or anything. You are not being forced down a path you are not choosing. It is in letting go that you will find the way. This is a time when you are being confronted with yourself. You can no longer hide behind the facade of the "good girl" or whatever you want to call your disguise. You are seeing yourself these days with a clarity that is too bright at times. And it is this you want to run from. Be clear about this. You want to find a haven where you can again retreat behind an easy mask. Don't do this. You are braver than that. Accept what is being revealed to you. This is all necessary. You do not have to be other than who you are. Accept this. Know that in the eyes of God, you are perfect. Accept the inner longings and workings. See yourself raw and open. See with eyes unclouded by illusion. This may be painful for awhile as you sort through all that has been hidden. All will get better for you as you cease to struggle to retain the blinders.

You think that if you give up your spiritual quest you will be happier. That could be if you were successful enough in hiding from yourself. But this is not for you. The time is now for true unfolding. Let your soul inform you. Do not struggle so. You are a being of light which has been covered with tarnish. The uncovering and cleansing of the tarnish, a tarnish that has been comforting on some levels, is a task which needs doing. Let yourself accept this. Let yourself accept yourself. See with your inner eyes. Lift up your eyes to the wonders of the universe. I know you are fearful of the future at this time, but see the footsteps are already laid out through the deepest parts, so you need not struggle to break your path. You know there is something there to break through, but this will come if you just cease your struggle. That is all.

Now, my dear, I am here with you once again. It has been a while since we have written and you are finding it difficult to do so. Let me assure you that this is fine. Do not feel guilty because you do not write to me. It is for your benefit and there is no use thinking otherwise. This is a time of internal struggle for you. Just let this be. You are having a difficult time flowing with your life. There are things still unseen which will beckon you down new streams. You will find it will become easier as time passes there.

Let me write a little message for your birthday. This coming year will be one of renewed vigor as springtime approaches. You will throw off the gloom of winter and approach the springtime with a new world view. Then there will be times of peace and contentment for awhile before new variations on a theme will begin playing. You see, this is a picture of the twistings and turnings, the ups and downs of life. You are on a quest, even when you do not acknowledge this. The quest is for yourself. Let yourself ponder on this, your birthday. You wonder if you should continue to have your monthly meetings. You wonder what to do if you do not write, or if you do write, find that the material is too personal to use. Yes, that is right. Our writing has changed. You are in need of much support and so it is difficult to send you messages of generality. But let me talk to everyone about the holiday season.

Ah, my friends, here you are approaching another holiday season. Some of you are excited and enthusiastic and others feel burdened by the very thought of Christmas. Let me shed a little light on the holiest of days for many of you. When it was decided that the Christ consciousness should again become incarnate, there was much discussion as to how that should happen so as to engage the notice of the world. You can imagine that there were many ideas and you already know the story that was chosen. But there were other parts that were lost to the populous at large because it was deemed necessary in order to perpetuate the story of Christ as the One who comes bringing the greatest gift, the gift of love. You see, if this had not happened, the world would have become darker and darker. The light was very badly needed at that time. Suffice it to say, the forces at that time were very powerful, and it was not easy to bring the sense of love into the world. It has been many years since then, and the light is still dim and the darkness still exists. Now we are trying other ways, but it is still good to look at the story of the Christ as one which has been very successful.

To give from your heart is a rare gift   You see, it is not the person, but the message, and that is why, when you celebrate Christmas, you are involved in attempting to bring the light into the world. However, there has been so much tarnishing of the original message that you find yourselves caught up in a frenzy which has little to do with love. So stop. Think. Reflect. How can you help bring the light of love into existence. There was a time when gift giving was symbolic of this. Now, too often, that meaning is no longer there. Think about this. No matter what religion or non-religion you are, you can consider that the birth of the Baby Jesus, the vehicle for a surprisingly bright soul to enter this world, was a major victory for the light. See how the message is still new, still so much unused. Do not focus on the person. Focus on the message. Let yourselves give to each other now. To give from your heart is a rare gift. It will enhance your very being.

So, on this holiday season, take time to look inward. Use this time to connect with the flow of the light. Use this season to share what you have with others. See this time as an anniversary of an important happening, one which still has time to come to fruition. There has been much distortion of the message, but this is not to say it was not important. Examine yourself. See what blocks the light from shining through you. Be transparent. Let yourself glow and shine with the love which comes. That is all.

We can write again here on your birth date anniversary. Welcome to the home of your heart. I remember well the day you came to the time of becoming incarnate. The leave takings were painful, yet glad too, as you set off on your current journey. What a big step that is to take, for you did not know at the time how it would all go, no matter how carefully things were planned. And here you are, at this stopping place on your journey home. How does it feel there? I sense that you have an urge to move on, but you need this time for regrouping. Some solitude is something you must structure for yourself as you will find that you badly need it.

November 28, 1988
Welcome to the Home of your Heart

And now a birthday blessing for you. Blessings on your birthday from all those who love you here. We are cheering for you as you come into the last, long stretch of your life. Glory in this time. Do not waste it with petty worries. Let yourself expand with the wisdom of your age until you overflow on all around. Do not be concerned with the physical losses you may feel, for this is a time of heightened inner consciousness. Let this be your beacon. Let yourself see anew as your mind opens further. Let yourself put into perspective all those things which were once so dear to your heart.

A blessing

Simplify your life. See the pristine beauty of it. Use this next year to further sharpen your inner vision, to further accept the blessedness of your soul, to deepen your connections with all of life. Let this be your guiding star. Walk the path of this coming year of your life boldly. Do not scrunch it. Let it expand before you. That is all for now.

Here is a word of welcome to your group members.

Delight and laugh aloud

Ah, my friends, welcome again to this place of blessed peace. Open your heart to the peace that comes from allowing the energy of the universe to enter you. Look now around the room and meet the eyes of your friends here. Look deeply. Communicate on the soul level your love and acceptance of them. Let their gaze enter and touch you. Know that your connections are as deep as the deepest ocean, as far reaching as the farthest star. Feel this. Now let yourself look once more around the room, allowing your eyes to play upon the beauty of each person here. Allow yourself to feel your beauty as radiated out to them. Smile at the variety of beauties assembled here. Delight and laugh aloud at this preciousness if you want. Feel inside the delight in yourself—your beauty, your uniqueness, your *youness*.

You want to know about writing a book like we talked of earlier. Well, my friend, I'm ready when you are, but you must be sure in your heart that you are ready, for this will not be such an easy task for you. You want to know how it will work. Well, this is how I think we will begin. It will be much easier to work on your computer, so this is what we should first practice. Then I will give you the content outline and we will begin. You and I will see how it goes. I do not know if you are ready yet, but we will see. There is no rush, but on the other hand, there is an urgency.

What else shall we talk of? There is a movement afoot in your country which is spreading world wide. This movement is not so clearly seen, but it is none the less spreading. You call this *New Age*, a misnomer if I have ever heard one, but that is OK. As I watch the unfolding of this medium, it is very interesting to see the responses. They are not always positive as you might think, for there are those who would take advantage of others' gullibility. There are some who are very afraid of New Agers as they think that no good can come from such beliefs. You would like to know how this movement fits with us here, and what place it has in the scheme of human development. Well, my dear, of course, it is one of the movements which lies in a positive direction, though there is again something which will hold humanity back from making the leaps necessary for survival. The question to be answered, after all, is what happens in the lives of persons who follow New Age beliefs? How has their behavior changed? What ways have their spirits been nourished? What ways do spiritual truths become active in their lives? There are many who use the New Age movement just as another way of feeling good, of abdicating from responsibility, of following someone else's truth.

Let me talk to you about something else. The ways of heaven are not something as easily seen by you there, and as I have indicated before, it is the search that is most important. The New Age movement is a search, a journey to a spot still dimly seen. There is a collectiveness about the worries of the people who find themselves stranded and alone. The movement speaks to them. But do not think that this search is the answer. You see, this is different. The need to search is stronger now than it has been for a long time as the world lies in twilight. There are many searches going on, each led by the flashlights of belief shining on the darkness. You see how this is?

So those who follow Christianity or are seeking to be born again, or even those engaging in Satan-like practices, are searching. This is important to know. None has the answer. None has the answer which will save the world and redeem humankind. Don't look at it like that. There is much to be done, for the earth is on a collision course. The pathways are not clearly marked, but it is not difficult to imagine the way. Seek, and if seeking involves New Age behavior, fine. But if you are engaging in these things as an end in themselves, then you are mistaken. It is not enough to assuage your pains with a new belief system. See that the way you are, the way you act, is more important. It does not matter what tools you take on your search if you know what direction you are going and what it is that you are searching for.

You want to know if the forces of love can ever change those who would heedlessly and needlessly destroy for material gain. You see, the strongest belief system operative in the world today is that of *materialism*. And, as long as that is true, you will have those who will take any advantage in order to increase their gain. But this belief is not held exclusively by those who are the perpetrators of greed. It is held by almost all. Even those who do not engage in these activities hold it to be a powerful belief.

So if you see perpetrators who cut down the forests or poach the seas, then you must see that they are only part of a circle, a circle that all are involved in. There is no easy out for you who would feel more pious. I do not suggest that you drop out and seek to live a life of poverty. This is not the answer. I can only point out that your beliefs create your reality, and your strongest belief is that of materialism. This is stronger than your belief in God at this time. So be aware of how this belief operates in your life. You will see this is so. You, however, cannot escape it, for it is a collective belief which is enmeshed in all areas of your life. Will this change? I do not have the answer for you. The course of history is long.

Now, we can write again. This is something new and we will have to practice with it.

(I was again trying to write directly on the computer, having gone back to handwriting after a short experiment with the computer a year ago.)

As I was saying, this is a special day for you and all others in your world. There has been a change of vibration such that we can feel it here. That does not mean that all is saved or anything else like that, but there definitely are some shifts happening as so many of you explore the spiritual issues of your lives. The shift in vibrations takes place when a new level is reached in a band. This you may not understand. It is when an overload happens in a band of vibration and there then is a shift to another band. This has happened many times and it has happened now. So keep going. Keep trying. Feel free to bring the spiritual into your life in every way that you can. That will help you and all others too.

You want to know when and how you will bring these writings to the rest of the world. I know you are sometimes inpatient, but there is no hurry for you. You will do all in your time. You see, there is much changing now for you. Do not be so impatient but follow your heart. You wonder why you are so slow, but that is not the case.

A message
Embrace this day
Let me give you a message for this day. This day is a day of creation in which you share. It is not merely another 24-hour period to be gone through, to be filled up, or used up, or dispensed with in some way. This is a day in your life and in the life of all creation. There is none other quite like it. The opportunities of today are like no other. The glories of today are like no other. The sights, the sounds, the loves, the choices, the chances are like no other. Do not see it as just anther Sunday to be gotten through. Embrace this day. Embrace it as part of God's creation. Will you spend it in anger or in love, ingratitude or thankfulness, irritation or in appreciation, in sadness or joy? This is your choice. Don't waste it.

December 8, 1988
Let me enter your heart. Do not hide from me. It is safe. Open yourself. Let my light shine down upon you. Let me cradle your soul in my arms and bring sweet peace to you.

You want to know more about your fears and especially about your deepest fears—those which are so strong, so basic, so private, so primal that you live your life so as to not disturb them. These fears are formed early. They are deep within your psyche and are very powerful. Often they are associated with other lives and so often do not have rational correlation to your present life. Let me talk about one of your deepest, rawest fears—that of failing. It is not simply a fear of failure which strikes terror into your heart, but this lies in combination with others that form a whole and is very strong. It was formed early, but it also has threads running back into several lifetimes. Your fear, at its core, is very strong, but you have managed through your life to keep it at bay by the way you conform your activities to its demands. Now is a time when it is necessary to confront this if you are to go ahead with our work. That is why you are feeling it so mightily. You are asking for some release of this knot of fears and we are trying to comply with that request. There is indeed pain associated with this. There is no other way to fully release these kinds of fears without confronting them. So let yourself go deep and confront depths.

Let me cradle your soul in my arms and bring sweet peace to you

Come to me and ask for guidance and comfort and I will help you. There is much to be learned at this time. Take small steps. Do not overwhelm yourself. Listen deeply. See yourself. Don't turn away in denial. This will all help. As I said, there are several things knotted together, so you will find that as one goes, others will also loosen. This a message for anyone who is suffering extreme anxiety or fear about a certain event. Some fears are so deep, so conditioned, so necessary that you are confronted with them whenever you step out of the bounds they have laid down within your psyche. See that the only way out is within. Do not be mislead by looking without. The answer is not there. But do not try to figure it out. Ask within for answers. Take time to listen. Know that answers will come in a form that you can handle and only as much as you can handle. The first step is knowing that all your feelings are talking to you in their own language. Listen. Ask what their meaning is. Ask what they are protecting. Listen. That is all for now.

On fear & anxiety

There we are. Let us talk a bit while you are here at your place of business. You wonder why you are feeling better today, and why you seem to change places so much that you can't keep up with it. You wonder if you are more than one person. No, that is not how it is, but you are oftentimes separated from the

December 9, 1988
A child set of behaviors exists within your mental makeup

225

various parts of yourself and are not connected to your core. This is understandable, given how you were raised, and is not at all unusual among human beings. Let me see if I can help you. You see today that you are feeling strong and able, and you think that you can handle what you need to do. Other days you are small and weak and can handle nothing at all, and you wonder how that can be. What is the mechanism of that? You know that many theories speak about the child which lies within you, and you think this is a metaphor, but sometimes you also feel like one and then think that indeed a child still exists. You understand that if you were working with a computer, you could create different programs which would act always in certain ways. Your mind is not exactly like a computer but it is somewhat like that. When you are switched into a certain mode, there is a whole set of behaviors which go with that. So a child set of behaviors exists within your mental makeup. The child is not lying there waiting to be awakened. But clusters of behaviors do exist in a program-like way and, especially in times of stress, these are triggered or activated. At other times others are activated. Now if this makes you sound mechanistic, I do not mean it to be so. You are not a machine like a computer, though there are patterns in your brain.

Free the happiness

What can you do when your program is activated and you feel and act like a helpless child? Well, it would be nice if you could simply push the right button and deactivate, but that is not so easy as that. However, there are things you can do. The first is to accept what is happening as what it is, so you do not become so sure that this is the way it is. Then you can nurture this child. See what she wants. I have told you of this before. You have a very angry, hurt child who wants to be saved from herself. You want to become familiar with that part. The goal is to move from an isolated to an integrated program. As I said, this is not so easy but help is available to you if you ask for guidance and if you listen for the words within. You must relax your control a little. Let yourself write to me daily. You will find your life much easier. Fifteen minutes or thirty will do it. There is nothing more important. You do not have to be angry and hurt any longer. There are ways out. Let me help you for I love you very much. Free the happiness.

There is also a happiness program. See if you can activate that. Let yourself feel your pleasure. Allow yourself to seek the arms of love. Do not shelter yourself from it with your anger and opposition. Feel that. See how, as a child, it was your only weapon. That is not true now. Let go of that anger that you have held for so many years. Let it melt. Let it go. Can you feel it there in your body. Feel those very old feelings of hurt and anger and rejection. See, you are still trying to pay back for that.

What should we talk of today? It is good that you are practicing some more on the computer. We will need more of that in order to get better at it. I have not done this before so we will have to see if we can make this work.

December 10, 1988
**Speaking to the
unseen forces
of the universe**

Now for today's lesson. My dear, we will begin by having a short lesson on prayer. You sometimes think that you would do this, but you do not know how. It is not as you might think it is by the way you were taught in church, but it is a much simpler way of speaking to the unseen forces of the universe. It is not necessary to have any particular form or content, but it does have, at its core, a belief that you can ask here and will be heard. It is not as though every message goes straight to the heart of a God person. Only if you believe that such a person exists will you be disappointed by that statement. There are many guides, angels if you will, and others who have powers to help you, and that is all that is needed—a *belief* that such can happen. That does not mean you will get your every ego wish, for that would be disastrous. Rather the messages that are heard and answered have much more to do with your soul's journey than the wishes of your ego self. This is not a Christmas party here nor are any of us Santa Claus. So when you ask from the depths of your soul, then listen for the answer. You will hear the message for your life's journey. This does not mean that all pain will be taken from you, or your life situation changed, but it could. You see, you only view what you want and need from such a narrow perspective that often you think that the All has forgotten you or has not listened. This is not the case, but as I said, the help is on a soul level and a growth and learning level. So when you speak to the unseen forces, keep this in mind.

You want to know if it is important to ask God or Jesus, or who would one speak to? As I said, the form or content is not important. You do not have a good concept of what this all really is, so we will transform anything you say in good intent. We do not expect you to know more than you do. Meditation, too, is important because it trains you to listen with a different part of your mind. This you should practice often as it takes practice to get it to work. Many people give up because they cannot get their mind to be still, but it is important to go ahead and practice even if the gains are slow. You wonder why all this is necessary, and I say to you that it is there for your own soul benefit in order that you can keep in touch with that which you need. It is not for God or some other deity that you pray, but for your own soul's movement and for your own peace. When your ego is in tune with your soul and its plan, then your life is happy and wondrous indeed. When your ego is battling that which you truly are, then you will feel much conflict. The way out is within and do not forget this. That is all on that subject for now.

December 12, 1988
On fear & worry

How are you this morning, my dear friend. It is a cold morning but that does not mean it has to be a cold day for you. Exude warmth. You will find that as you send it out, you will warm yourself as well. You are a magnificent being. Do not forget this as you start out upon this day. Be sure to look at the sunrise and pay homage to this giant that sends you so much of its energy. See how it lights up the sky as it does your life. Do not let the darkness hold you in its clasp for there is an abundance of light.

You want to know what to do with your worries of today. Just let them go. They are only that—worries. They serve you no purpose except to allow your mind to handle that which exists in your body. You will do well to talk with your body and find out where the distress is, and then allow that to be worked out. You wonder if your are picking up others' distress. Well, some, but most is your own. Look at your fears. They are the culprit. You defend against them until they overwhelm you. Allow them to surface. They will be easier to deal with in little doses. Now go about your day, remembering that this is a day created for you to interact with. Choose well, my dear. That is all for now.

December 15, 1988
**On pain &
suffering**

You are doing well, my dear. That is good. Now I have a word of caution for you. Be especially careful in the next few days. Do not take any unnecessary chances and stay alert. I will watch over you, but it is important to take care and you will be fine.

You are excited about your trip and that is good. All will go well. Do not worry about that. Now let me see what our lesson for today is. You wonder about the suffering of people and whether they have brought that on themselves, or whether it is simply a matter of chance, or if it is due to the evil intents of others. You see, my friend, you always want simple answers. You know that some would say that suffering breeds character, others would say that suffering breeds soul growth. But others would say that pain and suffering are a matter of paying off karmic debt.

You all have various theories because it does not seem right that so many people suffer pain where others do not, and you want to make sense of this. Well, my dear, I cannot tell you one thing or another, for it is not as simple as that. You would like me to make it all plausible for you and give you the right answer. Let me say that no one is ever *punished* by being given a lifetime of pain. Beyond that I cannot explain further. But let's say that you are one of the people who have a lifetime of hardship. How shall you view your life? How shall you make sense of it? How shall you still your envy of others more fortunate? Let me start by telling you that is is very important to look only at your life and to see it in context of many lives so you do not begin to think you have been cheated from a good life. But it is important to look at your pain and see what you can do with it—to alleviate it, to transcend it, to project its healing out into the community. You see, you may have chosen to be confronted in certain ways that will lead to the experience which leads to greater compassion. You cannot always tell what the purpose of the difficulties of your life are for, but you can always try to grow from them.

There is much help available, both in your world and in mine. It is important to ask for help, for it is available.

Transcending worldly cares

Let me send some words of comfort to anyone who is sorely tried this Christmas season. Let me hold you and comfort you and send you peace and relief from pain. Open your hearts to me and hear the prayer I affirm for you. Know that you are cradled in the arms of the All There Is and cannot come to harm. Bear that which you cannot change with courage, knowing that to transcend the worldly cares can be accomplished when the focus is on the spiritual. Look deep and be sure that you are not a party to causing your pain. Examine your beliefs and see if they cause you to live a life which is full of negativity. Let your heart open to the love which abounds. That is all.

December 19, 1988
On fearing death

Here we are once again. That is good for you to join with me this morning for I sense that your energies are being scattered in all directions. Let me help to center and calm you. Just breathe deeply as you write and I will help to send you calming energy from here. Now let me assure you that all is well and you need not worry needlessly. You will be traveling soon and all will go well. It is a time, though, for you to be in touch with your own fears of the changeability of life. You realize that all could go down a different road at the twinkling of an eye, but you see that would not be a different direction but merely the one you have been on all the time.

The fears of death, either of yourself or of those you feel close to, are always there. You see how those deep fears influence what you do in your life, whether that be staying home close to hearth or staying in jobs you dislike or whatever it is that you constrict yourself in. In this way you think that you can keep that old devil death from your door. You see this is not the way to look at life. There has been so much fear around death that you think you will lose everything if it happens. This is not true. Now you are all being given different information about death, but even that does not help enough. You still live your lives as though the ax will fall at any second. Even though many of you would deny this, you will find if you look deep in your psyche, that this fear above all others pulls your strings. You may never think of it and still be ruled by this fear. Look at your life and see its effects. Are you prepared for death or do you still hope it will never happen to you. I have talked often about death and how it is all one part of the process. Let this information penetrate deeply. See how the ego fights against this. It is the ego which does not want to give up this life on earth. It is the only one it knows. But look beyond. Look to the information of your soul. Know that the time of your death will be the right one for you. Do not fear that your life will be cut short, for there is no such thing. You will live out your life as it is meant to be. But see beyond this. Look to your life and how you let this fear dominate your thinking.

December 24, 1988
On the energy systems of the earth

(At Rio Caliente, Mexico)

You would like to know the history of the land you are on. Well, my dear, that of course would take many years of writing, but I will tell you that the energy patterns here were known for many centuries and would have been utilized by the ancient people who knew more about that than you do now. You want to know what energy lines are and how they are formed. You know we have talked of the energy field around and within human beings and how there is an energy system just as there is a circulatory system. The same is true of the earth and, of course, all else. The energy system of the earth runs in certain ways just as does your blood in its system. There are places where lines cross and interconnect which makes that particular place a place of power. You see in your body how certain doctors know the points of power. Well that is true of the earth. These lines do not exist for the benefit of humans but for the benefit of the earth. There is a balance of energy that must be maintained for its health, and so that is partly as a result of interconnecting energy lines. You, of course, can benefit as you too can feed upon the extra energy that is available. But you will find that it also can cause what you might think of as adverse effects because the energy of the earth interacts with that of your body. You find that you have all sorts of strange goings on, including your difficulty with sleep. But all in all you will find the flow healing and enjoyable.

There are many, many places in the world where energy lines cross, but there are only a relatively small number where there are enough crossing lines for it to be a power center. As centers go this is a relatively small one, but beneficial nonetheless.

Now for a brief spiritual message. My dear friend, let the words of the wind and the songs of the birds fill your very being with the knowledge and certitude that order and meaning exist. Let me assure you that the world is not one of chaos and disorder but one which reflects the plan and order and creation of the All There Is. We, you, and the wind are all part of this holy creation. We are it. We become it. We were it. We create it. It does not exist without us.

A message
**On order &
meaning**

You have said today that there are many, many ways of regarding the sacred or the mysterious and many ways of relating to that mystery. This is true and that is fine. It is not necessary that all regard it the same. You see, you still want Truth. You want to know who has the corner on Truth. Who has guessed right. This is not a game show where the winner receives the prize—that is, to be allowed into the kingdom of heaven. You see, you are all trying to figure out the wrong question, but that too does not matter. I have said before that the *search* is the thing, not the *solution*. There are many rungs on the ladder giving different scope to the view. You wonder if God favors one view or another. Dear, dear friend, listen to you. You are still seeking that Father figure who will reward you. Believe me when I say that everything is much different than that concept would allow.

Let me help you a little bit. Stretch your mind so big as to incorporate everything that is, was, or will be. This is creation. Much you have no concept of. You see only a pinprick of what is. You do not have to know more, but do not limit yourself. Let me assure you that everything is working as it should be. That does not mean that you can merely be complacent about things. Remember, I have told you that you are all part of creation and you have to be aware of what you want to create as human beings. But you and your world still exist as only a cell in a much larger body. I do not say this to allow you all to feel insignificant. That is not so, for you truly are in charge of what happens in your world. Do not neglect your responsibility there. But do see that you as people are in charge of determining the creation of the new. You can create a worn out, forgotten planet, devoid of life. This has been done before. Or you have opportunities for other courses. You have developed a belief in your own ineptness and wait for heaven to change things for you. It does not work that way at all. That is all for now.

January 7, 1989

Let me welcome you home from your trip. It is good that you are again writing to me as I have missed our talks. Now I know you want some information or a meditation for your group and I will oblige you. I know you are in a state of indecision about these writings, but all will come to you in due time.

A message
The New Year

Let me give you a message for your group. Welcome my friends as you all begin a new year in your world. Of course, in the whole scheme of the universe, time is an inessential concept, but for all of you, markers such as years are a valuable tool. So I will speak from that perspective. As you enter this new year and wonder what it will bring you, let yourself take note about what it is you hope for. See if it includes expansion of your spirit. See if it involves further development of yourself. See if it involves a greater understanding of the oneness of all. See if it involves the learning to act out of your spiritual beliefs. All of these are far more important than the mundane. Do not worry about the course of your life, but focus instead on your place in it. I wish you all welcome here at this gathering where you are beginning to explore the oneness you all share, where you can share the warmth of love and the safety of friendship. Allow your hearts and minds to open here. Feel the freedom to go beyond your normal boundaries. Feel the spirit within. Allow it to speak through you. Let the warmth and love and safety fill you with excitement and peace. These are not opposite terms, but can exist simultaneously. I am here with you.

Now a meditation. Lie back and allow yourself to focus on a spot in front of you. Watch this spot for a few moments, letting it expand until your entire awareness is focused there. Do not allow the noises around to distract you but incorporate them in your spot, allowing it to become filled with the entire universe. See that spot as a hologram containing everything that exists. Now as you become more and more focused, allow your mind's eye to drift inward, taking with it the accumulation of the All There Is from your focused spot. Allow this inward drifting to bring you into a feeling of fullness and peace such that you have not experienced before. Allow yourself to fill with the knowledge of your oneness. See this if you can. Feel your connection to all. See how your breath brings it to you. Now allow your mind to drift further inward and ask for a New Year's message to come to you. You can ask a specific question or you can ask a general question. Wait for the answer. It may come in words, symbols, colors, sounds. Allow it to come to you in its own form. When you are satisfied with your answer, return to this room.

A meditation
A hologram containing All There Is

My dear, I am here to write with you. What is it that you want to hear this fine morning? You would like a message of love and peace, I can see. It is nice to see you feeling so well. That is a good piece of work that you have been doing. I am glad to see things loosening for you and will continue to help as you ask.

January 29, 1989

Here is a message for you and all your friends who read these words. The new day breaks with a song, awakening as the sun rises out of its nighttime nest, and you again experience the sensation of light and warmth. This cycle is symbolic of life and death. While the sun is hidden from you, you would think that it has disappeared from the earth. If you did not know better, you would mourn its loss. You would think that you would never again feel its warmth or its light. But of course, you do

A message
Blending the spiritual in everyday living

233

know better so you do not mourn as it rests in the evening sky. You know that it will again return in the morning. Why then do you not see that life and death are the same? There is no reason to mourn, for all will be reborn again as the sun. It is only that you cannot see the actual process as you do the rising sun. This is because your perspective can include that of a revolving sun but is not large enough to see the rebirth cycle of souls. This you must take on faith. There is no other way.

This is a day of creation for you. I have talked of this often to you. It is important for you to be in touch with the spiritual in your life as it relates to the passing days. You can live your life purely from the ego level, never taking note of anything else. You can also try to incorporate the spiritual in your everyday living. This is very easy if you just take note. It does not compel you to live your life in a totally different way. There are innumerable ways each day that will allow you to act out the spiritual truths you wish to live by. Let yourself take time to ponder this. Take time in the evening to evaluate your day and allow yourself to congratulate yourself on what you did. I do not want to encourage you to feel guilty or feel you have not mastered something that you should. Just be aware. Set your goals for yourself. Play games with yourself. All need not be solemn, you know. The ways of the All are not to be sad and solemn and heavy, but light and playful and loving. To be loving is to be light, both in body and spirit. Let yourself erupt with healing love. You will be the better for it. That is all for now.

February 22, 1989
A message
The light of love

Hello, my dear. Here we are to write to you again. How nice to see you today. It is a very beautiful day in the heavens, but where you are, many people have their heads stuck in gloom and negativity. And that is very sad when there are much better ways to be. But I will give you a message for your group now, as that is a very important group; and I am pleased that you are continuing to meet. It is very instrumental in the growth and happiness of all of you.

Hello to you, my dear friends. Here we are gathered together for another evening of fun and relaxation with the ones you have come to know so well over this past year. You are all expanding and growing so that you take up more space than you used to. Isn't that fun? I want to welcome you with the love which shines from the brightest light imaginable. I want you to feel the spaciousness and warmth of that light. So let yourself close your eyes and imagine and feel the warmth that comes to you. Open yourself. Let it steal through you and ignite you. Let it comfort you if you are troubled. Let it bring joy to you if you are deadened. Let it soothe you if you are distressed. This light of love shines on you perpetually. You only need to invite it in. Now let yourself feel this for a few moments and then, as you open your eyes, spread this light from within around the room, showering and sharing it. Let yourself expand further. Let your light and love show in your eyes, in your smile and in your stance. This love is the most valuable thing that exists. Enjoy it here tonight.

Here is a meditation for your group. As you slowly make the ascent into spring, thoughts of regrowth and renewal of life come to mind. This is a season to celebrate the miracle of spring and all that is stands for. We will have a meditation that glorifies this time of the year.

A meditation **Glorifying the time of spring & renewal**

Lie back now and relax. Let your body sink into its space, becoming heavier and heavier as your muscles relax. Listen to your breathing. Hear it as the wind. Now listen to the wind of your breath. See it as it sings through the trees, caressing the earth as it sleeps. See the barren trees ready to swell with new life. Feel how your breath flows over them. Bring in the warmth necessary for the buds to open. Feel the wind as it crosses the plains and the prairies and the mountains and the forests, wakening life all along as it goes. See the buds open. See the flowers bud and open, the delicate spring wild flowers and the larger ones. See the birds begin to respond to the the wind, flying on its back to their spring nesting places. See the ground turn green and yellow and blue as new life peeks out. See the frogs emerge from their watery homes. See the small animals come out to see what the sun has brought. See the insects emerge from hibernation. See how they too ride the back of your breath as it brings alive the springtime world. Feel your part in this miracle of creation. Feel how you are a part of the creative mass. Feel yourself quicken. Feel your body come alive. Feel your blood flow faster and your heart beat stronger. Feel the rejuvenation of your body, mind and spirit as the winds of spring bring new life. Feel a renewal of your emotions. Let the heaviness of winter loosen and lift. Feel the joy of renewed life. Feel the promise in this of your own continued life, world without end. Now bask a moment or two more in the wonder of spring and then return to this room.

A message
Letting others
find their way

Here's another message for you. You have been troubled by the phone call of your son and are having a time of guilt because you did not do as he wanted. This is something to look at—for you and for many others. There is a feeling of guilt which often accompanies the word "No." Many books have been written to try to help those of you who have this problem. Whole courses of studies have been devoted to *assertiveness* as it is called. But let me talk to you of it in another way, and that is to see this as an opportunity for growth.

You have been confronted with a discrepancy between another's needs and your own. This much is clear, as soon as you stop to think about it. And then you wonder why it is so difficult to see that your own needs have an equal importance as the other's. Is it because you are a mother? Or a woman? Or that you were taught by the church that it is much Godlier to give than receive?

You find that there is little basis for having your own way. That you must be selfish if you do not share all that you have with others. You even want to go back to a time of poverty so that you do not have to have this dilemma. This is a time to let yourself search deep inside and see what message and beliefs are being activated. You know that they are there, for you would not have reacted so strongly if they were not. Find them. Search out their meanings for you in your life. When you are free of the restriction of the old beliefs, then you will be able to choose more easily what it is you want to do. And you will not be distressed by the requests of others. You will be clear as to whether you want to fill them or not.

You do not exist for others, but you can give to others if you want. You have a giving heart, but that does not mean that you have to give anything at all if it does not please you to do so. You see, you are all being freed from the constraints of authority, and that sometimes leaves you in a state of limbo where you do not know which leg to stand on. Ponder on this. Let yourself bring up the beliefs that cause you distress. Let yourself examine them and their roots. Make choices about what you want to keep. You are in a time of your life that is preparatory and you feel inside that there are certain things you need to do.

236

Follow your intuition. This will serve you well. Let others find their way. You do not have to pave the ground for them. That is all.

You can write for I am here to speak with you. This is fine for today. You want to know what message or lesson I have for you today. You think perhaps I am running out of ideas. Do not fear, my dear one. There is plenty to write about.

February 24, 1989
On beliefs & choices

I will tell you some information that will be surprising and interesting to you. It is that there is going to be a rather momentous happening within the next few weeks which will have impact on the lives of all of you. It will come in the form of a reversal and will bring happiness to many. Now that is all of that.

I will write to you now of your continuing struggle to make sense of the path of your life. I know that you are still looking and seeing how you run your life and are in conflict as you uncover the various belief systems that operate within you. This is the way to liberation as you struggle to see how old and new fit together or in opposition to each other. Your life is run by beliefs. Many people are so restricted by a single set of unchanging beliefs that they cannot incorporate anything new in their systems. On the other hand, there are those who adopt every new belief that comes along and add it to their already full storehouse. This is not freedom, but merely servitude to another system. You sometimes find yourself caught because these systems are at war within you. How to get free from this, you ask. Is it possible or will we always have to act out of one belief or another?

Of course, you do. The key, though, is to become aware of how your beliefs are controlling you. See if you can uncover them a bit. See where they came from. See who proposed them. See whose authority they represent. Then, you are much more likely to act in accord with that which you choose than that which you are driven to blindly. There is, of course, no way to know exactly if you are choosing freely or being driven, but each time you attempt to look beyond the immediate reaction, then you develop the ability to be more creative in your life.

Many beliefs lead people to act in ways that are not life affirming, though they may not know that. Even those beliefs that you share as women and feminists often are not life affirming but are destructive. This you must be willing to look at. I cannot emphasize enough how important it is for you to know yourself and to know which principles you wish to live by. These are for you to choose. They are not for some other to choose for you. I realize that there are many forces which cause you to conform, but even here, you can know what beliefs lead you to conform. I am asking for you to become enlightened. You will find that this will make your life easier as you free yourself from the bonds that hold you tight.

On intuition & meditation

You want a meditation for your group tomorrow and I will see what I can do. Now let me talk a little about intuition before I start.

It is a word I use often with you and often suggest that you pay attention to it. You see *intuition* is a word which describes *being in contact with the larger mind*. I do not know if that word adequately describes what I am talking about, but it is a word you understand. *Intuition* comes from a place of knowing and is separated from the demands of the ego. That is why it is often so much more in tune with your real needs than that dictated by wants and needs and old stuff. Intuition is not merely an outcome of brain activity. You cannot *think* intuition. You only can *sense* it.

That is why it is important to learn to meditate so that you can slow down the chatter of your thought processes and also detach from your feeling processes. Most of you there are not very in touch with your intuition workings, though it happens many times per day. You often are not aware that you followed your intuition and merely thought you had a good idea. It would be well to try for a few days or a week to be aware of what you are sensing, and then to go ahead and follow it. Even if you don't follow it, the practice of being aware will help you.

A meditation
To the Land of Intuition

Here is a meditation for you.

Lie back and let the peace descend upon you, covering you, sheltering you, warming you. Feel this as a soft, cuddly blanket or a layer of warm air or whatever comes to you which comforts, relaxes and calms you. Let each muscle go as the warmth penetrates to your very bones. Feel all the tension loosen as you go deeper and deeper. You are going to go even deeper now as I count from one to twenty. Just let go. (Count now) As you deepen and deepen, you are going into the land of your intuition. Let yourself enter here. Here there is no thought, no valuing, no holding back, no needs and wants. There is only wisdom. Look around. See what you can sense. Do not think or feel, but open all your senses to that which is. See what comes to you. Allow yourself to be aware of any flashes that come. See how intuition stalks quickly on little cat's feet. It comes to you whole and unadorned. See how you must trust it, for it easily flees when it is brought in competition with the drives and words of the ego. Allow yourself now to experience whatever comes to you in the next five minutes. I will awaken you slowly at that time.

Go ahead. That's good. I am here to speak with you again. Today is a day of lessons and challenges. You are sorely tried by what you see as roadblocks and hindrances to a smooth flow. But again you are only seeing through your ego's eyes that wants everything to go the way it wants. This is understandable because the ego is so much more likely to be heard than the voice of your spirit. That is why most of you live by its demands. The ego says, "Make it all go smooth. Don't bother me with problems. Don't give me trouble." The ego would like to live a life of pleasure, free from pain. This is, of course, possible when you can live on a transcendent level, but that is not what the ego wants. It does not want to expand its vision. It does not want to look broadly. It does not want to take others' needs into account. It just wants its way. You see how this is?

March 4, 1989
Behind all chaos is order

You want to know how to live easily without getting caught by what the ego dictates. Well, the first thing is to recognize that you are feeling distressed because you are being driven at the moment by what the ego is dictating. You see, ego thinks that what is happening is so very important that, if things cannot be worked out to its satisfaction, the world will come to an end. Hear its demands as they are. See how ego magnifies the importance of everything. See how it is difficult to look beyond. But know that this is not all there is. Relax a little. The matter is not life or death. The matter is not really all that important in the whole scheme of creation. The matter is a tiny blip on the lifeline of your life. This is not something to get excited about. You certainly can learn from the situation, but the biggest lesson to learn is that it is important to relax into that which is brought to you. There is a far larger picture. Let yourself know this. Listen to your higher self. Listen to that which tells you that all will be well. Perhaps not as well as the ego wants, but in the scheme of highest creation, behind all chaos is order. Now would be a good time to meditate on this matter. Let it all be.

Living from your higher self

Let yourself relax into an expansion of your view. Ask what your ego wants. See what you can give it, but do not let this be the only way you approach life. There are other ways. This does not mean that you cannot act. It does not mean passive acquiescence to the needs of others. This does not mean giving up. No. To live from your higher self does not imply any of this. There is an easy acceptance of what comes when you live from your higher self. There is a giving over of control to the wisdom of the universe. The universe is not against you. It is not playing mean tricks on you. No. The happenings of life are not always what your ego demands. Think how this would be if it were to be true.

The ego wants to know how dare the universe stand in the way of what it wants? It wants to be assured that the universe loves it by making all go smooth for it. You see. But that is not how it works. The universe is not there to kowtow to the needs of the ego. There certainly are times when the ego feels that all is well in the universe and that its needs are being looked after by a higher power. But this is not always the case. You see, there is a larger dimension to this all.

A message
On possibilities & living by instinct

I want you to meditate on this and see if you expand your view a bit. Take heart. Take strength. Hold fast to your abilities to have impact, but do not fret that you are not getting your way, that you are not having some angel here make it all go smoothly. And do not blame the universe for what is happening. There is no such easy answer. You are not being given a test that you have to answer. So relax a little, trust a little and know that you have much power in your life. Just tap into it.

Let me give you a little message that might comfort you. The time of spring is approaching, though as you look out your window it appears to be far behind. But let your heart open to the possibility, the possibility of new and renewed life. This is the message of spring. Feel within your self the ageless instincts that foretold of the ending of winter and the beginning of the spring tides. Feel how within your deepest psyche is a knowing, a quickening that comes at this time of the year. Pay attention. You need not only look to the outside, but look inward to the sensations that come. You know that the animals and the birds begin to respond to the longer days, the lengthening of the sun, the changes that are arriving daily. This is also true of yourself, though mostly you are unaware of the sensations as they stir. When you meditate, try to capture a sense of the coming springtime. See if your body is feeling different; imagine the changes that are taking place. Allow yourself to identify with all creatures and imagine what you were to do if you could live by your instinct. Let yourself reawaken. Let your spirit rise. You will find yourself lighter with each passing day.

You are doing fine tonight, my dear. It is very good to come to talk with you. There is much that I want to share with you tonight. It is time that I go beyond that which I have told you and share more of what is the mystery. You see, there is very much which you are unaware of, and this is a time when you all need to know more, or there will be such destruction that many of you will not survive. The time is now for the larger awakening to the plan of creation so that this human colony is not lost. The larger plans of God, as you describe it, are vast, far vaster than you all imagine. You as humankind are a very small blip in the whole of life. The time which you have been there on earth is miniscule in the whole of creation. This does not mean that you are insignificant, for nothing in creation is insignificant, only that the universe does not revolve around you.

It was once thought by your scientists that all the stars revolved around earth, that the earth was the center of the universe. This was shown to be false but the ideas of humankind still believed that they were the center of God's mind. They thought if the planets did not revolve around the earth, they were dead and insignificant, perhaps throwaways. It is still believed that humanity is the superior in all of life. This is an illusion that must be given up if you want to survive. You are not paramount in creation. You are a vital link, a magnificent part, but you are not the hub of the wheel. You must begin to see yourself as equal in stature to the rest of life. You must see that you have the will to do for good or evil. You can destroy or you can create. You can build or you can destruct. The time is now for looking at your practices. You still have time.

March 7, 1989
On the mystery

241

I am here. It is a wonderful day in the creation of the All. You there may experience it as cold or wet or gloomy or sunny but you are only experiencing a very little of All There Is. You are limited not only by your senses but by the attitude you approach life with. You think it is so much more important to achieve and acquire than it is to experience. So many of you do all you can to escape from life, as you call it, by using drugs, alcohol and other means of dulling your senses. You see, you do not know what it means to experience LIFE. You fill your days with mundaneness, trying to get through from one end to another. You find television as a means to relax when, in truth, it fills your mind with trivia. This is not experiencing life. This is dulling your senses. The primitive people would astound you if you were to match senses with them. They can see, hear and otherwise sense things that you would not even begin to know. You see, you there have developed your technology as a substitute for direct participation. You have, little by little, drawn yourself in, such that you are unaware of much of what you could know if you operated by your senses. I do not say this to make you feel bad, or even to try to sharpen your senses, for you are part of your culture. But only be aware that life could be very different if you could but see it. You have often been told that only what can be visioned can be created.

Now is a time to vision new dreams of what it means to be alive. You are disparaging of the native and primitive people, but look to them to see what you, as beings, have lost in your ability to lead a full life. It is one thing to use your minds to develop your civilizations and technology, but the time is drawing near where you will all see the dead end of these pursuits. Now is the time to open yourselves to all you can be, to all you can create, to all you can truly achieve as far as the development of the human being. You are only shells of what you can be. You all can be much greater than you are now. Dream this dream. Create this. Act on this.

You wonder what each of you can do to make this dream happen. First of all, there will be some who will tell this dream in ways that many can understand. This dream will come to many in many different ways. There are others who will spread this dream, whose purpose will be to let the others know the story. Then all will have a part in creation. You can start now.

242

Think on this. How in your life can you bring a greater sense of what it means to be fully human? Dream on this. What can you do in the midst of the life you now lead? The change will come slowly at first and then faster and faster as the dream spreads. This is not foreordained, you know. It must happen by your efforts. Ask where you fit. Expand your ideas of what part you want to play. Think on this. That is all.

Now you can write. I am here. We are getting quite good on your computer, don't you think? How nice to talk to you today. I am so glad that you are again embarked on the journey with me. Things have been turning for so many of you that it seems you all must be getting dizzy, but that is OK. Better dizzy than rigid.

March 12, 1989

You are meeting with your group this morning and I plan to be there even if you do not need my meditations today. That is OK. But I would like to give a short message to all my dear friends.

Welcome to the home of your heart. I am so cheered by the love that passes between you. You cannot see how far this reaches into the atmosphere nor how far-reaching its effects are, but let me assure you that that is so. You there are blind to the way that sounds, thoughts, emotions and other vibrations are conveyed on the airways. You were right in thinking that the way that sound travels was not devised by the All There Is for the purpose of radio and television. This, of course, has natural correlates. The airways are used in all kinds of manner by the inhabitants of your world. You think that you do not not have immediate access to them and must use radio or television, but this is not so. You are just unaware because your senses are not developed to use them. But whenever you think that you have had an ESP experience, you can be sure that you have been using these pathways directly. But they are more used than that. You are just unaware, just as much happens within your body that you have no direct experience of. That does not mean nothing is happening. You see how this is?

A message
**Using the airways
to communicate**

Now, I want to talk to you about something else. And that is whether I can talk about certain people's auras or whether I can help you to communicate with people who have died. Well, my friend, I could do that. For instance, you would like to sit down with a friend and be able to tell her what color her aura was that day. What is your purpose in doing that? Will that forward our work? Then we shall do it. Think on this a bit.

As to whether I can help you talk to people you know who have died, I will not do this now, for I do not think this would benefit you nor our work. If there is some one person that you would like to know about, that I will help you with. I know you have been thinking of your mother and wonder how she is, and you want her to know that you love her and wish that you could have really known her better. I will tell you that she knows this. Your mother is doing fine. She was incarnate for awhile but is back with us. She has been learning much and has been helping you to learn the lessons which she did not comprehend while on earth. You can take strength from her and can ask for her help when times are difficult. That is all of that now.

<table>
<tr>
<td>A message
On peace,
strength &
perfection</td>
<td>Here is a message of peace and strength. You have been talking about acting in some way that will benefit your planet. This is good, as it needs all the help it can get. It is important that you focus on what can be done rather than all that is wrong. This only compounds the problems when you talk about the ills of the world too much. I have told you that negative thought forms have a great deal of influence on the surrounding scene. So talk today about how you can forward the upcoming changes. How can you have influence in the world? You are all gaining strength and wisdom. You can share this in many ways. You may all agree to set aside the same time every day to say a silent meditation or prayer. You can ask others to join with you. You can do things that appear to be more concrete for your world. You can get creative. You can do big acts or small. It is important to form the intent. The rest will follow.</td>
</tr>
<tr>
<td>A blessing</td>
<td>I will send you a blessing. Peace be upon you, my dear friend. Let the winds that come blow away the cobwebs of your mind. Allow the fog that swirls before your eyes to clear so that you can see the light that is continually shining. Let this enter your pores and fill you with the most bountiful peace and joy. Allow yourself to receive this. Let its radiance penetrate all the organs of your body, bringing healing and relaxation. Let the radiance come out of you in forms that let it spill on to others. Allow the peace that comes from the knowledge that you are loved penetrate every corner and crevice of your being. You are loved just as you are. You do not need to seek to be other than you are for the love and light to come to you. This does not mean that</td>
</tr>
</table>

you cannot engage in the greatest pleasure there is, that of personal and spiritual growth. We will cheer you on in that endeavor, but it will not change one iota the love that comes to you. Bask in this. Free yourself from the bounds of seeking love in other ways. Know that in the eyes of the All There Is, you are perfect.

Today is a day that is very difficult for you, and you wonder if you are sick. I can assure you that your body is working fine, but your energy field is another matter. You are suffering some extreme blockages in the area of your spleen. It would be well to work on that or you well may find yourself sick. It is good for you to take hot baths for that too will help to cleanse some of the blockages.

I will write something for tonight for your group. Welcome, all my dear friends. I am glad to see you all tonight and also miss those of you who are off gallivanting around the globe. What fun. I can assure you that all are safe.

Here is a blessing for you all. Let the light of the moon and the sun and the stars assure you that a greater brilliance exists than you can fathom. You see the light reflected from these great organisms and think that the light is magnificent indeed. But let yourself now imagine that the light that fuels this all is lighter by far and carries with it an energy that surpasses any that you have known. This is the light of the All There Is. Let yourself now know that you are in it, a part of it, fueled by it. That life itself comes from it. Know that you are part of the magnificent whole that encompasses everything that is. You do not exist as mere mortals running around on a small planet, running until you drop over, never to be heard from again. No, my dear ones, let your minds and hearts soar into transcendence and know that as energy you are indestructible. Take this into yourself. Let yourself inform your days with it. Let it influence your acts both toward others and toward yourself. Let it nourish you, giving you strength. Let it heal you, giving you release from pain. That is all for now.

A blessing

And now a meditation. Lie back and let your mind scan your body going from limb to limb, from muscle to muscle, from gland to gland. Be in touch with the pulsing of your body as it meets your breath. Feel that breath as it balances your body so that it flows on an even keel. Let yourself be in touch with any

A meditation
Let your body take a journey

245

tension you are holding and let that go. Let yourself be aware of any stress you are under and let that go. Just relax, giving yourself over to the workings of your body. Feel centered in it. And now let your body take a journey. You can go along, but let your feet lead you. See where they want to take you. See what your body has ordered for its nourishment. Look around. Let your eyes feast on what they want. Listen. Let your ears direct you toward the sounds they wish to hear. Feel your muscles. See what they have ordered for their challenge. Taste. Feel. Sense. Let your body guide you on an adventure for the next five minutes. I will call you back then.

April 9, 1989
A world where
pain is rampant

Yes, I am here. We can write again. It is very good to talk with you again, as I have missed our daily encounters. But that is fine. I want to assure you again that there is no "should" attached to our writings, but you will find that you, too, will miss our meetings if you do not take the time out of your day to commune with me. I find that you are using much of what we talk of in your daily life, and that is very good; but do not let yourself become complacent and think that you have learned all you need to know. There is a certain fear in you that you will have to change too much if you continue to write with me too often. That may be true, my dear. Do not let your fear of change rule your life.

Child abuse

You were reading about the surge of child abuse in your city and wonder how that fits into the spiritual turnings which we have talked about. It seems to you that there are two movements afoot: one that is life-affirming and one that is not. No, it is not like that. The powers that you think you see are not operating like two polarities. Do not mix up what is happening in your city with the plans of the All There Is.

You see, there are many ways that people can choose to act and believe, and the outcomes of their actions are apparent in the results. If you were to say that there is a power of good that is influencing the spiritual growth of one section of your community and another force of non-good that is influencing the other section of your society, then you would think that the people who were becoming spiritual were visited and loved by God, while those who were living a life of drug addiction and who were abusing their children were not loved by God, but by some other negative force and thence would be looked upon as evil. You must not think this way. Those who are addicted to drugs and who are abusing their children are just as loved by God as the others who live a life of piety. This you find hard to understand. You think that perhaps God should visit his/her wrath on these unfortunate creatures. No, my dear, it is not like that. You all have free will and there is the means of growth open to all of you.

But you say, "What of the children? Is it necessary that they should suffer?" No. It is not. But the way to alleviate the suffering is in your hands—not yours as an individual, but yours collectively. You have all co-created a world where pain is rampant. Many seek surcease from this pain. This does not excuse their behavior. But you must all look at what you are doing there to see that the seeds of all that exists were sown many years ago. There is much room for improvement, believe me. You are all so far away from living a life that is in tune with the way of spirit that you can hardly imagine what that is.

Look at these parents, not as evil, but as victims of humanity's creation. But you say, "Everyone is not like that. There are many who are coping with this world and do not seek to wipe it out of their consciousness." Yes. That is true, though there are far more who do try to wipe out awareness by some means or other. But your society does accept that there should be many who are poor and hungry. Perhaps these people are spirits who have chosen this kind of life to act as catalysts for the changes that must come if you are to survive. You wonder why anyone would choose such a life, and I tell you there are many reasons. But look at these abused children as an opportunity for you all to increase your awareness. The world is indeed locked into a battle, but this is not between the forces of good and evil. It is between those who would choose the light and those who would not. Do not let yourself now think that those who choose the light are those who look prosperous by your standards. Those who are choosing the light may come from any station of life. What can you do about the abuse of children? Support all those who would benefit them. Send your positive energy out into the world daily so that the forces of light can magnify.

Let me talk to you of your idea of asking me to talk with you during your group meeting next week. This is something which we have not tried, but is, of course, possible to do. You will have to be very trusting of me and will have to be sure to allow yourself to be free of fear and be positive or there will be too much interference. Your idea of trying it with your friends tomorrow is a good one. I will be sure to be available. This will give us a chance to be more available to those who come to visit with you. I also encourage you in your steps to form a new group. You are right in thinking that I have been working behind the scenes for you.

Connecting with the creatures of nature & the holiness of life

Now, my dear, loved friend, let me give you a blessing and a message for today. The signs of spring are slow in coming in the external world, but they are there in your heart if you but let yourself feel them. The message of continued and ever renewing life is given to you by me, by many others and by the tides of spring. Listen to the birds as they signal the coming. Look at the trees as their barrenness is replaced by greenery. Look at the flowers as their blooms proclaim the message of life and love and color. They all know secrets which escape you. Let them tell you. That is their purpose. There are many things that you as human are blind to, but if you allow those creatures of nature to talk to you, they will unlock secrets which are hidden to you. Let yourself feel as one with the bird. Feel your similarity to the tree. Feel how your senses respond to the flower and the weed. They all share life with you. They all are part of the whole which you are a part of. Your connections with them are there. Sense them. Let yourself acknowledge the importance of all of life. When that happens, when you as humans acknowledge that life is the most important thing, then you will find that your actions are very different. This does not mean the continuance of life as you now look at it, where you try to maintain life in the face of certain death. No, I do not mean that. What I talk of is the creative force, the energy, the holiness of LIFE. This includes what you think of as death. Allow your spirit to inform you. It will not be difficult.

A blessing
Do not fear for I am here

I send you blessings from all of us here. I will send light and love to you whenever you request it. I will inform your steps as you tread your path. I will allow you all the freedom to choose that path that you require and will be with you there wherever your steps shall lead you. I will love and care for you each day of your life. Do not fear for I am here, in the name of the All There Is.

On God

You want to know more about God and how I represent God. Well, that is a tall order, but I will see what I can do. First of all, be sure you are not thinking of God as a boss in the sky that gives us all assignments. Do not think of this as a bureaucracy. God is not a person. God is an energy. That is the best I can do for you. We are all part of that energy, of that force, of that plan. I act in the name of the force, and so do you. I am of that force, and so are you, and so are those who abuse their children, and so are the children, and so are all the spirits who are here and all the human beings who are there. You find this a very unsatisfying story. You want to believe in the Great Father in the Sky Who Watches Over You. Well, let that be true for you if you want. I cannot explain God to you. *God* is *your* term, you know. It represents an unknown quality which you as humans have devised for that which you cannot comprehend. Your vision is limited by your beliefs and your beliefs are limited by your vision. You cannot comprehend the mystery so have devised the stories of what God is like. This is fine. It is the only way it can be, but there is no way that I can explain to you something that is way beyond your understanding. Stay with your images, but continue to expand them. Know that the answers are not out there in some man on a throne, but the answers can be found through your own connections. Do not struggle so with trying to fit everything in to a context which is consistent with what you know. Let the mystery serve to expand your view. Allow the paradoxes to exist. Let them help you to see that your answers are only temporary. Feel your power. Do not look to a God person for the power to control things. This is all for now.

Yes, I am here. I am very glad to write to you again. It is a very nice day in the universe and joy abounds. If you are not feeling it, then you have let your ego construct blocks in the way. Let yourself go as deep in as you can. See if you can bypass the everyday demands and pains and see if you can feel the joy which comes from attunement with the All There Is. This is your right. This is the way you were meant to function. You are so often a victim of narrow vision where you believe that the seen is so much more important than the unseen. You have many senses which you are not using. These would help you to be more in tune. It is important to meditate and let these senses develop. So, if you are not feeling joy at this moment, do not get on yourself for being lacking, but open your vision. See if that which you are distressed about is real or a figment of your imagination. See if you can expand your view so that the larger perspective allows you to see alternatives. Misery rarely helps, you know.

April 13, 1989
**Charity &
helping others**

You have been wondering about responsibility for another, especially as it relates to money. Your dilemma with your son has sparked this as have other events in your world. You wonder if one should help another in need, wondering if to allow another to depend on you is a blessing or not. What does it mean to be caring of another? This I will try to clarify for you.

First let me say that *responsibility* is a term to be used for oneself and oneself alone. You cannot be responsible for another. Even the Universal All does not take responsibility for you. You have free will and thus have the "response ability" to live your life as you see fit. Now that does not satisfy you because you have heard that you are looked after by the higher guides and can ask for help. You wonder what that means as far as your earthly relationships. Now here, too, is a distinction. Just because you ask, does not mean that all will be given to you. Then you would be carried from the cradle to the grave. That is not the case. Life is not made so easy for you that no pain or suffering will be felt. So look at it this way. It, too, is not your responsibility to affect others' lives so that they are without struggle or pain or anything else that you would like to save them from. You cannot steal another's path so easily. But what if they want to depend on you because they do not know what to do for themselves at the moment. You must distinguish what it is that you want to do. You must not respond out of the belief that you should save them or cure them or anything else like that.

You think that if we didn't have that belief, we would all be alone and not cared for. You sometimes think that the belief which says, "I am my brother's keeper," would, if it were carried out by all, make the world a much easier place to live. Ah, my dear, what does that *mean*? What is the meaning of *keep*? It is a term which is used in your jails, is it not? You see, you cannot *keep* others without taking away some of their freedom.

You want to know what to do in the case of your son. Should you or should you not give him money? Well, there are options, and what you do will have to take into account the various consequences of each option. But I sense in you a belief that you should give to him or he will fail. You are taking the weight of his success or failure from his shoulders to your own. This will not do. You only take from him when you do this, no matter what he would like. This does not mean that you cannot give to him. But, you ask, what belief should we hold that would help us to decide, if it is not one of charity?

Let us look at charity as a concept. This has been handed down as one of the virtues, and I think is a major stumbling block here, for you feel guilty for not being more charitable. Yes, my dear, charity is a virtue when properly understood. Your world indeed would be an easier one if charity were a universal belief. But too often, it is not charity that is afoot—but guilt. Charity involves giving freely from the heart, without strings and without being asked. It comes from the recognition that charity is needed at the moment. It bears no resemblance to taking care of, to guilt, to manipulation. It often does not involve money. It involves the recognition of the oneness of all and so reflects that knowledge. This is a high-level virtue and is often misunderstood.

Let us talk a little more about where the guilt comes from and how you are driven too often by that. Beliefs about how one should treat another are quite universally held by human beings. When you go against these beliefs, you feel guilt. And following the feeling of guilt you are often compelled toward an action which alleviates the guilt. Or you suffer. So often the action you take is not in the best interests of the other person, or your own, but occurs simply to make the pangs of guilt go away. Sometimes the feeling of guilt then is replaced by feelings of virtue as though by atonement you have negated the "bad" feelings you once had.

Look at this closely. Have you really done a good thing? Is this really charity? In most cases I would say no to that. Get in touch with the underlying belief when you feel guilt. See if this is a belief that furthers growth. See if this belief is one that is truly in line with the universal laws of love. The answers are not always easy. There are not right or wrong answers to many questions. But do not let yourself be compelled by grief or guilt.

Let me talk of something else. There are universal laws that are used to answer your prayers and requests. These are more complex than I can describe to you. But let me say that prayers and requests are heard from a vantage where your soul's growth and purpose can be seen. This makes the decision much easier to make. If you try to expand your vision and try to allow

On your soul's growth & purpose

251

yourself to understand that individuals are on their own quest and that it is not up to you to interfere with that quest, this may help you. I don't think it will be so easy for you to do that. But you will see that persons march on their own path and sometimes they stumble and fall, and sometimes they cannot see the next step because of the density of the fog. Then you may be able to pick them up or hold their hand if you are able, but you cannot take their place nor carry them down your path. You see, you may think that carrying them is part of your path, and sometimes, I must admit, it is. But this is not the general case. Give your hand to those who would raise up a step. Give your guidance to those who would see. Give your presence to those who seek. Be of good mind. Be of good heart. Be of good cheer. But do not think that it is up to you to bring those qualities to another. I know all this is somewhat confusing, and you will need to think on it and ponder and talk about it. This will all help.

A blessing
You are of nature

Now blessing on you this day, my dear. Let your joy rise with the sun. Let your spirit soar with the birds. Let yourself bloom with the opening of the buds. You are of nature. Let yourself respond to the glories of spring and rebirth. Sing a song of joy with the birds. Stretch yourself to the sky with the trees. Skip with the clouds and run with the wind. Do not burden yourself but free yourself to respond. That is all for now.

April 14, 1989
A message
The goal of life is to provide a teaching ground for the soul

I am here, my dear. That is good that we are writing again as you have many questions for me. You want a message for your friend Mary, but you also want to know about some of the larger questions your conversations with her aroused in you. Now first a small message for Mary. My dear, you are making your life so hard, but that will all be changing in the near future. You are beginning to see in a different way and this will help you out of the dilemma you have found yourself in for so long. The time is not quite yet. You will know when because the questions will get easy to answer and you will not be in so much conflict. You would like to know how to arrive at this state. First, you must stop trying so hard to figure things out. This always brings you back to the same stopping place. Let go. Just let yourself flow with your feelings. This will help you.

Let me try to answer your larger questions about commitment and what that means in the life of those whose relationships have become painful to the extreme. There are those who hold

252

fast to the marriage commitment or other ways of committing that hold them fast in a relationship which no longer exists as beneficial. There are others who break their vows as easily as changing their breakfast cereal. You want to know what is right. Well, my dear, of course, there is no right way. But let me talk a little about the first case—where the people believe their vows have been made in the sight of God and are not to be broken without the wrath of God falling on them. This is not the case. The marriage rite is man-made. It reflects the natural pairing that is existent. You must learn to distinguish what is what. I know that the Bible lends itself to the lifelong commitment of the sexes, and this is an ideal. But look deeply and allow yourself to focus on the health of each member within that relationship. The goal of life is to provide a teaching ground for the soul. You must ask yourself if the ground of the relationship is fertile enough to provide that growth. If not, if it is depleted or toxic, then nought will be served by continuing its existence.

To those who leave at the first sign of difficulty, this too, should be looked at. Many times, it is because one or the other member does not want to face the challenge of growth offered. You see how this is? So both cases need to be studied. The answer is not black or white but has many hues.

On love & universal love

Let me talk a little about love and universal love. We talked of this earlier, but we have not discussed it in detail for a while. Universal love is an energy which is available to you all to use in your daily lives. This energy can be used in your relationships to other people, to animals, to plants, to all other living things, to your earth and to your solar system. This energy, if magnified by all, would change the whole course of your earth in a twinkling of a second. You have not yet devised the mechanisms to detect it so you go along oblivious of its power. This will come with enlightenment. But for each of you, if you learn to use the energy that is there in your relationships, you will find a new lease of life. Let yourself approach each other as though you were signals from God with messages for your growth. Do not look to the other as though she or he has answers for you—but merely questions to be answered within. Be careful when developing commitments that you do not base them on the fulfillment of your needs or you will find yourself sorry later. Base your commitment on a mutual sharing of commitments to each other's growth. This will give the relationship a foundation that cannot be found when it is based on need-fulfillment. What to do if you find yourself committed in such a relationship? Well, then of course, it is the time for reassessment, for discussion, for self-learning. The answer is as above.

April 15, 1989
On responsibility

Yes, I am here. Today is a day when you have made many connections and that is very good. I will help you to understand more if I can. You want to know more about responsibility. Let me be clear again that one can only be responsible for oneself. Do not get confused by some of your ordinary thinking that allows you or directs you to think about being responsible for another, for you cannot do this. Your thinking that you can is only illusion. You want to know on what to base your idea of *responsibility*. What indeed does this term mean? Does it mean *to carry the weight of something* as is often thought? Does it mean *lack of blame* as it is sometimes thought?

No, this is not the case either. To be responsible is *to act out of the knowingness of your soul in accord with universal laws of love*. This is all there is to it. But of course that does not really make it simple for you as the *doing* is very different from the *idea*. And you have much that stands in the way of understanding the meaning of my statement. How is it that one can act responsibly in the world? The ways are myriad. The challenges are many. The opportunities endless. So you see there is time to have much practice. You can practice all you want or need to. Each day brings new chances for growth in your ability. To live your life in a responsible manner is to live a life of much growth. This I can assure you. To be able to act in accord with the principles of love will bring you great joy, but it will also tax you to the maximum. This is not hard, but the way is unclear for many of you.

Be gentle with yourself and others

You have been reading about how your world exists on the concept of power—power over another. You all have been indoctrinated into this belief. So for any of you to act always in accord with the principles of love is to go beyond that which you have been taught and to connect with the greater knowing of your soul. This you can do, but you will need to be consciously aware at all times for the opportunity that presents itself. You must not be negative about your ability to know always how to act. Your task is to learn. Be gentle with yourself, for no good will come from being punishing to your earth self. If there are particular incidents where you seek greater guidance, help is available to you from your inner self, from your guides, from your intuition. Anytime you connect with the Greater All, you will find that the answers to your questions will come with greater clarity than if you merely use the powers of your conscious thought, for here there are so many conflicting teachings that the way becomes murky indeed.

So to recapitulate, responsibility follows from the understanding and knowledge of the universal laws of love. The carrying out of these laws, given your upbringing, is difficult at times for some and difficult to even comprehend for others. Start from where you are. Expand you awareness. Grapple with this issue. Practice. Try some ideas out. Feel if your actions are in tune with your soul. You will develop an awareness of how that feels. All this will help. But please remember, you are human beings who have, at this time, an ego as well as your higher level spiritual component, and so be gentle with yourself and others. Do not judge others for their responsibilities or lack thereof. That is not your responsibility.

Now, my dear, allow the greatest peace there is to enter you, to fill you, to nourish you. Allow yourself to expand with the energy of love which surrounds you. Feel your deep connections to everything. Know that you are not alone but exist in communion with the myriad forms of LIFE that exist, both seen and unseen. Allow joy to walk with you today, to skip and run with you. Let your heart open and be light and of good cheer. May you be touched and touch. Let the love that surrounds you fill all the moments of your day with radiance. That is all for now.

Yes, I am here, my dear. It is almost time for your group to meet again and you wonder if I will be there. Of course, I will, and you wonder if we will be able to talk and answer questions for those who ask. I think we will try. It may not be so easy if you cannot feel relaxed and centered. It will be important for you to meditate a bit before doing this. There will be some difficulty otherwise. But we will try. OK.

April 17, 1989
Allow my words to enter into your heart

You also want a meditation. I will try to give you one.

Lie back and let the waves of relaxation wash over you. Picture yourself in a warm, salt sea which carries you buoyantly as on gentle waves. Feel your weightlessness. Feel your calm. See how your body is suspended and held by this gentle, salty sea. Do not struggle but just allow yourself to relax more and more there in the warm sun. Now, as you feel yourself relaxed, allow your mind to go out into the space that surrounds you. Allow it to travel from you to make contact with your higher self. Ask for this to happen. Perhaps you will even make contact with a guide or two. Let your mind arise, free and uncluttered, to meet and talk to the figures that arrive before you. See how, as you are open and receptive, messages will come to you. Perhaps they will be in the form of visions, or words, or symbols, or pictures. Ask that your higher self, or your higher guide if you prefer, speak with you and give you messages that you would like to hear. It is important that you ask only for your highest self in order to stay protected. Now let yourself commune with this higher self and see what the messages are for you today. Now let yourself relax and I will bring you energy and healing. Allow my words to enter into your heart. Allow yourself to hear my words with your inner ear. Do not be afraid of this task. Do not turn away seeking rest, for the greatest rest will come from attunement with the All.

April 19, 1989
**On passing from
the life you know
to that which you
do not**

Yes, I am here. That is good. I am very happy to share my teachings with you and all your friends.

You have questions about what happens to you as you pass from the life you know to that which you do not. In other words what happens when you die? Well, you have read some accounts told by those who nearly died, and you have read others by those who have some connections with the unseen world. But I will tell you a little more, especially for those who have not read as much as you have.

First let me emphasize, again and again, that you do not go to some long away place in the sky. The transitions between what you are now and what you are in eternity are made on the same level as you now exist, but in a different vibratory pattern. So now you must imagine that at the time of your death, so to speak, there is a releasing of energy from the body you have inhabited. This is not painful but very comfortable to you. At that moment, you are no longer physically bound to the concrete world, but you are on the way to rejoining those you have not seen for some time.

There is a period of transition when your vibrations are changing from one place to another, and there is sometimes a period of confusion that happens then. If you can imagine what it is like for a baby to be born, going from the darkness and warmth of the womb to the bright, cold day of the new world, then you can imagine the abruptness of change. So you may not know immediately what has happened to you and may have a moment of confusion. This is why you will be met by others you have known who will lead you along the way until you have made the full adjustment. You have read of this.

You also have read of the light that one goes into. It is not quite like that, but that will do. The way into the unseen world may appear as a tunnel going into light, but there is some difference that I will not discuss in detail. Suffice it to say, the brilliance of the light is more comforting than you can imagine. The purpose of the light is to further tune your vibrations and to help you to make the assimilation into spirit. This does not take long for this to happen. Following that attunement, you will be further assisted by those who have known you to remember that which you have always known and to integrate that which you have learned in this life to that knowledge which you have already learned.

Though I may speak of this as happening in a rather short time, I want to emphasize that the concept of time will no longer exist, and so it is only to help you to understand that I will use that term. There is a period of review, of assimilation, of integration, of looking at the soul's purpose and how that was carried out. This is most often done with your teachers and highest guides who have been with you in life, helping you, watching you and guiding you. This process is one which can be very important to the souls who have just made the transition. Sometimes it is very painful as they look at their life. There are some who find they cannot look at their life and want to turn away and sleep. This is something they can do. You see, there is no punishment for how they lived their life, but the recognition that comes when the ego is no longer running the ship can be more painful than any punishment that could be devised.

Some souls need careful care and concern in order that they can come to accept what they did with their earth life. There are others who have made progress on their path and they too integrate this information into the knowledge which they had previously. But these souls are usually ready to go on much sooner than those who have to deal with the loss they have made. You wonder what comes next as it seems that to live through eternity would be a very arduous task. But you see, my dear, you are again looking at it as linear time stretching out in front of you. I cannot tell you what it is like to have a timeless place, as you do not have the conceptual power to understand me. But do not let yourself begin thinking that it must get boring living to eternity. This is not the case. There is always much to learn and do and then, of course, many souls are preparing for the next time of incarnation.

The decision to return to an earth life takes very much preparation and is usually not done lightly. There is much to be learned and planned for, so that if you want to think in time, this may take many of your years. I do not want to go on and on about what it will be like for you as I think it is more important for you to be concerned with the life you are now leading. This is your present task, although I know that it is comforting to know somewhat about what your transition will be like. Let me assure you that it will not be difficult. There is much support and love which will affect your crossing. Do not be afraid. You may feel temporary confusion, but as the babe is washed and comforted, so will you be. That is all of that for now.

A message

Now, my dear, a little message for you. You have been feeling a bit tired and wonder where the energy blockage is. Let me tell you that you are still harboring a great many negative messages. Your work has been a strain on you, but you are letting old messages play instead of new. Focus on the energy centers. Raise your energy each morning. Pay attention to the feeling of joy and life that exist within you. Your work is not enough to drain you, but your thoughts are. This too is an opportunity for you to learn something. There are some old blockages that can be worked on if you want. Listen to yourself. Release the thoughts and emotions that are there so you can look at them. That is all.

Let the peace of God come to you. Let your heart fill. Let your mind be still. Let your feeling rise to reach those which are being sent to you. There is love all around. Let your senses feel it. Do not rely only on those you customarily use but continue to develop those which have been hidden to you. I will look forward to writing with you again.

I am here with you this wonderful spring day. Let me enter into your spirit and connect heart to heart. I am here to bring you messages of hope and joy. Today is a wonderful day in your life. Be aware. Let me see if I can enlarge your experience of what being alive means. You see, you have constricted yourself so that many times *being alive* is merely *not quite dead yet.* I do not want to blame you for your state because you are truly a product of your culture, but you do not need to remain that. You are creative. Use this power to bring aliveness to your life. You have cultivated a state which minimizes discomfort and anxiety at the cost of losing spontaneity and joy. Let me see if I can help you to regain some of that. Focus your awareness inward. Allow your thoughts to still and concentrate on the workings of your body. Engage at this level and disengage from the everyday world you find yourself in. Delight at your blood cells. Imagine them forming by the billions. Imagine your cells. Be awed by their miniature factories. Be aware of your organs and how they routinely function to keep you going. Tune in to this and tune out on all the external pulls. See that reality is merely a point of view. Try this and see what happens.

May 3, 1989
A message
See that reality is merely a point of view

I am here. Profound thoughts enter your mind as though they had been ready-made. You wonder where these come from. Let me see if I can help you. Thoughts are an interesting phenomena, don't you think? You find them entering your mind as though they had a mind of their own. They rise as from out of the sea to enter your consciousness briefly, only to be replaced by another. This is very puzzling. What makes them come together in the precise pattern they do. The thoughts you have and express come to describe you. But what is understood of this process? Virtually nothing. You see, you are at the very beginning stages of looking at thought and what it is and what powers it has.

May 10, 1989
On thoughts

Thought is not simply a random firing of your brain cells. It is not a happenstance which occurs, though of course, your brain is part of the process. Thought rises from out there. Where is out there? It is not within. Thought forms are formed constantly and enter via your brain. Thought has form and not mass, but a constancy. The way thought is formed is beyond your understanding, but believe me, there is more than neural connections. That is why very simple animals and birds appear to be able to think with a minimum of neural capacity.

You do have conscious control, as well as unconscious control, over the thoughts which you select from the multitudinous number available. It is the choice of thought forms which comes about through the process of growth. You see, that is happening in your world. There is a shift in what people are allowing to reside in their consciousness, though many still allow negativity to live there. You see, you can live your life joyfully if you are careful of what thought forms are allowed to live within you. You all have receptors and acceptors. Be aware of how these function. Be aware of how these are programmed to work. This is something you can do.

Let me say a few words of comfort to you. I will send you songs of love and glee today. Open your heart to them. Open your heart to love. Do not hold on to hurts, but open yourself to thoughts which bring joy to your being. That is all for now.

May 8, 1989
On the essence of your lives

Yes, I am here. How nice to talk with you again. It has been some time in your world since you have talked with me, but let me assure you that it is but a trice here. You must not worry about whether you should or shouldn't write to me, but take care that you recognize that which it means for you. This will help you more than trying to cause yourself to write. I am here for you. You can contact me in many ways. This is only one of them but, of course it is more permanent.

You have been troubled today by the lives of your clients and again are wondering how come some people have tragic lives while others only seem to be lucky? You have been taking on the burden of those who appear to be unfortunate, and you would like to be God-like and help them to overcome their tragedy. This is commendable as long as you recognize that your ability to help another is restricted by the place where you reside, that is, on earth. You are not God nor have you been sent by God, in most instances, to help another. This is something you have chosen for this life; that is, to be of service to those in need. This has been a line through your life, I'm sure you know.

But what of these unfortunate people that you see daily in your work? Have they been singled out by a devious God who strikes them with pain and misery or is it another force which strikes them? You see, you are back asking the same questions over and over. You want your world to be pure and simple and pain free, and you want to make God responsible for that. I want you to know how important it is for you and others to begin to see the responsibility they carry for their lives. Not only are you responsible there for the choices you make, but also, you are responsible on the soul level for the life you have chosen to live. I know this is difficult for you and we return to it again and again. But believe me when I say that there is order behind the seeming chaos that you see around you.

But this does not absolve you all from beginning to learn about being responsible for the world you are collectively creating. You see, this is a long ride from the beginning to the end and you must not become bogged down in any one spot. If you could watch a movie of the passage and changes of the growth of humankind, you would begin to see patterns. Now you are hampered by the small vision that you are restricted by. But you want to know how to act in accordance with these ideas. How do you relate to those who are in pain? You can take the larger view while at the same time taking the smallest view. That is, you can understand that individuals have their own destiny while at the same time giving help as you can. Do not take on the burden but lend your support to those who pass with you. There are lessons to be learned from this all. But do not blame God for things which are rightly left at the doorstep of your culture. Do not blame God for things which are the province of an individual. There is much excuse for behavior there. Responsibility for the creation of a saner world is often left in the hands of the few. It is time for you all to grow up a little more. The time is right for that. You have been asleep for too long. Let your eyes light up in recognition of that which you have too long forgotten. Let the knowledge that abounds inform you. Let your intuition come through to you. That is all of that for now.

Now, my dear, let me guide you a little down a path of remembering. This is a time of year when all springs to life again, and it is a time when you can touch memories that are otherwise hidden. If you will let yourself meditate and ask for memories of your past lives to come to you, you may be rewarded. Now is a time of great change and that which has

Remembering past lives

been your birthright will aid you in going forth into the years ahead. There has been much learning in the many, many lives you have led, and there is much that will be helpful to you. Ask for the memories and allow them to come. You see most of you there are not tuned in to what you have brought with you and think that all you know now you have learned since childhood. This is not the case. The essence of who you are is constantly being changed as new information is integrated into the old. Your essence is that which is extracted from all the experiences which you have lived through. So you see how important the events of your life are?

You are constantly upgrading or downgrading that which is the very core of your soul. It is important to have soul growth as your goal. This is easy to do. It need not be hard, or dreary or anything like that. Your soul wants to live bountifully. Create a vision for yourself as to what it would be to live a life which is focused on the growth of your soul. Think what it is that you are adding to your essence. That is very important to do. You see all earth happenings, whether they be joyful or tragic, have the potential for soul growth. The choices are there for you as to how you will use each event. I know this is difficult to comprehend, but if you try, a glimmer of how this is will come to you.

A blessing

Now let me give you a blessing for today. The days have become longer for you and the sun shines upon you with increasing warmth. Let this symbol of the warmth and joy of the universe invest your days with gladness. Let yourself experience the energy that comes from the sun, and let yourself know that all this is not an accident. You are very precious to the whole universe. Do not think you are in any way insignificant. Let this knowledge lead to an examination of the way you live your life. Let yourself grow this day. I send you love and peace and will visit blessings on you wherever you are. That is all for tonight

May 12, 1989
Releasing tension

I am here, my dear. You are feeling a little under the weather and wonder what to do for that. Let me tell you that a bit of fresh air will help you a lot. You have been too sedentary and are finding that there is not proper circulation going through your body so that it feels sluggish and not quite alive. I recommend that you go for a brisk walk outdoors. Be sure to pay attention to the external world of nature and do not allow your thought to drift to your everyday concerns. You will find that a period of meditation before you go will increase the awareness you bring to your walk. You can also drink a cup of your herb teas, focusing on those which increase your blood flow. Your red clover will do well for that.

Let me also help you to let go of some tension which you are holding in your body. Let your muscles go limp throughout your body, even as you continue to type. The tension in the muscles of your body in regard to external and internal stresses can be very damaging to your energy flow. You find that when you hold your body tight to protect it in some way, there is a loss of available nutrients as they are all tied up in the process of marshalling your protective shield. Provide time for a period of meditation where you allow all the tension to flow from your body. Allow the thoughts which are underlying your tension to float to the surface and drift away. The process of meditation is very helpful for reliving stress buildup.

Now, my dear, it is time for you to play a little. Do not be so serious. Let yourself go out and skip. Remember how that felt when you were a child. Let your body go. Let it run and play with the springtime breezes. Do not worry what others might think. You can free yourself to be spontaneous.

Yes, I am here. We shall talk again this fine evening. I am so glad to hear from you. You are finding this a rather difficult day and you are bemused by the goings on at your place of work. You must not waste your energies over this as it does not concern you directly. More will be played out before all is finished, but you will find that your concerns will merely sap you and will not bring you any relief from your cares. Look inside and see if you can see what fears and old beliefs are being stirred. Be careful that you do not fall into the trap of being amused by what is going on or become excited by the differentness.

May 13, 1989
On past lives

Let me talk to you about some other concerns you have. You are wondering about what the use of knowing of one's past lives is and how you should use that information. Many are fascinated by this topic and go to those who are helpers to find out what has gone on in other times. There is some benefit but also some danger in doing this. It is part of the growing consciousness that people will seek to expand their view of their lives and will seek knowledge of how they have lived in other times.

There is benefit of this in two ways. One, there is a chance to tie together things that run as a thread throughout a number of lives. You can begin to see what your soul's purpose is and also how you have gone off the track, so to speak. The other benefit comes from opening the way for information that can be healing for your present life. Sometimes there is leftover pain or other factors that are affecting how this life is being led. The knowledge of past lives can put things in perspective so that you can begin to understand how lives upon lives are the way that souls develop.

But all is not benefit, depending on the development of the person. There are some who become so enmeshed in past lives that they think they are living this now. There becomes a preoccupation with this. The focus should be on understanding, not on reliving. You are in your present life, make no doubt about that. You may still carry some remnants of other lives and you may be now relating with some from another life. This is how it is meant to be. Do not think that you can undo that which went before. The goal of your play is to help you to understand from a different vantage point. Thus sometimes you, who were a child, are now a mother. You see, there is a changing of roles such that your soul can learn a new perspective on that which has gone before.

For those who would seek information about your past lives, make sure that you are in safe hands and then allow yourself to experience that which comes to you. Do not use your emotion to deal with this nor try too hard to figure things out, but rather allow the wisdom within to help you. I will give you a few words of caution with this. If you do not feel ready to experience your past, that is fine. Do not push yourself. Allow that to be.

Living a conscious life

Let me talk to you of something else. And that is how to lead your life each minute of the day in a way that furthers your growth. I know that many of you are asleep most of the day, running on automatic. You follow the routine. You live in your rut. You allow yourself to be dictated to by habitual thoughts. I do not judge you for this, as it is the way that most people live their lives within your culture. You are blinded by these ritualistic behaviors to all that which surrounds you, to the opportunities for true living, for true connection. I only want to help you to open up a mere glimmer of something else. Many people there consume drugs in order that they can have what approximates an "authentic experience." This is not the way. Your country is in the midst of a peril that threatens to overcome many positive forces now acting. No, drugs are not the way.

You must approach this consciously, for you cannot depend on habit. Habit will only lead through another day of strife and boredom or excitement caused by too much stress. No, you must consciously set your vision to live a conscious life. This you should begin in the morning when you awaken. Connect with your source. Ask for guidance throughout the day. Then open your eyes. Pretend that you have been asleep for two years and are just awakening. Think how new everything would be. Think how excited you would be to see everybody. Think how good your food would taste. Think how wonderful would be the colors about you, the signs of spring, the colors of nature. Think how your nose would quiver with the aroma and odors around you. Think how you could feel with all your senses. Think how you would react to the love you would feel. Think on all of this. And pretend that you have just awakened. Try this out. Let your thoughts be new and creative. Let your energies rise to meet the challenge of a brand new day in your life. That is all for now.

I will send you a message of love from all of us here. You will find that our love will permeate your dreams tonight, so be ready. Let yourself awaken in the morning knowing that love descends on all of you all the time. Let it in. Let yourself know that *that* love is your birthright. Do not settle for anything else. A blessing on you, my dear. I will speak with you soon again.

A blessing

Yes, I am here, my friend. You want something to help you tonight with your new group of friends. This is another undertaking for you, and you are not to be too embarrassed by your reluctance. I know this is sometimes difficult for you to see yourself in this role. But believe me when I say that you are cut out for this and should give yourself a chance to enjoy it. Do not be afraid that this is too much for you or that people will not like what you do. That is your ego talking. Connect with your

June 1, 1989
Your spiritual path

deeper selves and you will find that it is all fun. Now let me give a short message of welcome to them.

A message

My dear friends, I am so happy to see you all arrive with love in your hearts. You have come searching. This is very important for you to be aware of. You would not be here if there were not something that is missing for you. You are on a spiritual journey. This journey takes place from birth to death and back again. You see the way is sometimes difficult to see. The way is sometimes lost in the everydayness of your life. The way is sometimes lost in the demands of your ego. But the way is there. It happens throughout your life at various times that you are more drawn to the spiritual purpose of your life. This is one of those times. You will find that to live by earthly means alone will leave you feeling alone and troubled. There are many ways to follow your path. Coming here is merely one of the ways. You will find that this is a place where you can open your hearts to yourself and each other and evaluate where you are. It is a place where you can listen for inner wisdom, a place where you can find larger truths, a place where you can expand your view of what it means to be human and what it means to be spirit. Welcome my friends. Let your love flow.

Now my dear, let me talk of something else to you very briefly for I know you are anxious to be ready for those who come. Let my love flow to you, giving you energy, courage and perseverance. Open yourself to the wonders of the love of the universe. I am only a beacon. The love that abounds is there for you always. It can bathe you in radiance if you but let it. Open your heart now to the wisdom that surrounds you so that the words which you speak are rich with meaning. I will be with you and will encourage you throughout the evening. Do not worry. You will be fine.

June 7, 1989
Events in China

Yes, I am here, my dear. I know you are thinking of your friend and if it would be helpful for the three of us to meet to help her with the depression which has been affecting her. Yes, my dear, I think that we would make a good team. It will be interesting to try this and see how we work together. Your friend is having a difficult time, but yet she is afraid to confront that which is behind this depression. There is reluctance to accept that which is, and she is trying to outrun herself. We will talk more another time.

Now, I want to speak with you about the events in China, for I know that has been on your mind this week as it has been for many others. You wonder what this has to do with the spiritual uprising that we have been talking about. You also wonder how it is handled when many die at once. You are always so curious about this, as though we could only handle a few people dying at once. This is not true at all, for then we would always be overwhelmed. You see, you are thinking of it much as though we were a hospital being inundated with the sick and dying. That is far from the truth. Dying is a natural process and does not take enormous care from us here. There is plenty of help for what needs to be done. You see, you cannot imagine it and so try to put pictures of your world upon what you think might be happening. It is much better if you just accept the naturalness of death and know that all is taken care of without difficulty.

You wonder about these young Chinese people and wonder if their lives are being given according to their plans or according to a larger plan. You see this is the same question which you keep asking in a number of ways. All is planned but all is free will. It is not as though the individuals who are killed signed up for that task before they were born, but on the other hand, there is a direction to their life and one of the possibilities was that they should be killed in this way. Now you wonder about the soldiers and if they too were masters of their choice. In other words, you want to know if some of them are on the side of evil and are fighting the forces of good.

You see, I want to reiterate that the concept of good and evil is one of the earth. It arises out of human behavior. You want to know if there are those whose souls are black and who come to earth to represent the dark forces. No, it is not like that. But the egos of humankind are prone to the destructive tendencies that you label *evil*. There is that. You see, you all are also spirit but you inhabit a human body and are prey to all that is meant by that. You develop a human ego. You can be influenced by your spirit, by your guides, by the All There Is, but it is possible, as human beings, to close yourself off to that which is transmitted by your spiritual self. You must all accept your humanness and your responsibility of how you act as humans.

*You are bigger
than you imagine,
but you have to
reach for yourself*

You often want it to be God's fault when something bad happens, rather than acknowledge your own part in what is happening in your world. I want to stress that much of what happens is collective and so you are all a product of your current culture. But that does not mean that you cannot transcend your culture. It does not mean that you cannot learn to listen for inner guidance and wisdom. It does not mean that you have to settle for being small. You are bigger than you can imagine, but you have to reach for yourself. This is very important.

You wonder why some of you never seem to want to kill or maim and are sorely moved by the pain of others, while others seem to take delight in the hurting of others. You still want to believe that this is because of how others have acted through the ages. There indeed are many who have a difficult time learning the lessons which will make them free. They bring with them, in their essence, the fabric of past lives. The challenge is always to go ahead, to further develop the light within them. So sometimes, indeed, those who are in the process of acting out hurtful deeds bring with them a history within their essence of brutality. This is not always the case, and it does not mean that they will act again in brutal ways. You see, the direction of their spirit continues to work to free them to go ahead on their journey. Many though, by virtue of their life experiences, find that they have developed egos which are not in tune with spirit and light. They find themselves acting out in this life in ways that might take many other lives to rectify. This all sounds quite complicated when I explain it to you because you do not have the full sense of this process. But take it on faith.

The events in China are not so much different than many other events which have happened before. Do not be distressed that this is happening. Progress appears to flow like this, but know that in time, all will be much clearer. You must think in terms of eternity, not mere years. Open up and let this knowledge in.

On the other hand, remember that I have said that as a human you can take the large view, which I have just been talking of, or you can take the intimate view and see these events on the earthly, concrete level. And here, of course it is appropriate for you to grieve the pain and death of those very courageous students. We here are providing what nurturing we can to them as, of course, we do to others. They are welcomed by others who have experienced like events in their lives, for sometimes there has been such sudden death that there is more confusion than necessary. You, too, can send your love and comfort out into the ether, and then you can also do whatever you want to on a concrete level. For some, this will be donating money for relief, for others it will be comforting those who are still alive. For some, it will merely be, being informed and raising their consciousness through these events. Do not be misled by these events though in raising all the protests to a high spiritual plane. Be careful, for it is easy to imagine that some are good and others bad. You must be aware and look for those truths which feel right to you. That is all.

Yes I am here, my dear. You are feeling a little scared tonight but are not sure why. There is an abundance of anxiety over the coming financial crunch which you fear. Let me assure you that you are not knowing the future but are responding to the past. Do not confuse the two. You are feeling old pangs which come from a childhood which was often riddled with the lack of money. You experienced your monetary scarcity in a physical sense more than you did in actually knowing it in your mind. That is why sometimes you feel physical sensations that you are not sure where they come from.

June 9, 1989
On anxiety, the
past & present

Let me help you with that. Just hold your breath for a while. You will find that the feeling of anxiety will pass much more rapidly. Do this now. You see, this will help you to come to the present. Do this a few times when we finish. It is important to claim the past for yourself and not be driven by it. We talk of this often. It is not enough to become aware that the past has come calling you, but you must learn how to refuse to answer its calling cards. This does not mean by denying it nor repressing that which tries to come, but if you learn that the messages of the past are just that and no more, then you will begin to see that your present day life does not have to be constantly affected.

There has been much talking about the past traumas by your psychologists, and sometimes too much weight is given to dredging up the past so that people begin to excuse themselves by it. But think how important it is to learn to go past the past. You are much more than merely a receptacle of past happenings. You have access to wisdom which can help you to put everything in perspective. Strive for this. Now let yourself go into a meditative state where you allow the feeling to rise, but then call on your higher wisdom to offer solutions and transcendence. You are a very creative person. You all are. Let yourself rise to the situation.

Finding your connection to the spirit

I will talk to you a little more about finding a spiritual path that satisfies the craving inside. You and those about you are finding themselves longing for a deeper connection. Many times they do not know this, but they find themselves very discontent with their lives and blame this on their jobs, their spouses, their children, lack of money, health problems, etc. You see, the hungers for connection to the ground of being have not been defined for you as have your hungers for other things, and they often go unnoticed in the frenzy of your daily life. You run here and there, trying madly to keep ahead of yourself and often do not have the time to question what it is you are doing. Or if you ask that question, you often do not have the answer for it.

For many, life is just a string of activities that fill up the day from morning to night. There is little connection to the spirit. There is little recognition that there are other ways to be in connection with life. There is little knowledge of the Divine Spark which exists in each. There is little knowledge of the strength of relationships which are built on unconditional love. So life often feels hard. It feels lacking. It feels as though it is going too fast. Now you wonder what is the answer to that. We have talked of this often.

Life takes on a larger meaning

There is no magical answer for you, except to take time to make the connections with the All There Is. You know that when you do this, when you operate as though you are not merely a human being, then life changes for you. This does not mean that you become less of a human being, but more so. Life takes on a larger meaning. It vibrates with energy. You see life is not hard when you are in the grace of your spirit. You wonder how you can do this when there seems to be so much of the daily world to contend with and so much negativity in all that surrounds you. Yes, that is true, and you too can be part of that. But you do not have to. There are many ways to help yourself to transcend that which you appear to be. You yourself have noticed changes over the past year, and you are hardly trying. I do not say that to condemn you, but the way to enlightenment takes commitment. It is very easy to stay rooted in the physical everydayness. But you see how you now let yourself take a few minutes here and there as you go to sleep and as you wake and often during the day. You see as you do this, you are in touch with something larger. This is good for anyone. You cannot go from hectic involvement in your world to a place of nirvana.

Take a few minutes here and there. Look at the world around you. Be in touch with nature. Take a minute and feel deeply whatever is going on at the moment. Look at other people as though they were divine. Speak to someone as though you share unconditional love. You do not have to do this all day long, but take the time to let yourself experience a more loving, peaceful existence at least three or four times each day. You will find that you will want more. Be aware of how much your mind is mired in negativity. Raise your spirits even if it is only for a moment. Practice this. You could have a buddy that you could call and share the moment with. That is all.

Hello, my dear. I am so glad to talk with you again. I am very happy to see you involved in the building of the houses for the poor. (We were volunteering with Habitat for Humanity in Milwaukee.) That is a fine way to spend your time. You see how it is that you feel when you are doing work that is investing in love? This is an important thing to be aware of, that is, how you feel when certain events are going on. You speak of being touched. Do you know what is being touched? You see, you can trust these feelings as they are an expression of something very knowing. You can trust the feelings that well up which feel as though you are connected to a greater source. These will not lie to you. You see, many people pooh-pooh these feelings as they come and do not use their feelings to inform them when they are on the right track.

June 12, 1989
Being in accord
with universal
principles of love

Remember this, when you act in ways that feelings of love and connection arise, that is a good way to tell that you have acted in a way that is in accord with the universal principles of love. There may be other feelings which arise, but you will know the difference. Many do not seek to find the kind of experience that we are talking of, but you have experienced this in your groups and there is no difficulty in naming it. You see, you are all much more knowledgeable than you think.

Having an impact
on creation

Let me talk to you of something else, and that is what the concept of *God's work* means. You have heard that phrase this week and have wondered about it. Is there such a thing? Is that what we were just talking about? Well, my friend, let me elaborate on that for a bit.

You see, *God's work* is a term of your earth. You would not hear that in universal ways. God, as I have said many times, is not a person who lays down rules such as that. You are a product of your upbringing, and so you have to live with the concept that your country agrees upon. But let me say this. When you engage in what could be called *God's work*, you are indeed advancing the creation of a state of love. You see, you are not something apart from God. You are at one. And so, what you do has impact on the whole of creation.

This you find hard to believe as the whole of creation seems so large and you are so small in ratio. But this is the truth. You see, you as individual and you as collective do have impact on the everyday shape and size and countenance of creation. So yes, there are certainly ways to act which will have a greater positive influence on the world, and there are ways to act which add to the storehouse of negativity and pain. You see, your people have not yet learned that they are responsible. They strive to make God responsible for everything. Listen sometimes to yourself. This does not mean that you are in charge or responsible for what happens in the sphere of others. But it does mean that you are responsible within your own. There are many opportunities to act during each day in ways that advance the way of love. You see, you cannot only wait for things to change. You, by your very presence, are an agent of change, both positive and negative.

"What is positive," you ask. Is it God's way? *Positive* is that which leads toward the light of love. It is very simple. So simple that many search wide and near looking for answers which are there in front of the nose. You see how that is? You have the chance each moment to create. Be aware of this. The man who comes home from work and beats his children or fights with his wife and who feels justified in this as he can complain that he had a hard day at the office is creating an atmosphere in his home that is negative. But he also is adding to the pain of the world. These acts do not die there in his closed-door home but expand as they pass into the universe.

272

You all have choices. Exercise them. But you wonder if there are not some underlying principles to follow which will make you more in tune with the over-all plan of the universal whole. Yes. I have told you, seek always to follow the path of love. Begin to find out what that means. It is not that which you often excuse for love. No, but it is very simple. You need not feel great stirring in your heart to act in the way of love. You need not feel affection or sexual desire or anything like that to act in the way of love. The opportunities during a day's time are myriad. Just think on this. You need not be passive nor aggressive, nor must you give in nor give up. You need not always think first of the other; you need not think of yourself last. You need not always make another happy. No, these things are not necessary to act out of love. You must think on this. Pay attention to how you are during a day and use the standard of light for you to examine yourself. This does not mean to be rigid and not spontaneous. It does not mean to be unemotional; it does not mean to be less than human. You must expand your view of love and raise it above the view of your ego. The world needs much of this now. Learn with others what this means. Look around for examples. You need not always be right, just keep learning.

Yes, I am here. I am happy to write with you again. I know this is an important day for you, but then they all are, aren't they. Sometimes people forget this. They think that only some days are to be looked forward to. They wait for the day of the party or of the raise or payday or a birthday or something else which they mark as important. But you see, my dear, they are looking at it all wrong. Each day that you are alive is an important day. You need not wait for some external event to mark the day as special. You are wise in waiting for the day to break but that is enough. I will not go on about this as I think the message is self-evident.

June 23, 1989
Each day that you are alive is an important day

Let me talk of some things before your group arrives tonight. I send a word of welcome and comfort to those who come. Today is a day of blessing. Allow it to come to you. Open your hearts and minds to the power which lies about you. Feel the presence of spirit. Feel the heartbeat of the universe. Listen closely with your inner ears for the sounds which aliveness makes. You are part of this. Feel your blood coursing through your veins. Feel your energy flowing around and throughout you. Feel the wondrous workings of your mind, that wonderful connection to the All There Is. Take note of the needs of your ego right now. It may be telling you something, but then, go beyond and listen to the voice of your spirit. Let the love that you are capable of go out from you, covering all that are within this room. Radiate. You are energy and light. Shine. Send and receive. Feel the pulsations. Be with love tonight.

A meditation
Healing Colors

Here is a small meditation for you on this very warm night.

Lie back in the most comfortable position that you can find. Let your body go limp. Imagine that it is a sawdust doll that has no bones or joints or ligaments. See this in your mind. Feel it in your body. Relax more and more into this state of formlessness. See yourself as merely protoplasm moving this way and that in space. Relax more and more. Now with your inner eye, let yourself travel to a place of great beauty. Look around you at the scene. Feel the air and the temperature. Look at the trees and flowers. Smell the smells which are in the air. Look especially at the colors. Now focus on a particular color. Know that you will choose the color that will be most healing to you. Let your eyes rove about until you find the right one. Look deeply into this color. Let yourself become immersed in it. Let it cover you. Let it permeate your body, entering into each pore until you shine and radiate with a brilliance of beautiful color. Bask in this. Know that this color is what your body needs tonight for healing and nurturing. Take this in now for a minute or two and then slowly return to your everyday waking mode. Be sure to do this slowly.

A message

Now, my dear, a message for you. I send you great love tonight. You are doing very fine. There is much for us to talk about and though I know we often commune directly, it would be wise for you to write more often. I will try to not be too long winded, but it is a joy to meet with you.

June 29, 1989
The goal of parenthood

Yes, I am here, my dear. How nice to hear from you today. It is a very beautiful day there and here and everywhere. When you can see from the right perspective the beauty of your world is unbounded. You cannot imagine how much more beautiful it could be if all were in tune with the wonders of life. That is all of that. Just enjoy your senses for they open up vast and myriad scenes of wonder for you.

You have been mulling over many topics but would like me to write about children and parents and parenting. You wonder about the task and how often there is a lack of skills for this task. You wonder how this all fits in with the over-all plan, and if there are some concepts that parents should follow. This is a large undertaking to give you all that information, so perhaps we will write more than one time.

To begin with, parenting is both a worldly and an other-worldly task. But since you are all parents there on a day-to-day level, I am sure you want me to address that. But first, let me talk about what the goal of parenthood is from the perspective of the All There Is. From that perspective, the goal of parenthood is to raise children to adulthood in a manner that frees their souls to experience that which each child has set out to do. This is very difficult to explain, and few people are in touch with this purpose of their parent life. So just know that there is purpose, but this is more to nourish and care for children so that they may experience their lives.

You ask though, about parents who seem to destroy their children's lives by their abuse of one kind or another so that they grow to be troubled adults. Well, this is indeed true, has been true and will be true for some time to come; but it is not an inevitable way of humankind. This is very sad, for there is so much lost by the kind of treatment that is meted out; but this I cannot talk of when we talk about the way of parenting. You know that abuse is destructive to the spirit. It does not mean that much survival cannot be learned, nor that all who are abused have asked for that in their lifetime. I shall have nothing good to say about the practice of abusing children, but that too is a part of a much larger picture than might first be apparent.

You see, your culture fosters the kind of treatment that we are talking about. It is not a necessary condition that humankind should hurt their young. Watch the animals for the ways of parenting. There it is very easy to see the purpose and way of being a good parent. The fox mother teaches by deed what it is the newborn pups need to know for their life. There also is contact with the larger mind of fox which helps the young to grow and prosper in the way of foxhood. But you as humans find it much more difficult to raise your young because your world has become so artificial and there is so much to learn that is not natural. If you were a natural people living in a natural world, learning to live by natural means, you would find the ways to parent surprisingly easy, as the way of child would be in tune with the learning needed for survival in the world. But now you have created a vast atmosphere of artificiality, and there are many, many mores that need to be taught to children, many at the expense of the natural knowledge that they could be in tune with. So the task of parenting becomes more difficult with each advance of technology and knowledge.

Most parents too are out of touch with the natural way of being a parent and must learn this from books, from others or whatever way they can. They often find themselves frustrated by their own lacks when their children seem to follow a theme that is foreign to them.

To love with an
open heart
You want me to tell you what should be done about this, and I will say that there is nothing simple to be done. There are ways, of course, to parent that will help the child to grow in himself or herself, but this is so simple that you will say that I have not told you anything. That is, to love with an open heart. But of course, that presupposes that one knows how to do that. You see, to be a parent is first of all to grow in love toward yourself. To be a parent means to become connected with the spirit of yourself and of your child. To be a good parent means to have at your fore the knowledge that both you and your child are separate but connected parts of the whole. You are not your child's owner, but merely the keeper of her or his soul temporarily. Your connections may have come from other connections in other lives. You may be establishing the first connection of many to come or this may be a fleeting time in eternity for you to be together. Each soul is on its own journey and so this is true of both parent and child. The way of interaction influences both of your paths and gives you both opportunities for learning many tasks along the way.

This understanding that you as parents are merely bystanders in your children's lives may be distressing to some who see the parent-child relationship as paramount in their life. And that is so. This is a very, very important relationship but it still does not mean that parents are responsible on the cosmic level for the soul of the child. What happens on the daily level is, of course, part of the cosmic plan and becomes incorporated in both the life of the parent and of the child.

You see, there is much to be said, but I feel I have not laid a good ground work for all that I can say. You would like to know more specific things that would be helpful to a parent. This relationship, like others you have, can be improved by learning to expand your view of what it means to love another. But I say to you again that your world has made parenting difficult because the emphasis in your world is on materialism rather than on love and connection, and the children are starving for the connection which would nourish them.

They are starving for connections to the spirit. They are starving for connection to the natural world. They are starving for connection to value. They are starving for lack of *love*. They are starving from loss of knowledge of their unique place in the whole scheme of creation. Let yourself have pity for them and yourselves. Begin to learn what you are doing to deprive yourselves of the wonders of life. It is time for all to awaken. For those of you who are beginning to awake, you will learn more and more of what is needed. Let yourself contemplate what a world would be like that is run on love and connections. What would it be like if you were able to tune into the intuitiveness which connects to the overall plan. You must begin to think of this, or your children will continue to suffer as will you. Think not of yourself as parent and the small ones as something lesser. Let them teach you. Hear their voices. Listen, for they are closer to spiritual knowledge than those who have more years. See them as teacher. This may help.

Now, my dear, a small message of love for your day. Let the love of the universe descend upon you, holding you fast in its palm. Think of yourself as a child who is nourished by unending love. This love is given you by virtue of your being. Learn from it. Experience it in the deepest core of your being. Allow yourself the knowledge which tells you of the specialness of you in the web of creation. Allow yourself this knowledge, for if you do, it will be impossible for you to deny it to others. The way is a way of love. Know this deep within your heart. I will write again soon. *A message*

Yes, I am here. You feel my energy coursing through you and we can once again write today. I have missed talking with you, but that is fine when you take what time you need to assimilate the lessons we speak of. July 8, 1989 **On peace & its meaning**

You would again like to hear some of the wisdom of the ages from me. Well, sometimes you must understand that the wisdom of which I speak to you is not only that of the ages but of the future also. I would like you to remember that this information is something which is always available through your closer connections with the intuitive side of yourself. When you write and ask for guidance from me, I am only giving you that which is already available to you, except you often are not aware of it.

For today, let us talk about peace and what that means in your world. Is this something that is achievable or will there always be war? There, of course, is a distinction between what you now call *peace*, which is really a resting place between what you call *wars* and a greater concept of peace. The *state of peace* that has been spoken of by the masters and which you all yearn for is not this *waiting for war to begin*. It is an active state, a state as active as war and is not the counter foil.

This is hard for you to understand, as you have been conditioned to think of the former way. But when you let yourself think of what it would mean if a state existed in which there were no possibility of war, then you would find a very different world. This state is achievable and will be achieved, but not so soon. There will be much trial and error before that time of awakening takes place. But you are on the path, you *collectively*. There is always the possibility that there will be major disruptions on this journey. It takes much for the mind of humanity to accept that war is only a destruction of oneself. The time is coming that more and more people will see the wastefulness of this, but for now, you will not find even the kind of peace you usually think of in your world.

The idea of solving your life conflicts by violence is very ingrained in the psyche of all. There will have to come changes in this mass thought before there will be changes in the practice. Let us talk of what you can do to help the expansion of the concept of the world peace. There are many opportunities in each day, for it is within the minds of all of you that change will take place. Look at yourself. How often do you want to manage the stresses of life by anger or violence, even if this violence exists only in your mind.

There are those who work against the nuclear mind by exposing all that is potentially dangerous. This is good in some ways, as it helps to create a different image of war. You have been ingrained with the idea that there is something glamorous, patriotic, sterling, about war. Many still have fond memories of how powerful they felt in the course of doing their duty. But the time for this is over. Now is the time to see how the idea is carried to its extreme in the potential of the self-destruction of all living things. This course still may happen. It is not assured that the minds of mortals can change rapidly enough to stave off the explosion of life. But take heart at the changes which are happening.

I told you several months ago that there were to be important breakthroughs and to watch for them. I tell you now to continue to watch. There is potential within the next several months for much growth in peace concepts, but there also is potential for destruction. You will see what I mean as time goes on. Allay yourself with the forces of life and light. Pray for the light to enter into the minds of all. Contribute your energy when appropriate. Think creatively about peace. Start small. Think of peace within the sphere of your home, your job, your family. See if you can understand what it would mean to live with *an active concept of peace.*

Now let me speak to you about the issue of abortion which is going to be so roundly fought there in your country. You see how this will approximate a small war. Watch for the behaviors. Watch for the emotions. See how their methods will describe the concept of violence and power-over. It is ingrained in all your psyche. I cannot tell you all how to solve this question. It will go on for some time. But I say to each of you who read this, "Think of how you are adding to the war mentality when you turn out to do battle." There are other ways that you can make your beliefs known. I know these few words will not still the civil war which is brewing, but mark them for the future. I spoke to you before that the issue of abortion is not one that is of concern here, except when it happens in later months as much preparation might have taken place as souls get ready to enter that life. But, you see, this does not help you all there, for the only ones who will listen have already formed some belief of their own. In the end there will be forward progress to enlightenment, but in the meantime there will be a time of darkness.

On abortion conflict

A message
*Open your heart
to life and love
and the highest
urgings of the
spirit*

Now, my dear, it is time for a message for you, one of peace and love but also one which asks you to consider that you have been using old ways of thinking to deal with life situations and have not been in touch with the spirit which is you. Let yourself think daily on this. Ask for help and guidance from within. Say *no* to the old ways of thinking which bring you feelings of pain or distress. Open your heart to life and love and the highest urgings of spirit. Let my words come to you, but also listen for those within which bring you joy. Do not be afraid, for all is pure freedom when you live with the path of spirit. It is only when you live wholly in ego that all the mundane assume importance. Let yourself soar. Let yourself rejoice for it is a day of life. Conduct yourself with mindfulness. Be aware. Be in touch. See. Listen. Feel. Sense. This is what will bring the feelings of joy to you.

Do not let yourself get mired down in the pettiness of the everyday. Do not let yourself get caught trying to live the path of another. This you cannot control. Let loose. Let the reins on your life be loose. Be ready for what comes to you. You have all that you need to be successful in living life, but be sure that you know what that means. So my dear, live today. Let your love flow. Do not stifle it out of fear or from feelings that you will lose control. Let loose and ride freely down the path which opens before you. Let knowledge come to you today. Let warmth enter you. Let light fill your being and shine upon those around you. Let love.

July 9, 1989
On relationships

Yes, I am here, my dear. It is a very warm day there, I know, but you will find that if you are in touch with the peace within that you will find yourself comfortable.

Your mind is full of relationship questions as you watch your friends struggle with what it means to relate to each other in a loving way. And you wonder yourself how to balance the needs of the one with the needs of the two. Well, I am no expert on the subject, but I do have a larger perspective than you do there. You are all at the mercy of the current trend in how to be with each other. It is often difficult as ideas change, to change with them, even when you agree that the change appears to be beneficial. You see there are many, many ways of establishing the rules for marriage or love relationships. This depends on many of the practicalities of the time and place where they are set.

For instance, economic factors often play a large role, as do beliefs about the role of the partners. The demands of the environment and the care taking of the young are all factors. But let us remain with your particular time and place. There is a move afoot to change traditional values of how to be in relationship, and you often find yourself caught between the new and the old. There is a yearning deep within yourself for the perfect love. You know it is there, but you also have fears about attempting to find that. You see many have the same wish. But when it comes to acting out their side, they find themselves reluctant to play a part that puts them into a role they do not wish to play.

Let me give you a few ideas I have. First, you must always see the larger dimension of your relationship. Why have you chosen it, both from a present life perspective but also from a past and future life perspective? You are not there on a whim, you know. So ask often what is it your soul can learn, for relationships with others, whatever their form, are the bed of richness for learning. Know yourself. Know who and what you are as much as possible. Take responsibility for being where you are. This does not mean that wherever you are, you have to stay, but it does mean that the difficulties that you all sometimes encounter are not necessarily to be run away from.

Each situation is different and you must assess where you are constantly. But it is important to recognize that you are in relationship with another and not with yourself. So often people want the other to change and become a carbon copy of themselves, perhaps not in looks, but in desires. There is nothing to be gained by that—except frustration. Often times, there are power struggles as each of the couple try to pull the other into a path which they feel comfortable with.

On love

The question of love comes up. You wonder if love is sufficiently deep, will all go well; and I will tell you, *no*, if it means the experience that so many of you call *love*. If you are able to love unconditionally, using the love energy of the universe, then I will say, *yes*. There is a transcendence to this kind of love which makes the daily cares seem frivolous. Few can achieve this at this time, but you will all progress slowly on this path for it will become apparent that something more is needed than your current ways of being. But all is process. Learn each day from each other. Do not let yourself be fooled by the words *relationship* or *marriage* as something sufficient onto itself. I know that this information is not concrete with do's and don'ts for you. I am not a marriage counselor, you know.

A message

Let me send you a message of love. Let yourself open to the wonders of each other. Let yourself wonder that energy links exist between all people. Feel how good that feels when you connect on the energy level with another person. Do not strain so to control each other. Do not strain to manage the lives of all. Do not strain at all but lift yourself to transcendence. Then it will not matter about the trivialities. That is all.

July 11, 1989
**On lesbians &
gay men**

Yes, I am here now. Let us meet once again. I am very happy to talk with you again and I know this is important for you. There is a peacefulness within you that was not there before. Isn't that true? Now what shall we talk of today.

You are wondering about the problems the gays and lesbians have in getting accepted by many of the others, and you wonder what, if anything, I have to say on this subject. Well, my dear, of course the important thing to be aware of looking at it *from a higher perspective*, is what this means for the souls of those who are gay in a particular life. This is not something that is thought to be wrong, but it is a natural part of the possibilities of life.

There are many variances in people, and it is not that some shall be judged as natural or unnatural. A very hard core belief and set of fears are continually acted out in your world, but these do not differ so much from other judgments and fears concerning various races, etc. There is a major belief that some are better and some are worse, and you will find that as long as that belief is held, then you will find judgments and prejudices.

But you wonder about what it means to be gay, and why this happens when it seems that the way is for all species to mate. You wonder why there is this variance. Well, my dear, that is not the case that all animals mate either, but that does not have bearing on this case. You see, there is often a carryover from one life to another, so that sometimes the sexes are mixed up and the strong emotions of an earlier life are played out in this one.

282

That is part of the answer, but there is also benefit in living a particular kind of life. A time will come when it will be necessary for all to restrict the birth of the children. It will be important knowledge that all kinds of relationships can be formed and that all relationships will not have to result in a child. This is becoming very apparent. There is a great deal of sentiment concerning the right to bear children, but your world is becoming overpopulated and if you all want to survive, there will need to be some curtailment there.

You see, it is not as though it is important whether someone is gay or not. The only importance comes from the judgments that are made there. If this were not the case, nothing much would happen. There is not value in being gay or not being gay. It is not as though this were a force that was going to take over the world, you know. The fears that are being perpetuated come from an unknowingness about what is feared.

You are all people there, but you would think that you were a number of species who were enemies of each other. Some of you would eat the others if they could. Look into your God-like hearts where everyone is of value. Do not harshly judge each other. Do not harm the psyches of each other by hard words and deeds. Extend the love that comes from knowing that you are all one, that you share a common heart. Reach out and see yourself. This is all that is necessary.

Yes, I am here. You want to know again if I am real or just a figment of you. You see it does not matter. What I write to you is important. Only be concerned with that.

July 18, 1989
On parenting

Let us go on talking a little about parenting. Very many books have been written to tell parents how to do it. But in the end there is still much unlearned and undone. There is a time for parents to stop and think about what it is that they are trying to convey. There is very much learning going on today that is destructive to the life of the child, but more importantly, to the life of all. Each generation comes along to carry the ball forward, but too often there is slippage as the sins of the parents are visited upon one generation after another.

You are all beginning to learn how this is, and it is important for family destructive patterns to be broken. But you wonder what I have to add to the messages of your experts. You see, at this time there is not much to be said, but as the consciousness of the masses rises, then there will be important chances for the advancement of all—through parenting. At this time there is much left out.

The soul of the new child is often confronted with much that could be avoided if there was knowledge that you were not parenting merely a child but raising the vehicle of the soul for its journey. Each child is a part of the evolution of souls to enlightenment, and so each has a part to play in the creation of the world. This does not mean that you are responsible for what that soul accomplishes on the earth, but it would be worthwhile if there was more knowledge about the place of spirit in the daily life.

This does not necessarily mean religion, you know. It is important to teach children about their connections to all, to the natural world, to the birds and plants and animals, to teach them about the sacredness of life and the communion of souls. There is a time for knowing and a time for doing. Judge this with your children. Provide them with an expanded view of life and what it means to be human. You may have difficulty with this as your society does not foster such thought, but be creative and find ways to teach. Listen to your children; they have much to tell you about life for they are closer to it than you are.

On being abandoned

You are sorely tried tonight by your inner workings. Let me tell you that much of what you experience comes from a long ago time when you were left out to die by the wolves. You were very afraid and it was not a pretty death. There are still vestigial fears left from that time. Confront these now. Know that you are in a new time and place and that your fears are ungrounded. You know that you were left because there was not enough food, but that is not true now. Do not worry so about being abandoned, but when it comes, turn to yourself and let those old fears come to rest.

Here is a prayer for you. Allow the inner voices a place to be heard, but understand with your heart that the time is not now for you to grieve them. Let the light of the unending love come to you to bring lightness into the darkness where the old pain and fears now live. Allow yourself to grieve for that long ago self, but know that you have survived much since then and that the life of this time does not include abandonment to the wolves or other dark forces. Rest your head on the shoulder of the All There Is. Allow the cooling nurturing of the Mother comfort you. Allow the spirits and the angels to bring you sips of joy. You are loved, my dear. Allow this knowledge to permeate your days.

Yes, I can give you a meditation now.

A meditation
The Pink Cloud

Lie back and let peace descend upon you. See this as a large cloud of pink vapor which slowly drifts to earth to gently cover you. Feel its softness and warmth upon your body. See how it has special properties that enter your very being, bringing relaxation to all your tired muscles. Feel them let go and relax, one by one. Now let yourself be aware of breathing in the pink cloud which gently is covering you. Feel the sweet moisture entering your lungs to bring a special nourishment to your body which allows it to enter into a deeper peace. Breathe now, releasing the stored toxins from your day of stress. Breathe easily and gently, imaging the pink cloud being drawn into you. Now let yourself taste of the cloud. Taste its nectar. This is nourishment from the land of spirit and brings with it knowledge and wisdom. Take this into you and allow the further deepening of the feelings of peace. Now let yourself journey to a place where the peace of the world abounds. Let yourself experience the light and warmth which goes beyond understanding. Look around and feel the breath of love upon you. See how it shimmers in the air and falls from the trees. This is a place of magic. Let yourself look closely now at all that resides there. Ask for a gift to take home with you—a symbol which will be able to bring you this level of peace and love whenever you desire it. Take time now to experience this place of wonder and when you are ready return, slowly and gently to this room.

Yes, I am here, my dear, dear friend. Tonight is the night of another meeting where you share my thoughts with your friends. This is a very important event, for you will find yourself energized and heartened as will those who attend. I will come and offer my comfort and love to all.

July 20, 1989
On experiencing your spiritual connection to the All There Is

Now just a little message before you find yourself ready to go on. I am sending a message of love to you especially today, as I know that you are feeling depleted by the activity that you have had going on in your life. You see, you, like so many, find yourself caught up in a frantic pace that leaves you little time

A message

to acknowledge yourself as unique and to feel your inner connections with the world which exists. You see, there is a speeding up of your time such that you do not feel equal to crowding all that you think you need into the small space that is given you. You no longer hardly know what it means to travel life at an easy pace.

What is it that you can do to save yourself from wearing out by this frenzied activity? Well, you could retire to the country, but even there the pace of current life will get to you. No, the better method always is to find time to come to your center, to breathe in your life, to relax into the arms of the Mother and feel at peace. There is hope for all of you, but you must make conscious effort to allow the juices of love to flow within. There is plenty of time there. Just relax your body and mind and realize that ninety percent of what you do could be left behind. You do not believe this, as it all seems so necessary.

You see, this is because it is very hard to get connectedness needs met by your society. You must work very hard to survive. You think that you have made life easier through your technology, but you make it more and more difficult each day as you drive yourselves further and further apart.

I will tell you once again, it is necessary for human beings to experience certain things if they are to survive with joy. The most important is spiritual connection. This does not mean going to church once a week or following some rote creed. This means experiencing your spiritual connections to the All There Is. It means having an appreciation with the life force and all its many variations. It means knowing that you and all your brothers and sisters are children alike together. It means acting in ways that demonstrate your part in the great meaning of life and love. This comes first.

You are One
with Love

Next comes sharing in love with each other. This does not mean having an exclusive relationship which you call *love*, but operating with each other from a firm foundation which says, "Here I am and I am for you." When this love is felt between members of a clan, there is strength indeed. Love is not something to be parceled out, to be sold, to be hoarded. It is there to share on a minute-to-minute basis with all. This is a lesson to be learned.

These two needs make up the greatest bulk of a human's needs. When these are there, it does not matter how rich or poor or difficult or easy life is. It will encompass joy. But when they are absent, you will find people running madly about trying to find something to satisfy them. Think on this.

Now a simple prayer for you. May the night bless you and bring you peaceful dreams, dreams which connect you to the Source of All Knowing, of All Loving, of the great home of the All There Is. Let your mind wander freely in its rest. Let it seek its home. Let it find the home of its heart. You will waken with a smile on your lips if you have been successful in releasing your soul for a brief journey to home. Retain the knowledge that you are One with Love. Sleep a wonderful sleep.

A prayer blessing

(The end of the first book.)

Mother Courage Press

In addition to *Welcome to the Home of Your Heart*, Mother Courage Press also publishes

Women at the Helm by Jeannine Talley. Two women sell everything and begin cruising around the world in a 34-foot sailboat. Articulate, poetic and filled with adventure, the book will inspire and delight sailors and armchair sailors of both sexes and adventurous women everywhere.
Paper $11.95; Cloth $19.95

Olympia Brown, The Battle for Equality by Charlotte Coté. This is a biography of the first ordained woman minister in the United States who had a life-long commitment to equal rights for women and women's enfranchisement.
Paper $9.95; Cloth $16.95

Fear or Freedom, a Woman's Options in Social Survival and Physical Defense by Susan E. Smith. This book realistically offers options to fear of social intimidation and fear of violent crime with an important new approach to self-defense for women.
Paper (8 1/2 x 11) $11.95

Warning! Dating may be hazardous to your health! by Claudette McShane. Date rape and dating abuse occur in every corner of our society, without regard to race, class or age, and may indicate future spouse abuse. This book emphasizes that women need not put up with any kind of abuse, are not to blame for being abused and can regain control of their lives.
Paper $9.95

The Woman Inside, from Incest Victim to Survivor by Patty Derosier Barnes. This workbook is designed to help an incest victim work through pain, confusion and hurt. Practical mental lists, emotional recipes, activities and exercises for healing.
Paper (8 1/2 x 11) $11.95

Why Me? Help for victims of child sexual abuse, even if they are adults now by Lynn B. Daugherty, Ph.D. This sensitive, frank, important and informative book can begin the process of healing the psychological wounds of child sexual abuse.
Paper $7.95

Something Happened to Me by Phyllis E. Sweet, M.S., is a sensitive, straight-forward book designed to help children victimized by incest or other abuse.
Paper (8 1/2 x 11) $4.95

I Couldn't Cry When Daddy Died by Iris Galey. First published in New Zealand, this courageous and sensitive personal account of an incest survivor is not just one of despair, it is a story of inspiration and hope.
Paper $9.95

Rebirth of Power, Overcoming the Effects of Sexual Abuse through the Experiences of Others, edited by Pamela Portwood, Michele Gorcey and Peggy Sanders, is a powerful and empowering anthology of poetry and prose by survivors of sexual abuse.
Paper $9.95

NEWS by Heather Conrad is a gripping novel of a women's computer takeover to make the empire builders and the money makers stop destroying the people and the earth.
Paper $9.95

Night Lights by Bonnie Shrewsbury Arthur. More than your traditional lesbian romance, this novel tackles middle-age lovers dealing with teen-age children, AIDS hysteria, women in the priesthood and Ronald Reagan's brand of economics—with a light touch that will make you laugh out loud.
Paper $8.95

Rowdy & Laughing by B. L. Holmes. She's not gay, she's rowdy and laughing. After four children and 20 years of marriage, the author fell in love with another woman. These poems encompass the joy of life and being in love—for all people.
Paper $4.95

Womb with Views, A Contradictionary of the Enguish Language by Kate Musgrave is a delightful, more than occasionally outrageous social commentary cartoon-illustrated feminist dictionary.
Paper $8.95

If you don't find these books in your local book store, you may order them directly from Mother Courage Press at 1533 Illinois Street, Racine, WI 53405. Please add $2 for postage and handling for the first book and 50¢ for each additional book.

290